Metanoia

Also Available From Bloomsbury

Present Tense, Armen Avanessian and Anke Hennig
Genealogies of Speculation, edited by Armen Avanessian and Suhail Malik
Speculative Realism, Peter Gratton
The New Phenomenology, J. Aaron Simmons
Philosophical Chemistry, Manuel DeLanda
Philosophy and Simulation, Manuel DeLanda
Introduction to New Realism, Maurizio Ferraris
After Finitude, Quentin Meillassoux

Metanoia

A Speculative Ontology of Language, Thinking, and the Brain

By Armen Avanessian and Anke Hennig

Translated by Nils F. Schott
With a foreword by Levi Bryant

BLOOMSBURY ACADEMIC
LONDON • NEW YORK • OXFORD • NEW DELHI • SYDNEY

BLOOMSBURY ACADEMIC
Bloomsbury Publishing Plc
50 Bedford Square, London, WC1B 3DP, UK
1385 Broadway, New York, NY 10018, USA

BLOOMSBURY, BLOOMSBURY ACADEMIC and the Diana logo
are trademarks of Bloomsbury Publishing Plc

First published 2014
Paperback edition first published 2019

Originally published in German as Metanoia: *Spekulative Ontologie der Sprache*,
© Merve Verlag 2014

English Translation published 2018
Paperback edition first published 2019

English language translation © Armen Avanessian and Anke Hennig 2018

Armen Avanessian and Anke Hennig have asserted their right under the Copyright,
Designs and Patents Act, 1988, to be identified as Authors of this work.

All rights reserved. No part of this publication may be reproduced or
transmitted in any form or by any means, electronic or mechanical,
including photocopying, recording, or any information storage or
retrieval system, without prior permission in writing from the publishers.

Bloomsbury Publishing Plc does not have any control over, or responsibility for,
any third-party websites referred to or in this book. All internet addresses given
in this book were correct at the time of going to press. The author and publisher
regret any inconvenience caused if addresses have changed or sites have
ceased to exist, but can accept no responsibility for any such changes.

A catalogue record for this book is available from the British Library.

A catalog record for this book is available from the Library of Congress.

ISBN: HB: 978-1-3500-0472-6
PB: 978-1-3500-0473-3
ePDF: 978-1-3500-0471-9
ePub: 978-1-3500-0474-0

Typeset by RefineCatch Limited, Bungay, Suffolk

To find out more about our authors and books visit
www.bloomsbury.com and sign up for our newsletters.

Contents

Foreword		viii
Introduction		1
I	Poetics: Principles of Lingual *Poiesis*	15
	The poetic function of language (Jakobson)	15
	The potentializing function of language (Guillaume)	17
	Poietic linguistics	23
	The myth of the arbitrariness of the sign	28
	Speculative poetics	32
II	The Analytic Circle: The Lingual Creation of a True World	37
	Triadic logic of the sign (Peirce)	45
	The *poietic* triad	54
	The linguistic turn, or the signified as predicate of the signifier	61
	S means X *by* Y (Kripke, Meillassoux, Harman)	75
	Lingual things and the ontology of individuals (Strawson)	83
III	Speculation: Aspects of a Poetics of Thought	87
	The speculative triad	99
	Subject—object—other: our methodical constellation	103
	Abduction as a *poietic* procedure	111
	Poeticizing philosophy	122
IV	Cognition: Metanoia is an Anagram of Anatomie	135
	The recursive structure of cognition (Metzinger and Malabou)	141
	The coevolution of language and the brain	148
	Aspects of universal grammar (Chomsky v Leiss): generative, extra-linguistic, cognitive	151
	Semiotics of the brain (Deacon)	154

Epilogue: The Whole Truth and Nothing. But the Truth! 161
    Matters ethical (and religious) 166
    Going beyond thought: temporality 172

Glossary 179
Notes 187
Index 203

Illustrations

1	Semiotic triangle by Andreas Töpfer	47
2	Semiotic triangle by Andreas Töpfer	50
3	Semiotic triangle by Andreas Töpfer	51
4	Semiotic triangle by Andreas Töpfer	52
5	Eco's Subterfuge	57
6	Rosa x Centifolia "purpurea"	63
7	"Maheka" "La Belle Sultane"	64
8	"Rosa Indica dichotoma. Le Bengale animating"	65
9	"Rosa Indica Caryophyllea. Le Bengale Oeillet"	66
10	"Slater's Crimson China"	67
11	Abduction in perception	123
12	Terrence Deacon's Semiotics of the Brain	157

All chapter opening images are from Armen Avanessian, Andreas Töpfer, *Speculative Drawing*, Berlin: Sternberg Press 2014.

Foreword

The book before the reader brilliantly deals with the theme of *metanoia*. Drawn primarily from religious language in the Christian tradition, *metanoia* is often mistranslated as "repentance". More properly the term should be translated as "conversion". *Metanoia* refers to a fundamental transformation of one's self, nature, thought, and world. However, it would be a mistake to conclude that the origin of this word indicates that this book is a work of theology. In the concept of *metanoia* Avanessian and Hennig discern a phenomenon that is far more pervasive than the religious register and its conversions, but that lies at the core of thought and language. There is a power of language, thought, and speech to transform both the subject and the world. How is it, Avanessian and Hennig wonder, that a book, a poem, a conversation, or a thinking can fundamentally transform both the subject and the world? We enter that book, poem, conversation, or trajectory of thought at one end and when we come out the other everything is completely different. Indeed, in such experiences we can scarcely remember who we were and what the world looked like before. So thorough is the transformation that it even transforms our retroactive selves and worlds. We see the past differently than we did before. This is *metanoia*. In a thinking that traverses speculative realism, new materialism, neurology, structural linguistics, and Peircian semiotics, Avanessian and Hennig seek to determine just how something like *metanoia* is possible. I will leave the book to the reader for the details of this account, instead using the space of this foreword to discuss both how we might think about the phenomenon of *metanoia* and some of the implications of the concept.

In what follows I will use language and games as a launching point for discussing philosophy. In linguistic circles it is a commonplace to compare language to a game. Take a board game. *A* board game has the board upon which it is played, the pieces with which the game is played, and the rules of the game by which moves can be made. Simplifying matters dramatically, the pieces of the game in language would be phonemes, while the rules of the game would be the syntax by which those elements are composed into larger units such as semes, sentences, paragraphs and so on. These would roughly be the paradigmatic and syntagmatic dimensions of language respectively. Competence here would consist in knowing how to make moves in this game; which is to say, knowing how to form sentences or engage in speech-acts.

We can think of philosoph*ies* as similar to games and languages in this respect. There is a Plato game, a Lucretius game, a Descartes game, a Hegel game, a Deleuze game, a Heidegger and Badiou game, and so on. Each one of these philosophies has its own "phonemes" or pieces that inhabit the game and each has rules for making moves in that game. One shows competence in any one of these games not when they can cite the intricacies of these philosophies chapter and verse, but rather when they can make a *new* move within those games according to the rules governing the game. Compare the Plato game and the Epicurean game, for example. Suppose we were to ask whether or not it is ethical to do the drug MDMA or ecstasy? Now clearly we will not find an answer to this question in the writings of either Plato or Epicurus (or Lucretius) because the drug did not yet exist and therefore could not become a topic of ethical reflection. It is likely that both Plato and Epicurus would be opposed to MDMA, but for entirely different reasons. The goal of Plato's philosophy is the purification of the soul so that it will separate from the body at death and go on to the world of the forms. We achieve this goal by living a life of intellect and by turning away from the body and the five senses. If Plato would be against MDMA, it would be for the same reasons that he rejects certain musical instruments, forms of art, and poetic meters in *The Republic*: they draw out the passions of the body, clouding the power of the intellect, just as the drum is among the anti-Platonic instruments *par excellence* because it evokes sensuous affects that lead our body to move involuntarily, emphasizing the body and its passions over the intellect. One need only think of the famous dance scene in *The Matrix Reloaded* to discern the power of the drum and bass.

Like Plato, Epicurus would probably be against the use of MDMA, but for entirely different reasons. In Epicurus the goal of the game is to live the most pleasurable life possible (because pleasure is the moral good) and to minimize anxiety as much as we can. However, while Epicurus treats the pleasurable as the moral good and the painful as the moral wrong, he nonetheless argues that we should avoid forms of pleasure that are either too much trouble to find or that cause pain as a consequence. For Epicurus, the question would then be whether MDMA is too much trouble to get or causes pain (psychological or physical) as a consequence or whether it increases anxiety. It is likely that he would see it as being a negative impact on all these fronts and would thus argue that the prudent person should reject it.

All of this seems remote from issues of *metanoia*; however, a few things are of interest here. First, we can talk of a philosophy as an "*alethetics*". For Heidegger, truth as *aletheia* is not a correspondence between a proposition or statement and the independent reality that it depicts, but is rather a *revealing* or *disclosure*. Where the correspondence theory of truth holds that truth is a relationship between a proposition and a thing or state-of-affairs such as the claim that the statement that a "hammer is a tool for pounding nails" if there exists a tool that is for pounding nails, truth as *aletheia* holds that this assemblage *presents* or discloses itself as something for the sake of this task; it gives itself in this way *prior* to any *claim* we might make about it. The hammer is given differently for, say, the physicist who might encounter it in terms of chemical and atomic composition, mass, position in space, velocity, etc. These are *different* forms of disclosure. As Avanessian and Hennig repeatedly remind us, disclosure is a dual relation between a subject or self and a world. The self of the physicist and the self of the handyman are different selves, but there are also different *worlds* revealed to each. In light of the foregoing, let us say that there is a deep *grammar* to each of these *fields* that differs in each case.

Compare three examples: the mechanic that works at a privately owned garage, the investor, and the Marxist sociologist. In each case, one and the same world—the garage—is disclosed differently. The mechanic enters the garage and probably notices the tools first. She grasps those tools in terms of their purpose and their use. The space of the garage—the field or board—is discerned in terms of the actions to take place in it. When the investor enters the shop, he probably pays little notice to the tools and certainly has little understanding or comprehension of what they are for. He might not really notice them at all except in a vague and fuzzy way. Rather, the garage is disclosed to the investor in terms of its potential for profit. What leaps out to the investor—and it does literally leap out in much the same way that a hologram leaps forth—might be the financial records, signs of waste, signs of efficiency pertaining to the garage as a business, and so on. "How much does the garage spend and how much does it bring in? What are some ways of increasing profit and diminishing waste?" For the investor, fixing cars is all but *invisible* in his evaluation of the garage. Where those that work in the garage might conceive this as their purpose and goal, the investor sees this as secondary to making profit. In some respects, the Marxist sociologist doing field research on labor practices under capitalism is closer to the investor than the mechanic. Like the investor, the tools about the garage are more or less a mystery for him. Like the investor, he might be particularly attentive to the financial records of the garage. However, unlike the investor our Marxist sociologist would be particularly attentive to what the working day is like for the mechanics and whether or not the way the wealth produced by the garage is justly distributed.

The mechanic, the investor, and the sociologist can all have a discussion with one another and believe that they are discussing the same thing when strangely they are talking about different worlds and different selves. The worlds that each are talking about, while overlapping in some respects, are nonetheless divergent. In each instance a different world is disclosed. There is a different field of truth. With Heidegger, we can thus say that with every disclosure there is also a veiling. Other worlds are hidden. In the disclosure of the world in terms of profit, the world of the mechanic and his labor becomes veiled or disappears. The investor is looking elsewhere and seeing a different hologram. And is this not what we perpetually see in philosophy? Each philosophy discloses a different world, yet simultaneously falls prey to the illusion—an illusion that could be called "transcendental"—that it is discussing *the* world. Perpetually we encounter the experience of philosophers talking to one another as if they were speaking about the same selves, the same world, the same rules for making moves, when all too often they are talking about entirely different things. Inhabiting a philosophy means inhabiting a field of disclosedness that reveals as much as it conceals.

What, then, does the concept of *metanoia* as developed by Avanessian and Hennig bring to the table? In approaching philosophy as something that is not so much *about the* world as something that *brings a* world into being, it seems to me that they present us with a sort of meta-philosophy or philosophy of philosophies. The idea of a conversion or transformation that brings both a new subject and a new world—a new field of disclosedness, a new game—into being suggests a new way of approaching philosophical discourse between different worlds or alethic fields. Rather than the focus being on which of the opposed claims might be true in the sense of a correspondence between proposition and reality—Plato or Aristotle, Deleuze or Badiou?—we might instead get the question of how to bring about transport or relays between these incommensurate alethic universes? In this respect, the project of Avanessian and Hennig shares a resemblance to certain themes in Laruelle's non-philosophy where we are to bracket the battle of the philosophers and instead investigate how philosophies posit their own worlds. The twist that Avanessian and Hennig bring—though not explicit in the text—is that of how to create transports between these worlds or evoke something like "metanoiac" encounters?

However, at the most profound level, I believe this text raises the question of how it is possible to make a move in a game—whether in language, politics, or philosophy—that changes the nature of the game itself; the field of the game, its rules, its pieces? In politics, for example, we often occupy ourselves with the question of how to make the winning move. What might go unnoticed here is that even where a move might win, even where it might bring triumph over our opponent, it nonetheless leaves the grammar of the field, the pieces and rules structuring the field, intact. In this respect, the deep structure of power remains in place; for power is not to be measured so much by which side holds the advantage, but rather by the *structure*—the rules, the grammar, the pieces— that preside over the game or the relations themselves. If, from beginning to end, there is one question Avanessian and Hennig's remarkable book asks, it is that of how it might be possible to make a move within the constraints of a game that transforms the very nature of the game itself: its grammar, its pieces, its field? Can the pawn make a move within chess that abolishes pawns, queens, kings, rooks, knights, and bishops, their opposition and their endless struggles with those of their opposition, bringing about an entirely new game with different pieces, different ways of moving, different ways of being affected, and a new field? Their answer seems to be yes and their name for this answer is *metanoia*. If such a thing is possible—and these transformations do indeed take place—then it would seem that true emancipation is not so much triumph over one's opposition as a transformation of the game itself. What strategies can we devise to accomplish this aim?

Levi Bryant

I see the world with new eyes.

After that, I was a different person.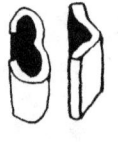

   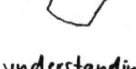

earlier perspective	difference	knowledge of the now	understanding
positions?	an earlier	to take up	is it possible

earlier understanding no longer possible

the world looks at us differently

Introduction

I have no knowledge of what passed prior to my fifth or sixth year; I recollect nothing of learning to read, I only remember what effect the first considerable exercise of it produced on my mind; and from that moment I date an uninterrupted knowledge of myself.

Jean-Jacques Rousseau

"*I now see things in a new light.*" We have all at some point had the experience of reading a book that changed us in a fundamental way. We are all familiar with statements like Rousseau's describing, and we have all said or heard others say about reading a book: "I was never the same afterward. . . ." or "Only then did I realize. . . ." or "Only since then have I. . . ."

Yet what do we really mean when we say something like "I see the world with new eyes"? Such statements implicitly acknowledge that our understanding now is different from our previous understanding. But can we ever regain the former perspective? To see the world with new eyes means that our thinking has changed forever. Not only that: to see the world in a new light also always means that the world, too, sees us in a new light and looks back at us differently.

The question can thus directly be answered in the negative: an earlier understanding is no longer accessible to a new way of thinking. "How could I ever think that?" "I have no idea what I was thinking!" "Of course I now see things completely differently." At most, something like an auto-hermeneutic act, a philology of the self, can reconstruct how we used to view the world. Understanding and not understanding switch positions. The new understanding overwrites the old one, that is to say, the new understanding entails not understanding (the previous understanding).

Because of this "overwriting," we no longer perform our earlier "readings" of the world. Metanoia is more than just a problem of understanding; it shifts an existing relation of thinking and world. Only in language does the world present itself to our thinking; between language and world there is no fundamental difference to obstruct thinking. To express a new thought also always means inventing a new language game appropriate to that thought. Language performs a differentiation of the relationship between thinking and the world. Language is not arbitrary, however obvious such arbitrariness may seem to contemporary theorists of language. Instead, each and every part of language is tied into an ever-developing system. Language develops our understanding of the world in the same way and to the same extent that it continues to develop itself. The principle of language is not arbitrariness but contingency. Language, in other words, develops within a continually changing framework of possibilities constituted by its ties to thinking and the world. That is why the possibilities of a new understanding are immediately tied to finding or inventing a new language.

Metanoia is a fundamental transformation of the mind. What does that mean? What happens in metanoia? We read a book and cannot put it down. We read a book and when we stop reading, we have changed. Once we have stopped reading, the world itself has changed because of our reading. Through metanoia, we become intellectuals; metanoia makes philosophers philosophers; through metanoia, literary scholars become the literary scholars they are; basically, metanoia has made us all who we have become. Metanoia touches on and creates the existential core of thinking. Without metanoia, that is, without having been a Deleuzian, say, or a Lacanian, without ever having understood everything (really understood *everything*!) in Jakobson's or Shklovsky's or somebody else's terms, we would not be writing this today, we would think something completely different—"we," this much is certain, wouldn't even be here.

Metanoia rarely occurs more than once a decade, and it tends to come with significant relocations, radical epochal changes, or the collapse of personal worlds. When in fact "the whole" shifts, the meaning of each and every part changes. Whenever this happens, the past suddenly is no longer what was, no longer what it was before, but that which returns as something that is not understood. Metanoia does not just (bring about) change—it institutes reality. Put succinctly: *Afterward, what comes before is different.*

In every metanoia, an elementary epistemological situation emerges in which the new subject and the world change at the same time. A third element—an other—always participates in this emergence that transforms subject and object equally. That is why thinking about metanoia compels us to go beyond a structuralist universe determined by oppositions: how thinking goes beyond thinking becomes intelligible only if we replace all descriptions of dyadic epistemic situations with descriptions of triadic epistemic situations. The engagement with metanoia furthermore compels us both to reformulate the connection of cognition and language and to understand this connection as the question of the mutability of thinking and the plasticity of our brains.

Language plays every conceivable part in metanoia, as an everyday phenomenon (in natural language), as an artifact (in literature), as a social practice (in speech), and, not least of all, as a mental structure and form of knowledge (as *logos*). Yet what metanoia confronts us with above all and in a unique way is the *poietic* function of language. How can we account for the fact that, in extreme cases, all it takes to change the world is reading a single book?

Mark Turner has suggested locating the connections between cognition, narration, and grammar in a "literary mind."[1] Metanoia can indeed only take place because thinking, language, and world already cooperate. An inquiry into metanoia necessarily leads to the question of how an ontology of language is possible.

This book is a philosophical book about why metanoia is possible and about the conclusions to be drawn from its existence. We do not capture metanoia by examining a clearly outlined corpus of texts (there may be texts that lend themselves to such an investigation, yet metanoia is not the effect of a group of texts that share certain properties). Nor do we encounter metanoia at the level of our knowledge, just as we cannot grasp it by reading phenomenological descriptions or by understanding historical facts. That is why this book can only be written at the level of our experience. The philosophical challenge in writing it is to develop a way of thinking that avoids falling behind this experience.

Metanoia is an experience, and as an experience it prompts us not merely to think but to think philosophically and thus to rethink, to think anew, to reflect anew, to rethink thinking. Yet it is not to be thought of as an *aesthetic* experience; more precisely: it may be perceived as aesthetic, but that tells us nothing about what happens in metanoia.

Perhaps it is its recursive structure (there is no other way to become a philosopher than to completely immerse oneself in a text that opens up the world) that makes it so difficult to reflect on metanoia. How else could we explain that a phenomenon all philosophers have been so familiar with has remained invisible for so long? Granted, we, too, are not writing *about* metanoia, we are writing *of* metanoia, writing of a thinking that changes thinking. We are interested in this change, and to this extent ours is a philosophical book that reacts to a problem, to an experience that makes thinking itself problematic. To reflect on metanoia is to repeat the gestures of a first philosophizing (i.e. to repeat what is at stake in the first encounter with philosophy).

A phenomenon whose meaning and magnitude have until now not been understood must first be conceptualized philosophically.[2] This approach is diametrically opposed to texts about experiences of metanoia that essayistically attempt to conjure up metanoia or try to get to its phenomenal essence by means of emphatic descriptions.

While we're talking about prevalent philosophical habits (and in the spirit of the biblical translation of metanoia: *repent!*, itself a translation of the Hebrew *shub*, "turn back" or "conversion"), we should make a further confession. Metanoia practically compels us to employ the usual philosophical hyperbole: insofar as we want to philosophize (in the emphatic sense), we cannot avoid proclaiming ourselves the first thinkers of metanoia. Of course we don't want to go to extremes, like so many philosophers have done, who were pleased to think of themselves as those who had overcome all previous thinking. Almost all nineteenth-century philosophers who convinced their contemporaries or metanoietically overpowered posterity had already convinced themselves that they were the last in a long, failed tradition and the first in a new one. (Has anything really changed in the twentieth century, at least there where philosophy does not resign itself to the well-financed administration of its heritage in the academy?)

Linguistic ontology between two fronts Once we are aware of the importance of metanoia, central debates between philosophical factions over the last few decades and up to the present day acquire a whole new significance. When we look at the disciplinary turf wars that characterize the past century, we see that the battlefield on which they were fought is marked out by the philosophy of language. (There is no relativism implied in our suspicion that the formation of different schools of thought may be traced back to different metanoietic experiences and different ways of being shaped by reading.) Just think of the debate between proponents of hermeneutics and of deconstruction or the enduring rift between so-called continental philosophy and analytic philosophy.

We, too, object to central assumptions of modern language theory (as well as of its postmodern variants that are barely different or distinguishable, not only when it comes to the central thesis of an "arbitrariness of language"). The nominalism of the analytic philosophy of language has led both linguistics and philosophy to a dead end, which is why it is now being revised by contemporary linguistic and philosophical theories. We follow those currents that seek to replace a thinking in terms of causes and effects with a thinking of functional relations between objects: on the one hand, contemporary speculative philosophy[3] makes temporal structures and events the objects of its ontology; on the other hand, a new linguistics of universal grammar prefers finalistic or functional explanations to describe the makeup of language. Both are united in their resistance to the thesis that language is arbitrary, a thesis that creates a rift between language and the world. This rift has led to an epistemological and linguistic immanentism cut off from phenomenological cognition and has confined the subject to a correlationalist hall of mirrors.

The lingual* construct—language—already contains an ontological thesis: the world mediated by language is made up of relations, not of objects. Because of its immanent knowledge, language can claim a higher degree of realism than our perception, which presents us with things alone. Language leads us right into the world if only because, to a degree that is difficult to overestimate, the world itself is a product of language.

The differences within the philosophy of language under discussion here are conflicts of interest between linguistic and philosophical discourses. A generalized semiotic theory that describes our common practice of constituting

---

* ["Lingual" translates the German *sprachlich*, which encompasses everything pertaining to language, *Sprache*, and is thus broader than both "verbal" (pertaining to speech) and "linguistic" (pertaining to the study of language).—Trans.]

the world as we are interpreting it, while we are interpreting it, makes one thing clear: philosophy demands of language that it objectivize truth and nothing but the truth. It has to condemn all literary creativity as an uncontrolled production of signifiers. Linguistics, in turn, is content with its insight that language exists and that it changes, which is why linguistics can dispense with the idea of objective truth.

From the point of view of the holistic semiotics we establish in this volume, we can see that such differences arise when semiotic relations are reduced to serve particular discursive interests. Counter to such reductions, we insist that semiotic relations always have to be thought in three dimensions and that they form a relational whole. As we will see, metanoia can only be understood by going through all three moments of semiosis. Metanoia radicalizes the *poiesis* that is proper to language, the opening up of a world through language.

Let us attempt a provisional (semiotic) definition of *poiesis*: Whenever I act in language (when I speak, when I write), signifiers glide, meanings shift, and the object to which they refer changes. Integrating the parts into a whole changes them; in the recursive introduction of ever-new parts into a whole, its structures become more complex. This also means that lingual recursion increases language's reality content and enhances its referential possibilities. This is what we encounter in our attempt to capture metanoia in the terms of philosophy (of a philosophy of language).

It is not by chance that *recursion*—the last lingual universal—is our ontological guide. Yet recursion is also a function of language that establishes higher cognitive levels. Language is a speculative tool for thinking the world because it consistently establishes recursive states on a higher level of totality. The task, in other words, is to grasp the "tool being" (Graham Harman) of language.

Othering as method Faced with competing discursive methods, we choose a procedure best called "switching cards." In addition to speculative ontology, the analytic philosophy of language, evolution theory, and cognitive linguistics (or, in Peirce's terms, speculative grammar), this also concerns hermeneutics and deconstruction, especially when it comes to the reading of texts, an all-important aspect for metanoia. Metanoia, in which understanding changes as a whole, demands radical hermeneutics. The hermeneutic circle, which Heidegger extended to describe a structure of being, explains how individual parts—in this context: elements of meaning—connect recursively in such a way as to form a whole, to make sense. The recursivity that becomes visible in hermeneutic circles is the key to our ontology of language.

Because the world is different after a metanoia just as I am different and just as the book I am holding has not remained itself—because there is metanoia—we need a method that allows us to think the interaction of subject and object as well as the changes both undergo. For this reason, the relationship between metanoia and a thinking of metanoia, too, is recursive, not reflective. In a book, we write of a book, in language, we write of language, we write of how we refer to the world being ourselves right in the world, and we think a change in thinking.

Put differently: in every metanoia, a method that changes (itself/us/the world) is at work. One could call it an active "othering." This is the agent of change in subjects and objects, and our theory must thematize it as such.

The spirituality of philosophy In his lectures on the *Hermeneutics of the Subject*, Michel Foucault traces this dimension of philosophy from Hegel via Schelling, Schopenhauer, and Nietzsche to Husserl's *Crisis* and comes across a spiritual dimension of philosophy that usually remains well hidden:

> In all these philosophies, a certain structure of spirituality tries to link knowledge, the activity of knowing, and the conditions and effects of this activity, to a transformation in the subject's being. *The Phenomenology of Mind*, after all, has no other meaning.[4]

Philosophy tends to repress the originary "care of the self" (*souci de soi*) in favor of an imperative to "know yourself!" (*gnôthi seauton*). And yet we see that the history of philosophy, from Descartes' *Meditations* via Pascal's *Pensées* to Kant's fundamental critique and Wittgenstein's mythical ladder, is populated with great rationalists whose works and ideas have triggered comprehensive metanoieses. This could be described as a symptomatic return of the repressed. Kleist reads Kant, Schopenhauer reads Kant, Nietzsche reads Schopenhauer, Thomas Mann reads Nietzsche (and Schopenhauer). And not just Thomas Buddenbrook, after reading

> Schopenhauer, asked himself the question as he mounted the stairs and sat down to table with his family, What is it? Have I had a revelation? What has happened to me. . . .? Was this message meant for me?[5]

"*The formation of the self, the Selbstbildung as the Germans would say*"[6] How is metanoia distinct from the peculiar self-reference of caring-for-oneself? And: "What is this identical element present as it were on both sides of the care: subject of the care and object of the care?"[7] Indeed, in metanoietic transformation, subjects become something objectively other, become objects for themselves: *That is what I used to be, this is what I am now.* Metanoia subjects us: but this does not make us a subject of truth nor does it turn us into an object about which we make true claims. Instead, metanoia turns us into the subject of a new truth, of a new objective whole of which we have become a part.

In this, in our immediate (subjective) incorporation of the new (objective) truth, also lies the reason for the radical immanence of metanoia. We always emerge with the newly emerging world, with the world as we newly understand it. That is why metanoia can neither be explained by going back to the forms of subjectivation of Antiquity—attempts at self- or transsubjectivation oriented at another world—nor by distinguishing between the Christian idea of a "break within the self" and a later Hellenistic-Roman preference for a "break with the world." When we say that, thanks to metanoia, our subjectivity becomes an object, we mean a shift that affects both the self *and* the world. *This world, the one and only, is the real world, and we are its true subject.*

Poeticizing philosophy The great philosophical turf wars of the twentieth century—between deconstruction and hermeneutics, between continental and analytic philosophy—have left all parties exhausted. The primary battlefield for these fights is (the theory of) language. Today, in turn, we all too often witness abstract counter-strikes, as if an ontological *tour de force* could cut the Gordian knot of language, thinking, and being. The long tradition of separating language and ontology, which reaches from Plato to Badiou, obviously is not yet exhausted.

Our switching of philosophical positions and our othering of these positions condition and reinforce each other. In general, we are pleading for "poeticizing philosophy." What do we mean by that? We seek to continue the critical momentum of the analytic philosophy of language to correct 200 years of an unrelenting aestheticization of philosophy. In concrete terms, we oppose an "inner principle" (Baumgarten) independent of language that would govern sensibility as a faculty of cognition (however much it may be framed by a teleology).

There is no cognition independent of language. Neither *aisthesis* (perceiving the world) nor *noiesis* (thinking the world) can be had without *poiesis*. That is why a theory of language cannot do without a *poetics* of thinking, without a speculative poetics. The *poietic* dimension of language, which has been overlooked not just by aesthetic philosophy, concerns its world-creating function. Without it, metanoia would be unthinkable. Our reflection on metanoia thus builds on the analysis of lingual *poiesis*.

To think about metanoia (or rather, to think metanoia through) thus compels us to speculatively grasp the ontogenetic capacities of language. What metanoia reveals is that thinking, world, and language are inextricably linked.

The starting point of the first chapter ("Poetics") is Roman Jakobson's reflection on the poetic function of language. Schooled in the poetics of the avant-garde, Jakobson describes this function as the superimposition of phonetic and semantic similarities on metonymic, syntagmatic similarities. In effect, the principle of metaphor here corresponds to the principle of linguistic metalanguage, which is the main focus of philosophical interest in what language knows.

We sketch a different image of language, one that is based on metonymy. We do not work with the principle of similarity, the concept of reflexivity, and the construct of a metalanguage. Instead, we operate with metonymical contexts, favor the concept of recursion, and take Gustave Guillaume's idea of *ontogeny* as our guide. Our theses aim for a metonymically recursive noetics of language that provides us with both a world and a concept of language, with a language ontology. Only knowledge of the principles of a *poiesis* of knowledge can give us any hope for gaining clarity on how metanoia changes our world.

The second chapter ("Analytic Philosophy of Language") examines philosophical discourses of the twentieth century to see what they can contribute to a realist theory of language. It adapts from them tools for describing how metanoia creates meaning: the hermeneutic circle, the sliding of the signifier (as postulated in deconstruction), the triadic relations of signs (described in semiotics), and a subject of meaning (articulated in the analytic philosophy of language).

A reading in parallel of hermeneutic and deconstructionist theses on language and meaning opens the chapter. By switching the cards between the two discourses, we radicalize the figure of the hermeneutic circle, thereby describing a deconstructive sliding of the signifier in which what shifts is precisely that whole from out of which the meaning of the parts is determined.

Semiotics describes all creation of meaning as a part-to-whole relation in which a whole becomes a part of a new whole. This takes place thanks to an interpretant that relates one whole to another whole (such that both become parts of the new whole). This process is usually conceptualized as a "semiotic triangle." This triangle, as we will see, is a reduction that is as productive as it is dangerous; it creates the enduring impression that all relations that constitute meaning ought to be identifiable (and thus comprehensible) in or by means of this triangle.

We trace the labelings and interpretations the semiotic triangle has been given in various discourses. In particular, we look at the "subterfuges" analytic philosophy (Wittgenstein, Quine, Davidson, Kripke) has believed to suffice for perambulating the triangle. We will see why the project of an analytic philosophy of language had to lapse into nominalism and why the realist impulses that initially drove it dissolved into a correlationalism of world and language. The reason lies in the presupposition of the world's facticity (in which language has no place) on the one hand and in the assumption that language is arbitrary (disconnected from the world) on the other. Quentin Meillassoux's concept of "factiality"—"*only facticity is not factual—viz.*, only the contingency of what is, is not itself contingent"[8]—help us to develop a realist ontology of language in which thinking, language, and world are not separate spheres that would exist independently of one another and enter into relation with one another as independent entities. At that point, we re-introduce the conception of a subject of semiosis, which we take from analytic philosophy and discuss in terms of Strawson's concept of individuals. Although it is initially but the bearer of a contradiction, the idea of a subject of semiosis has far-reaching consequences. The change of mind a subject undergoes in metanoia is and remains a change of meaning.

In the third chapter ("Speculation"), we take a look at the consequences that follow from our speculative ontology of language for a subject of knowledge. The point of contact between semiotic speculation and speculation in the philosophy of language is the realist insight that the knowledge we gain from semiotically obtainable part-to-whole relations attains a higher degree of reality than the knowledge we derive from our perception of things (and which exhausts itself in having to specify ever more precisely how exactly things and language correspond). We conceptualize a language-ontological triad that makes it possible to understand how lingual recursions are steeped in ontology and epistemology.

Next in our search for a procedure of knowledge that allows thinking to escape correlationalist reflexivity and speculatively to develop its relationship with the world, we encounter "abduction." The principle of this logical procedure of inference, first described by Peirce, is a methodical "othering" that will show us how thinking, by means of language, creates an object; how this object, by means of thinking, changes language; and how language, by means of the object, drives thinking forward. The subject does not remain external to this movement but is tied into it (as a cognizing, logical, and grammatical subject). In metanoia, the subject is even at the center of the movement. In radical forms of abduction, for example in what Umberto Eco describes as (meta-)abduction, we see the creation of a new paradigm that can only be attested to by the subject of knowledge. Its cognitive-ethical imperative is: "Follow your conclusions—become what you have speculated!"

The fourth chapter ("Cognition") critically discusses two approaches from the philosophy of consciousness to outline the cognitive aspects of metanoia: first Thomas Metzinger's theory of a recursive consciousness of the self and the world created for us by our brains, then Terrence Deacon's model of the semiotic labor of our brain.

The change of perspective imposed by metanoia leads to a theory of consciousness as that form of circular thought that creates an *I—here—now* origo. In Metzinger's theory of how consciousness produces the phenomenal world, the relationship between thinking and world is the following: in recursive loops, the permanent circle of personal, temporal, and spatial produces differential deictic information (on here & there, on I & you, on now & then). It is through externalizing the differences that result from continually comparing deictic information that we situate ourselves in the world.

Terrence Deacon's theory of the co-evolution of brain and language will help us to understand why it would be impossible for our brain to allow for access to the world if we did not acquire or construct triadic semiotic relations. Of central importance in this process is the interruption of dyadic (indexical) semiotic relations; an iconoclasm internal to the sign is the *sine qua non* of the development of both the brain and language. This explains why all kinds of correlationalism derive from an attempt to find that *one* perspective from which to understand the relationship between the world and thinking, thinking and language, language and the world and to "convert" these relations into unambiguous correlations.

The Epilogue ("Metanoia"), finally, attempts a phenomenological description of metanoia. Only at this point have we assembled all the conceptual tools to be able to argue on par with our experience. Only at this point is it possible to see why metanoia cannot be captured by aesthetic categories—what is at work in metanoia is the procedure by which thinking develops itself. Thinking grows, grows beyond itself, influences its preconditions, and creates new possibilities of thinking. We conceive of this self-affecting as a lingual one and we align it with the poetical to emphasize the necessity of a critique of language and the necessity of a poetics.

seeing   world

language world

world of language

thought

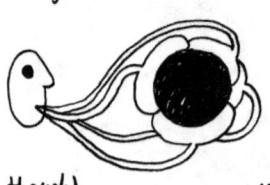

thought   world

Language unfolds our understanding of the world to the extend to which it develops itself.

I

Poetics

Principles of Lingual *Poiesis*

Please leave the concepts as you would like to find them.

Ph. Lathe

The poetic function of language (Jakobson)

Let us begin with the definition of poetry developed by the linguist and onetime futurist poet[1] Roman Jakobson: "The set (*Einstellung*) toward the MESSAGE as such, focus on the message for its own sake, is the POETIC function of language."[2] In the poetic use of language, the focus is on the message itself: either it draws attention to itself because something about it becomes conspicuous (a rhyme, say) or it foregrounds itself because it interrupts an otherwise continuous process of understanding ("I'm unable to pinpoint what this metaphor refers to").

Does this mean that we have to look for the poetic function of language in a refusal of or resistance to the "real" function of language? That would be in line with a modern model of poetry in which literary language has become autonomous and no longer wants to be a medium of communication. Using Marshall McLuhan's terms (and at the same time opposing the methodological implications of his thought) we could say that in the case of poetry—and only in the case of poetry—the medium is the message: language turns into its own metaphor.

For Jakobson, words in non-poetic language are chosen from a set of similar words and combined to form a sequence according to the principle of context (i.e. of contiguity). In a poetic sequence, in turn, linguistic elements are connected according to the principle of equivalence: "*The poetic function projects the principle of equivalence from the axis of selection into the axis of combination.* Equivalence is promoted to the constitutive device of the sequence. In poetry one syllable is equalized with any other syllable of the same sequence; word stress is assumed to equal word stress, as unstress equals unstress; prosodic long is matched with long, and short with short."[3] "Axis of selection" here is a synonym for the paradigmatic axis of language and "axis of combination" a synonym for the syntagmatic axis of speech. The principle of speech, then, is contiguity, the principle of language is equivalence.

Does this suffice to grasp how language functions in speech? Has Jakobson really succeeded in determining what the poetic function achieves *within* language? He thinks that an utterance is poetic to the extent to which the other functions of language are obscured by equivalences. Yet that only designates the characteristics of poetic language; it does not identify its function *for* language. In fact, the question of what this function consists in has not even been raised.

Metalanguage—metaphor—metonymy

The problem with Jakobson's definition of the poetic function of language is that its central determination makes the poetic function identical with the metalingual function: both are organized by equivalence. That is why Jakobson can only distinguish between the poetic and the metalingual function by way of their directionality: "in metalanguage the sequence is used to build an equation, whereas in poetry the equation is used to build a sequence." Jakobson's example for a metalingual equation is: "*Mare* is *the female of the horse.*" His example for how a poetic text employs similarities to build a sequence is the slogan from the 1952 presidential campaign, "I like Ike."[4]

In the definition of a mare as the female of the horse, the sentence serves no other purpose than to establish paradigmatic equality. In the case of the poetic text, however, we encounter similarities that serve to establish a sequence. On the one hand, therefore, the metalingual and the poetic function are diametrically opposed; on the other, they are similar in that they are both determined by the principle of equivalence. "Similarity in meaning connects the symbols of a metalanguage with the symbols of the language referred to.

Similarity connects a metaphorical term with the term for which it is substituted. Consequently, when constructing a metalanguage to interpret tropes, the researcher possesses more homogeneous means to handle metaphor, whereas metonymy, based on a different principle, easily defies interpretation. Therefore nothing comparable to the rich literature on metaphor can be cited for the theory of metonymy."[5]

But do we have such a good understanding of metaphors *because* they obey the principle of metalanguage? In that case, the mission of linguistics would have already been accomplished in rhetoric, and language would be thoroughly understood. Yet the problems we face in understanding language suggest that the truth of language has not yet been grasped. Do we not instead merely believe that we have understood the principle of language because metaphors speak to us with such immediacy? For it could well be that metaphors deceive us when they put on the airs of a master trope of language. Perhaps they only derive their power from acquiescing in the subordination of poetics to linguistics. And perhaps metonymy is much better positioned to explain the principle of language.

The potentializing function of language (Guillaume)

Morphogeny and ontogeny

Concurrently with Jakobson's investigations, Gustave Guillaume spent decades working in his seminars on a speculative linguistics that can also be called a *holistic* linguistics because Guillaume conceives of the potential and the actual as part of a single phenomenon.[6] Looking back, he said in 1956: "Like everyone else, I once spoke of the *morphology* and *ontology* of language. Now I prefer to say *morphogeny* and *ontogeny*."[7] This implies two things: First, Guillaume assumes that the being of language is founded on its grammar. Second, grammar is not to be conceived of as a fixed framework or definitive form. Just as language develops itself, so does grammar. We cannot, therefore, obtain a morphology of language without elaborating a morphogeny. The conclusion Guillaume draws from this is that language is to be described not in its (mere) being but only in its (constant) becoming, i.e. in its ontogeny, not its ontology.

It would certainly be wrong to situate the procedures and mechanisms of the development of language beyond language. While the reasons for the concrete development of a given language may well lie in an historical, constantly changing reality, this development can only unfold because language has a potentiality of its own that effects its constant adaptation.[8]

For Guillaume, *la langue* fulfills the function of language development. Speech actualizes two functions: on the one hand, it actualizes the structure of language, it actualizes itself as discourse, and it does so according to the rules of syntax. (There is an even simpler way to articulate the fact that speech actualizes the message: we speak to communicate.) Yet there are on the other hand additional aspects of Guillaume's language as process that necessarily accompanies the first[9]: speech [*tongue*] also has a potentializing function and, dynamically, it creates *la langue*. For Guillaume, *la langue* is a mental structure. It is not to be conceived of as an inner monologue, which, as the voice of thought, belongs to the three forms of speech (oral speech and writing being the other two). In Chomsky's terms, competence is more relevant to *la langue* than performance.

Every speech act serves not just a communicative function, nor does it merely actualize the paradigm or render it effective in some way. Speech also and at the same time has a potentializing function. This, in turn, creates a system of language, a second paradigm. The two paradigms encompass the virtuality and the potentiality of language. While language is given in its virtuality, the task of speech is to produce language in its potentiality. Every speech actualizes one paradigm and at the same time creates a new one.

Guillaume's concept of potentialization thus aims for a second paradigm that is not yet given. The virtual paradigm is actualized in speech. What about the potential paradigm? Is it *actualized* at all, even though it does not yet exist? Our argument here will rest on an overlap between tense and mode, time and possibility. The potential paradigm probably lies in the future of speech.

Aspect—Tense—Mode

It is not easy to conceive of how precisely the potential [*das Potentielle*] would lie in the future and yet form the basis of every speech act. Perhaps a sentence that expresses the course of time can illustrate the point: *The present was futural, is present*, and *will be past*. In this sentence, we can see how the futural aspects—once in the form of the adjective *futural*, once in the verbal form of the future tense—are distributed on either side of the present.

The relationship between potentiality and actuality in language has to be understood as a relation of language to its system, a relation structured by grammar. The relationship between potentiality and actuality can be characterized as a mode that becomes effective when it combines with tense. (Tense is a condition of mode like time is a condition of possibility.) Morphogenetically, the development of a tense in a given language always precedes the development of a mode (just as aspect in turn precedes the system of tenses). That is why potentiality can only be understood temporally. It is not already *given* prior to tense such that it would only need to be presentified. Mode is inextricably linked with the future tense. This means that the potentiality of language lies ahead of the actuality of speech in both temporal directions: it is both the possibility of a past and the possibility of a future, and it is closely tied to lingual *poiesis*.

The potentiality of language lies ahead of speech in both directions. This is the advantage of the concept *potentiality* over against the concept *paradigm*, which Noam Chomsky considers to be at our disposal as competence and performatively deployed in speech. Thus, the three relevant concepts are *competence—performance—potentiality*. We therefore do not have to look for an essence of language beyond speech (which would already virtually contain its possibilities of future development) but may instead presume a *poietic* principle immanent in language.

Actualization—potentialization—modalization

With regard to our later reflections, we have to note one more thing that points beyond Guillaume. To explain how the potentiality of language expresses itself in its development, we have to know how it affects paradigms. We have to be able to say how the futural (i.e. potential) paradigm affects the paradigm that is given. Evidently, the given paradigm thus changes and becomes a past paradigm.

But this temporal moment does not suffice as an explanation. It is hard to believe that a potential and futural paradigmatic element emerging in speech is simply archived and that it institutes a past simply by virtue of being archived. Nor can we presume that potentiality is actualized within the paradigms of language. The temporalization of language—and this also refers to its history—cannot simply be undone. Is it not the case, even, that the modality of language follows from its temporalization? We therefore call *modalization* the return of the potential paradigm of language to the paradigm already given. What this means is that the recursion we witness here is not just a temporal recursion but also, precisely, a modal one.

Inscribing modality into the paradigms of language amounts to no longer seeing the paradigm simply as given. Nor is the paradigm strictly identical to itself. In view of its variability and historicity, we can call it *plastic*. Such plasticity, to be sure, cannot simply emerge by inscribing something in the paradigm or by adding to it. Plasticity changes the paradigm *as such*. The paradoxes of a temporal order that come with this (the origin of time in the future, its home in possibility) have left their imprint in the history of literature and determine the development of language. Paradigmatics, potentiality, and plasticity unite in language; their combination allows language to develop itself.

Contiguity—metonymy—recursion

The relation of speech to paradigmatics did not go unnoticed by Jakobson. Yet the poetic function he describes only amounts to speech referring to an existing (virtual) paradigm by way of the poetic function. In this description, there is no space for the (potential) paradigm that *emerges* in speech in the first place.

But how can we think such a *poietic* function of speech? What are the procedures by which speech acts on the paradigm? First of all, this takes place by establishing coherence: the contiguity of speech is transformed into coherence. This is achieved thanks to a principle that connects lingual levels, namely the production of relations between parts and wholes. This principle is the principle of metonymy, the rhetorical figure that produces relations between parts and a whole.

In the construction of a sequence, the metonymic principle ensures continual selfconnection (i.e. the continuability of speech). The figure of metonymy unifies the two tasks of potentializing speech. It follows the principle of contiguity, thereby establishing a connection, and it translates this context into a synecdochal relation between part and whole. We conceive of the relation that emerges from this inclusion of parts in wholes as *recursion* and distinguish it from *reflexivity*. While *reflexivity* designates the metaphorical poetic self-reference of language, which is based on equivalence, we reserve the term *recursion* for its metonymic *poietic* self-reference, which is based on the production of part-to-whole relations.

Jakobson himself notes that such part-to-whole relations also connect the various levels of language. Recursion, therefore, not only allows for the emergence of a sequence from the organization of parts, which it relates to parts already organized; it also organizes these emerging contexts as parts in the context of a whole of language. Because it integrates sequences into higher-level lingual wholes, the metonymic principle also contains a moment that points beyond itself and creates paradigms. This moment, nonetheless, remains tied to the whole of language through metonymic part-to-whole relations.

Evolution

The *poietic* principle of language can be found at the origins of language and does not dissipate in the course of its history. Its significance is neither merely archaic nor simply historical. Indeed, the *poietic* function is the motor of the ongoing development of language. Without it, language would not be language.

In their 1928 structural manifesto, "Problems in the Study of Literature and Language,"[10] Jakobson and Yuri Tynyanov sketch the interweaving of diachrony and synchrony in reflections on language and the reciprocal dependence of system and evolution as a methodological perspective: every system presents itself as an evolution, and every evolution has systematic character. But this methodological perspective has not yet been cashed out.

In linguistics Gustave Guillaume has, as we've seen, made some suggestions for such a model that would frame the *poietic* principle in more precise terms. In order to establish a reference to reality that is able to adapt to historical change, language needs a development tool. This tool is the *poietic* principle. The effects of the emergence of a world of language are not just confined to the language experiments of the literary avant-garde. On the contrary: what we may call the onto-genetic realism content of language ensures that there is also something experimental in everyday speech.

When we say that language owes its evolution to a 'tool' that allows it to deal with reality in a consistently experimental way, we do not mean that language is merely a box of tools we make use of (better) to deal with reality. It makes a difference on which side of an actual speech act we situate the system: either in the past (as a toolbox), in which case it is only possible to speak of a poetic self-reflexivity of language, or in the future (as tool-making), in which case a *poietic* creation of language, and reference is also conceivable. Language, to continue the metaphor, does indeed provide us with tools. As speakers of a language, we indeed participate in the construction of new tools, a construction that can only take place through speaking, which allows a new paradigm to emerge. But we cannot use language to construct new tools at will. "Linguist-engineers," in Guillaume's somewhat polemical formulation, "do not exist, nor does a science for constructing language."[11]

It is essential to language that it unfolds, which implies its ability to adapt to new conditions. This, however, is neither an automatic process nor does language enclose itself. The relation or reference of language lets new relations to reality emerge—simply because language, in referring to itself, turns to itself as referring to reality—and provides for the production of new references. Just as self-reference is not to be understood as *art pour l'art* or a self-enjoyment immanent in language, lingual realism is not to be conceived of as a regression to the idea of a naive similarity of language and world. Language potentially refers also (but never exclusively) to itself and potentially refers also (but never exclusively) to the world. It is neither reducible to one of these poles nor does it get caught up in an infinite regress: in language, self-reference can only take place through recursion. It is precisely the most extreme of experiments undertaken by the avant-garde—as for example Gertrud Stein's famous line "Rose is a rose is a rose is a rose"—that demonstrate (as we will see) that natural language, because it is *recursive*, excludes such an infinite regress, such a vicious circle. A realist philosophy of language will therefore base itself on recursion as a lingual universal.[12]

Chomsky first described *recursivity* in the context of his universal grammar as a characteristic of syntax. More recently, the Munich linguist Elisabeth Leiss has attributed a more comprehensive function to recursion—the function of instituting reference—and emphasized its epistemological potential: "Language is then no longer a tool of expression that materializes thoughts. It is the interface that mediates between the world and our unfinished thoughts.... Thoughts, therefore, do not precede language, they are the result of recursive operations and perhaps of other universal lingual operations as well."[13]

In order to be able to develop and change its own shape at all, language has to recursively refer to itself. Self-reference does not come with a reflexive isolation of language from a world that would remain external to language (an isolation that would allow language to come into its own and that would allow poetic speech, according to the model of autonomy mentioned above, to emerge); instead, it serves the self-regulation of the development of language—neither reference to the world (or its objects) nor adaptation to the world is possible without self-reference. That is why from an evolutionary perspective, the opposition of reference and self-reference is merely an apparent opposition: there is no barrier between the domain of language and the domain of objects. Language refers to facts (which thereby become real objects in language) in the same poetic/*poietic* way in which it refers to itself, namely as a system of facts that exist in reality. Reference and *poiesis* cannot be had independently of one another.

Poietic linguistics

Guillaume and Jakobson

Let's recall the two tendencies of what happens in language according to Guillaume, which are "the tendency to potentialize which gives rise to tongue, and the tendency to actualize which gives rise to discourse."[14] In speech, the site of all lingual events, the actualizing and the potentializing tendencies are at work simultaneously. What is crucial for our purposes here is the process within speech that determines the construction of mental language *(la langue)*.

"In its totality, *la langue* is a vast construct, built according to a general law: the coherence of the parts within the whole."[15] Let us read this definition with a view to Jakobson and compare the description of language in its *poetic* function with the description of language in its *poietic* function. Both are possible only thanks to the double structure of speech, in which the actualizing function (which refers) and the potentializing function (which concerns language construction) are at work simultaneously. In the poetic function Jakobson, however, only perceives its reflexivity: in its poetic function, he holds, language reflects on itself and thereby brings out its self-referentiality.

What is *not* brought out in this reflexive determination is the *poietic* moment that creates lingual structures in the first place. Polemically, we might say that the function Jakobson conceptualizes is not a *poetic* function. Its fixation on the *perception* of relations of similarity makes it an *aesthetic* function. Perhaps this is the point we're looking for, the point at which Jakobson's fixation on aesthetics leads him astray, for a dominance of the poetic function of language in speech does not have to be understood as language turning its back on its referential function. The poetic function cannot be separated from the *poietic* function. That is why, from now on, we will use the term *poetic function* in this comprehensive sense that includes *poiesis*. (The same goes for the concept *poetics*.)

A look at language's turn back to itself, often invoked in discussions of modernism, clarifies the difference between our approach, inspired by Guillaume, and Jakobson's: in contrast to the reflexivity favored by Jakobson, the recursive structures of language are not non-referential but productive. Language creates its organism by means of recursions, by means of the recursivity inscribed in it.

Recursions thus create a whole. But this immediately raises the question of how language can be built from the part-to-whole relations thus created. We suggest that an explanation can be given by taking recourse to the operations of *selection* and *combination*, understanding *selection* to be the selection of parts from a whole and *combination* to be the integration of parts into wholes.

We may interpret the metalinguality of speech not just on the basis of relations of equivalence but also by starting with part-to-whole relations and all of their moments. As we suspected, this means to approach metalinguality from the direction of metonymy, not that of metaphor. The poetic function of language is a function that creates paradigms. The more the potentializing function dominates in speech over the actualizing function, the more clearly the paradigms of language itself, its virtuality and potentiality, are brought out. We also suspect that what makes metanoia possible is a *poietic* moment, which opens up a truth. In metanoia, the potentializing function of poetic speech dominates to such an extent that not only is a new paradigm opened up and established, this new paradigm also completely obscures the current paradigm or even replaces it; in any case it changes it fundamentally.

Jakobson reads Peirce

At the end of his linguistic career, Jakobson converted from a linguistics based on Saussure to one based on Peirce. The important aspects of this conversion once more have to do with questions of cognition and the systematic construction of a conception of language that turns against the modern dogma of the arbitrariness of language. The central point is the discovery of the triad of the semiotic elements *object*, *sign*, and *interpretant*. Relations between part(s) and whole are only possible in a model that contains more than two elements, more than two semiotic conceptions thought differentially.[16]

Parts-to-whole relations must consist of at least three members: a part, a counter-part and a third member. Only this third creates the whole in recursion to the first part. Reading the triadic parts-to-whole relation exclusively in terms of the oppositional relationship between a part and its counterpart necessarily loses sight of the fact that an oppositional relationship can only exist within a whole. Without the relation to the whole, an opposition could not appear as an opposition, it could not even appear as an incoherence—because *coherence* is just another word for *whole*.

To illustrate this point, imagine two arbitrary things, a moth, say, and a tree. Can we make a connection? Nothing easier, we can name an infinity of connections. Take just these four examples: (1) Both of these things, such as we imagine them, are material. Furthermore, (2) both the moth and tree are organisms. We can also establish (3) a connection between two ideas, that of a moth and that of a tree. And we can say that (4) *moth* and *tree* are two words in the English language. Now: which answer is correct?

Of course we cannot say which of the connections or contexts we can name provides the correct answer, once and for all—there is not just one possible correct answer. Yet whatever answer we do give, we always take one of the elements to be a part and the other to be its opposite. When we take the moth to be a part, we take the tree to be not-moth; when we start with the tree, we treat the moth as not-tree—and in each case, we treat the part as relating to a different totality, the totality of material objects, of organisms, of ideas, or of words in English.[17] To speak of part and counterpart (or opposite) only makes (!) sense within this triadic constellation. When, however, we absolutize this way of speaking and turn it into an opposition by 'forgetting' the third element, the totality—when we conceive of part and counterpart as a simple dyad by declaring *tree* to be the part and *moth* to be the counterpart *per se* and when we believe this *identifies moth* as *not-tree*—and then repeat the same operation with the elements *tree* and *rose*, we note, to our astonishment, that both *rose* and *moth* have become *not-tree*. Are we thus not allowed to distinguish between *rose* and *moth*? Are we deluding ourselves when we believe there to be such a distinction? Does it perhaps not exist in reality?

This confronts us with another general difficulty with dyadic relations. When we pick up again on a dyad, this repetition immediately leads to the ambiguities of irony and to a multitude of paradoxes (which have been exploited ever since Romanticism). In the end, oppositional relations are not potentializable. This, however, is precisely what part-to-whole relations achieve in the service of the complexity of the lingual whole: they can be introduced into one another without creating—as is the case in relation to opposition—a never-ending reciprocal reference that produces the "bad infinity" of metareflexivity. When, however, we introduce the element *rose* into the part-to-whole relation that initially consisted only of the parts *tree* and *moth*, then this new element simply becomes one further element of the totality *material things, organisms, ideas,* or *words in English* that previously only referred to *moth* and *tree*. Accordingly, the element *stone* becomes a further element of the totality *material things, ideas,* or *words in English* but not a further element of the totality *organisms*.

Leiss reads Jakobson

Jakobson's reflections on recursivity and on part-to-whole relations open up for linguistics the perspective of a universal grammar that could serve to develop a realist theory of language.[18] This is where Elisabeth Leiss picks up the thread in her reading of Jakobson's less well known later work, which leads her to a comprehensive description of language construction by means of part-to-whole relations—those relations in which we situate the potentiality of language: "Part-to-whole relations define lexical as well as grammatical semantics. In the mental lexicon, they organize the character-content of meanings in various gradations. In grammar, they are responsible for structuring the flow of sounds (or of material expression generally). The serialization or succession in time and space is separated into units that stand in relations of inclusion with one another: phonemes are parts of morphemes; morphemes are parts of words, words are parts of constituents (phrases), which in turn form the building blocks of sentences. Both grammatical semantics and lexical semantics are thus characterized throughout by a mereological structuring that takes on a different quality in each case."[19]

Language creates its systematicity through the recurrent introduction of part-to-whole relations. In repeated recursion, a systematics of systems emerges. Through repeated recursion, the system of language becomes increasingly complex. At the same time, it increases its opportunities for reference. The operation of recursion itself is material (i.e. metonymic and immanent). Language is a part of the world to which it refers itself. "We only reach the position of a realist theory of language when language not only optimizes human cognition but when it does so in such a way that human cognition does not take place independently of the object to be cognized."[20]

Within the framework of a realist theory of language, it must therefore also be possible to write a poetics of thought. We would like to underscore the poetic-*poietic* (i.e. a disclosing function of thought that lets things pass from non-being to being and crosses an ontological threshold). We would like to emphasize this dimension against the reflexive dimension of thought, suggested, for example, by the term *knowledge* (knowledge of the sensible perceived) or against the abstract and explanatory dimensions of thought often implied by the term *consciousness*; we favor the plastic qualities of thought, to form and to be formed through *poiesis*. This emphasis is marked by the term *noiesis*.

We are not yet in a position to determine the place of *noiesis* in a realist theory of language. But there is at least one fundamental relation of thought, language, and world that we *do* know about: knowledge is not independent of its object, thoughts do not precede language, meanings are not to be found *a priori* either in language or in thought. None of these relations can be summed up in equivalences.

This leads us to a paradox that raises a question fundamental for a theory of metanoia: to say that in a metanoia, the world changes, is that not merely to say that metanoia creates a world, a "new world" that replaces the "old world"? Is the principle of metanoia thus an arbitrarily chosen name for what we could also call "imagination"? This also brings us to a central point in the systematic development of a "speculative lingual realism." This seems to imply a self-contradiction. How is it possible to claim both a cognitive functionalism and a lingual realism? Such a concept of language—speculative and realist at the same time—only appears paradoxical if we accept the assumption that language is fundamentally arbitrary.

The myth of the arbitrariness of the sign

The opposition between a realist and a nominalist theory of language is particularly stark on the question of whether lingual signs are arbitrary. The common view is that language can only be understood on the basis of its arbitrariness. This is one of the dogmas of modern linguistics; without it, modern theories of language cannot be maintained. An overview of the many parallel arguments in its favor, however, reveals a number of inconsistencies. What becomes clear is that the principle of arbitrariness is itself an "arbitrary principle," a point already made by Roman Jakobson: "It is not at all arbitrary but rather obligatory to say *fromage* for 'cheese' in French, and to say *cheese* in English."[21]

A pragmatic theory of language that assumes the conventionality of the sign, for example, contradicts the thesis of the arbitrariness of the sign: arbitrariness and contractually guaranteed conventionality are mutually exclusive. The question of the arbitrariness of signs shifts and becomes the question of the arbitrariness of conventions. There is a similar problem with theories of correspondence in which signs are assigned their meaning by definitions. As soon as these definitions apply, the use of the sign is defined by the definition, and the question shifts to become the question of the arbitrariness of definitions. What is even more important is that it remains unclear which of the various semiotic relations are to be seen as arbitrary. Is it the relation between expression (signifier) and meaning (signified) or the relation between the form of the sign (signifier) and the object the sign addresses (referent)? Or are both arbitrary, perhaps even for the same reasons? Would the difference, then, merely lie in whether arbitrariness is situated between signifier and referent or between signifier and signified?[22]

De-arbitrarization

We will return to the arbitrariness thesis, but before we do, we would like to establish the concepts we use to avoid such arbitrary designations. Since language is systematically constructed from part-to-whole relations, we can designate it as *contiguous*; since the construction of language is determined by recursive relations, language can be described more precisely as *contingent*; the noietic function of language, finally, suggests that meanings are not to be conceived of as arbitrary but—insofar as they speculatively shape our thoughts—as *plastic*.

What obstacles does the fixation on the arbitrariness of language put in the way of thinking about metanoia? They consist mainly in a particular understanding of language as a practice. This applies even to highly elaborate theories of use such as Wittgenstein's: "The *meaning of a word* is its use in the language."[23] In assuming that use as such institutes meaning, theories of use once more enclose language in a nominalist immanence. They reduce all material acts in which speaking (thinking or writing) takes place to the fact that it is in material acts that this speaking takes place. In other words, they declare speaking to be a tautology and deny that there is anything contingent about speaking. The correct use of language would thus already be a use of language; it would make no sense to speak of language deviating from use. In this way, these theories produce not only a concept of language in which language is arbitrary—they also produce an arbitrary language. For such a theory of language produces—in Wittgenstein's terms and against him—propositions thanks to which those who understand them enter into language in order to then—when they have understood that propositions may produce nonsense as well—forget that the ladder they used had itself been produced.

A theory of language, aware of its ontological foundation, must not reduce language to a tool devoid of meaning, nor must it lose sight of the question of how language is connected to reality. The focus, therefore, must be on the potentializing function of language. The object of such a theory of language is the speculative threshold crossed by lingual *poiesis*: the threshold from reference to the referent.

A use theory of language cannot but deny that lingual creations *are* meaningful (and are not merely assigned meaning *ad hoc*). This denial ontologically reduces meaning to its instrumental function: meaning is not produced but is exhausted in its use—and since it changes according to how use changes, it cannot, from this perspective, but be arbitrary. (Such an assessment, incidentally, concerns not only meaning, which is the object of interpretation, but also fiction, which is easily misunderstood as a non-referential, intentionally arbitrary lingual creation.) To the extent that pragmatist theories of use deny existence to the products of lingual *poiesis* (such as fiction and meaning) they deprive them of any dynamic of their own.

The freedom of the sign

The preoccupation of linguistics with theories of arbitrariness can be abolished in a theory of meaning that describes language as a system of part-to-whole relations that recursively modifies itself. We will show how to go about this in a detailed discussion of the dimension of *Thirdness*. We consider talk of arbitrariness to lack foundation and thereby situate our discourse beyond modern debates in the theory of language. Throughout language, we find what could be indications of arbitrariness. Here are four of them.

(1) *The difference between acoustic language and the image* The way we are equipped anthropologically, hearing finds in the the mouth an organ to complement the ears. The acoustic material of language can be resolved completely into recursive part-to-whole relations. Nonetheless, our cognitive concepts of world and things are framed cross-modally: we make use of the difference between haptics and optics to construct our perception of space just as we use the asynchrony of hearing and seeing to constitute our ideas of time. Yet the power of non-acoustic data to inscribe themselves in language is limited; optical information (e.g. color, size, shape) hardly participates in shaping lingual signifiers.

(2) *The difference between thought and speech* For Guillaume, one of the problems of psychosemiology is that "an idea cannot invent a suitable sign for itself, but can look in the already existing semiology for a sign that might be transferred to it; because the sign has not been made specifically for the idea, it becomes suitable to it only by losing its former suitability. This is the way things develop. This is why the linguistic sign is arbitrary. Inventing it entails a loss of suitability: the new suitability is based on this loss."[24]

(3) *The iconoclasm internal to the sign* To construct triadic semiotic relations from dyadic ones, the dyadic relations have to be negated. We would like to think of this negation internal to the sign (whose emergence we'll examine in more detail in our discussion of Terrence Deacon) as iconoclastic. Such an iconoclasm internal to the sign is not just a generic necessity; in our view, the possibility that semiotic relations can be interrupted is both a condition of semantic innovation and a necessary tool for undoing the paradoxicality of relationships.

(4) *The openness of the cognitive horizon* The opening up of a new truth, which takes place in every *poiesis*, implies an openness of knowledge. This also presupposes a minimum of freedom for the sign. The experimental formation of concepts that a speculative poetics seeks to develop requires significations (i.e. denominations) that are not just found or reactivated but have also to be invented in creative procedures of inference.

In all these cases, it is possible to demonstrate, as we will see, that language is able to live up to what is demanded of it not because of its alleged arbitrariness but because of the contingency that results from the recursivity of language. Only this contingency allows for the sign's own dynamic, which, as we said, is necessary for *poiesis*. We would love to follow Daniel Charm's unrestrained courageous listing of the facets of meaning, "there are four *functional* meanings and a *fifth essential* meaning," and follow him all the way to the last, essential meaning of objects: "The fifth meaning is—the free will of the object."[25] A speculative poetics insists on the sign's fundamental freedom. It lets the creation of language exit from a given (virtual) context and makes a moment of innovation possible.

Can we find the point at which the lingual structure develops? Combining Jakobson and Guillaume, we consider the poetic function of language to be the function of a genesis of language in speech. What we need to describe the ontogenesis of language, therefore, is a theory of language centered on poetics. A poetics that does not simply overlook and ignore *poiesis* is not (just) a theory of how literary texts are produced or understood. It also asks about the poetic function of language (in the fullest sense of the word).

Speculative poetics

Knowing—experimenting—inventing

In everyday use, *poetics* designates an academic discipline. Its objects are literary works or the rules they are based on. This establishes the universe of literature by delimiting it from normal everyday speech. The kind of poetics we're looking for, however, aims for the poetic function of language as a whole, which is particularly salient in literary texts.

Once again, it is Jakobson who pinpointed this connection: "Any attempt to reduce the sphere of poetic function to poetry or to confine poetry to poetic function would be a delusive oversimplification. Poetic function is not the sole function of verbal art but only its dominant, determining function, whereas in all other verbal activities it acts as a subsidiary, accessory constituent."[26]

Up to this point, we could not agree more. Yet his focus on the aesthetic (instead of the poetic) function of language—"This function, by promoting the palpability of signs, deepens the fundamental dichotomy of signs and objects"—leads him to draw a conclusion different from ours: "Hence, when dealing with the poetic function, linguistics cannot limit itself to the field of poetry."[27]

We are not the first to cast doubt on Jakobson's definition of poetics as a subfield of linguistics. Yuri Lotman already thought "that artistic language is not a part of natural, i.e. colloquial language but colloquial language is a part of artistic language and that to understand the phenomenon of language, one has to understand art."[28] This aims at more than just an inversion of the hierarchy of poetics and linguistics: it implies that only poetics can give us insight into a truth that poetic creation opens up in language.

In lingual *poiesis* we witness the materialization of what Giorgio Agamben has described as the distinctive characteristic of the poetic: "The central experience of *poiesis*, production into presence ... the essence of the work—the fact that in it something passed from nonbeing into being, thus opening the space of truth (ἀ-λήθεια)."[29] Agamben traces how, historically, the poetic function (and that of literature, too) has increasingly disappeared. But we are less interested in this story of decay, which sets in as early as antiquity; we are interested in a contemporary or modern disposition: under the auspices of aesthetic literary criticism, the poetic moment of language has become invisible.

Ever since the advent of structuralism, literature has been reduced to the oppositional principles of poetry and prose. In its *totality*, however, it displays a common poetic—*poietic* function; it is precisely this function *for* language that we miss in Jakobson. It consists, *qua poiesis*, in instituting reference. This happens both in phonetic and syntactic shifts (which are characteristic of poetry) and in deictic shifts (which take place in fictional prose).

Poetry drives the realism of language just as much as fictional prose, both in terms of adaptation to the world that is to be designated and in our knowledge of language. Put differently: in shifting the references that always already exist, literary language produces new references and thus discloses the ontogenetic potential of language (or the potentializing function inherent in it) in a particularly clear way. A comprehensive reference of poetics to grammar not only restores wholeness to the concept of literature but to language as well.

Language is not merely a medium of knowledge of the world. Fitting as the metaphor of language as an interface of our relation to the world might be, it would be misleading to understand it the way a philosophy of media would (i.e. to see it as standing *between* our thoughts and the world). A poetics that is able to live up to this insight can only be thought as poetic speculation. It includes finding new rules for binding together parts that are already available. It also includes the production of new dominants from already existing relations by manipulating part-to-whole relations, in which parts that are dominants in a particular system are systematically interpreted as details of another system. One example of this procedure is what we call "switching cards."

Literature at large

Up until now, academic poetics has not asked what place the subject has in poetics or what relations the subject entertains with its objects. This suggests that the subjects of knowledge are to be found outside the field of poetics. For a speculative poetics, however, the positions of the subjects and objects of knowledge are fundamentally different. This comes with a change, not only in the object of knowledge but also in the relationship between object and subject: in a speculative poetics, as we will see, the positions of subjects and objects change.

One such othering concerns our approach to what we understand as literature and it concerns *that which* we understand as literature. A speculative poetics as we imagine it is concerned with *literature at large*, a literature *released*. The epistemic mission of literature is to develop language, which already implies an experimental approach, namely one that aims at *knowing literature* (i.e. knowing what literature is as well as the knowledge of the functioning of language generally that becomes effective thanks to and in literature). Our emphatic concept of (poetic) literature conceives of it as genesis of language. Poetics is the laboratory of lingual *poiesis* and literature furnishes us with lab reports of a becoming that would otherwise remain invisible. Opening up a poetic truth does not leave the subject unchanged; the object or the literary text also has to change in this change of perspectives.

A speculative poetics experiments with the scene of knowledge itself; in speculative poetics, knowledge appears as a constellation of subject, object, and other. In this constellation, the other has characteristics similar to those of the *interpretant* in Peirce's semiotics: on the one hand, it repeats the already existing constellation of subject and object (and even their opposition), on the other hand and at the same time, a new procedure of gaining knowledge appears in this triadic constellation. This procedure allows for an othering of the object of knowledge without exposing it to arbitrariness. Including such a procedure in the scene of knowledge is the precondition for knowing objects that have to be conceived of as constantly changing and can only be thought—and this is essential—as independent of us: in metanoia, as a radical cognitive shift, the subject of knowledge grasps itself in its changing—and thus also the world that surrounds it. This is the direction in which we have to keep thinking.

until the rose is really red although red does not occur

$\overbrace{}^{\text{redundance}}$
$\overbrace{}^{\text{tautology}}$
$\overbrace{}^{\text{meaning}}$

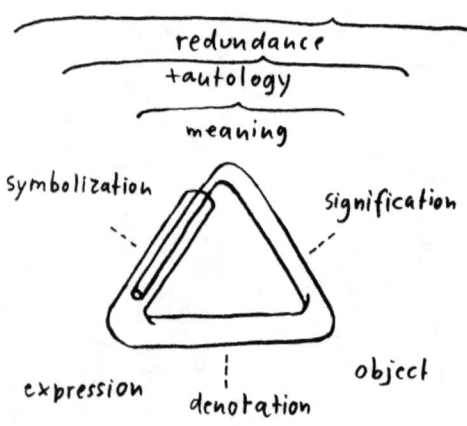

symbolization · signification

expression · denotation · object

Language changes the world

II

The Analytic Circle

The Lingual Creation of a True World

Sag zum Stück Holz: Du bist holzartig! Das ist gut, doch ist das wirklich schon Holzkritik?

Sag zum Stück Holz: Du bist dingartig! Auch das ist gut, doch wohl noch nicht Dingkritik.

Sag zum Stück Holz: Du bist wortartig! Das ist richtig gut! Nun fang mit Lyrik an, schau nicht zurück und bau dir das Stück! Das Paßstück—das nämlich ist das Glück!

Tell the piece of wood: You're wood-like! That's good, but is it a critique of wood?

Tell the piece of wood: You're thing-like! That, too, is good, but it's not a critique of things, is it?

Tell the piece of wood: You're word-like! That's really good! Now begin to write poetry, don't look back and build that piece! The piece that fits—for that's where happiness lies![1]

Ulf Stolterfoht

Hermeneutics and deconstruction

One of the most incisive debates in the history of twentieth-century theory was triggered by questions of sense and representation and caused two traditions in continental philosophy to clash. The debate between representatives of German hermeneutics and the French tradition—namely between Hans-Georg Gadamer and Jacques Derrida—and its focus on the fundamental question of meaning and understanding has occupied an entire field.

The concrete trigger for the debate between the two philosophers was the question of how literary or philosophical works are to be read. How are we to evaluate the interpretations that readers develop in the course of their reading? What role does understanding play in this? Here, we simply propose to highlight those aspects of the debate that have promoted knowledge of what would best be called *poetic meaning*. (We take its particularity to lie in the shifting or institution of meaning operated by *poiesis*.) In this context, we would like to emphasize the concept of the hermeneutic circle, which corresponds to our approach to the *formation* of meaning as the recursive production of part-to-whole relations.

The question of what the totality of a text would be was decisive in the debate between Gadamer and Derrida. "Since interpretation is necessarily ongoing, consisting of successive readings," Karin Littau writes, "Gadamer's 'inexhaustibility' principle presents the multiplicity of meaning *within* the horizon of possible understanding, and 'anticipates' therefore that 'the whole truth' of a text will eventually be revealed. For Gadamer, the truth of the text is 'whole,' therefore, towards and within which the multiplicity of *interpretations* must be oriented insofar as these are interpretations *of* that text."[2] Reading, too, can therefore be understood as the production of a part-to-whole relation. The process described by the hermeneutic circle clarifies the effect of a mental forerunning to the wholeness of a text. Yet this totality is to be produced in the first place: in the reading process, loosely assembled elements of a text are connected recursively; this continued recursion turns them into parts of an inexhaustible whole.

The hermeneutic circle

Why is this process often described as a circle? On the level of the text, we are dealing with the same recursive structures that serve to form sense or institute meaning on the grammar and vocabulary level. The only point of contention is what is meant by meaning. Hermeneutics conceives of meaning as the unified and individual meaning of a work. In our view, however, part-to-whole relations do not institute a noncontradictory unit, nor do they presuppose it.

When we read a text by recursively relating its parts to a whole, we always understand something; that, however, is not necessarily an understanding of the text as a work (of art), nor does it have to imply an appreciation of its uniqueness.

Hermeneutic reading is fooling itself when it believes the wholeness it has found—when the parts of a text begin to form a whole through repeated recursion to the text as a whole—is the wholeness of the text and when it takes its task to lie in actualizing this wholeness. Instead, this is already an effect of the metonymic, potentializing process of lingual poiesis. *Poietic* reading does not consist in filling in textual gaps or uncertainties but systematically produces symbolic semiotic relations or wholenesses. It is quite possible to free the hermeneutic circle from such misunderstandings.

Parts and whole form a relation without which neither the parts nor the whole would exist. This essential moment can be expressed as follows: the circle describes how relations emerge from the insertion of ever-new parts into a whole, an insertion that takes place as recursion in reading. As soon as we know of the existence of this whole, it acts as if it had determined the order of the parts beforehand, as if these parts had (in the process of reading) been combined in view of the already-given whole. As we see it, however, such a synchronization of before and after is not necessary; something changes with the emergence of a *relation* between parts and whole. This change, without which metanoia is unthinkable, incorporates everything that succeeds it as well as everything that precedes it. Our (in Deleuzian terms) *disjunctive synthesis* of hermeneutics and deconstruction can be described as follows: the movement that never obtains sense as a unity can never exhaust sense as a resource.

In hermeneutics, the concept *horizon* indicates the inexhaustibility of the wholeness of the text. As long as we understand the hermeneutic fusing of the horizons of the reader and the text to mean that the reader enters the world of the text to fill phenomenal gaps with elements taken from his world, reading serves the text. Every reading and every interpretation then works toward 'charging' the work with new facets of meaning that increase its wealth of sense and further the impossibility of exhaustive interpretation. Metanoia, however, demands a reversal of perspectives that makes it possible to see how language is capable of moving the world into a new semiotic constellation.

We have already said that the *poetic* function of literature is not a reflexive operation. It is not a mere turning of language toward itself. It is a recursive operation that crosses an ontological threshold. The same holds for the ontological foundation of the hermeneutic figures that allow us to further clarify our notions both of recursion and the circle. "This circle of understanding," Martin Heidegger writes, "is not an orbit in which any random kind of knowledge may move; it is the expression of the existential *fore-structure* of Dasein itself. It is not to be reduced to the level of a vicious circle, or even of a circle which is merely tolerated. In the circle is hidden a positive possibility of the most primordial kind of knowing. To be sure, we genuinely take hold of this possibility only when, in our interpretation, we have understood that our first, last, and constant task is never to allow our fore-having, fore-sight, and fore-conception to be presented to us by fancies and popular conceptions, but rather to make the scientific theme secure by working out these fore-structures in terms of the things themselves."[3]

Reflecting on the circle and on its interpretation by Heidegger adds three components to our understanding of recursion. First, then, Heidegger's description of the circle provides an instrument for a more precise description of the status of the products of recursive operations (i.e. of *poiesis*). The circular structure to which these products owe their unremitting productivity turns them into "existentiales" (i.e. objects intuition gives to itself).

The second essential moment consists in an agency or subject structure of Being constituting itself in the circle: "An entity for which, as Being-in-the-world, its Being is itself an issue, has, ontologically, a circular structure."[4] The third moment concerns the question of temporality, which we already touched on in our discussion of recursive structures.

What kind of temporality does a determination of objects as existentiales imply and what kind of temporality does a determination of subjects as understanding Being imply? Both—subject and object—stand in a temporal relationship to one another: the subject's relation to time becomes objective in Being, an object's relation to time endows the object with an existential character. Bound together and merging with one another, subject and object form a circle that stands in relation to a structure of meaning: "The 'circle' in understanding belongs to the structure of meaning."[5]

Determination of the circle in terms of tense-philosophy

All three moments can be recuperated by a philosophy of tense (i.e. by taking recourse to temporality as it is grammatically inscribed in all language). The temporality of the circle is neither a cyclical nor a postmodern metaphor of the future perfect. Nor does it suffice to think of it formally as always already having been. The paradox we're interested in (and without which there could be neither *poiesis* nor metanoia) is this: *what comes before will be different afterward*. Time enters the horizon of the event. This means that it is not to be conceived of as a series of points of time that form a chain and thus constitute a progression.

Understanding, however, is not only characterized by its actually changing reality (or by its finding the past "behind" it to be changed). We also see in understanding a strong temporality that is neither a continual progression nor an uninterrupted chronological succession. It results from the structures of language themselves and can be derived from them. As the temporality that institutes the circle is created by (recursive) lingual relations, we may also call this *lingual temporality*.[6]

Shadowboxing of deconstruction and hermeneutics

Given the productivity of the circle, Paul de Man's criticism of the idea that parts of text could come together in a "unity of sense" becomes obvious. In the whole that they form, paradoxical relations emerge in which the actualization of a moment of sense declares its complement to be impossible without being able to eradicate it. We take this insight from deconstruction seriously: in every whole, difference is maintained. The institution of sense through a circle inaugurates an inexhaustible difference of sense. In a part-to-whole relation without unity, individual parts are always lost, separated (as details), supplemented or doubled.

The usual juxtaposition of a hermeneutic thought of unity and a critical thought of difference ignores the achievements of both approaches. On the one hand, it ignores that in the *formation of the circle*, hermeneutics has described a central procedure of the production of sense in which difference (we could also say: contingency of sense) emerges in the first place. On the other hand, deconstruction is wrongly accused of being arbitrary. In fact, it brings out a unified (we could also say necessary) principle.

The reproach, voiced in German literary criticism in particular, that deconstruction embraces an arbitrariness of interpretation is thus based on a misunderstanding. In *différance*, deconstruction has a very rigorous figure (of thought) to guide it.

The extent to which this figure has become a rigorous methodological standard can be seen in the similarities displayed by deconstructive readings of the most variegated of works. These readings uncover a very specific structure of all (literary) texts, which is why deconstruction can rightly claim *différance* to be a universally valid concept. The reproach that such readings do not do justice to the uniqueness of literary works comes up short against the systematic way in which deconstructive aspects can be found in every literary text's construction of sense.

Drifting of sense and sliding of the signifier

"'Signifier of the signifier' describes ... the movement of language: in its origin, to be sure, but one can already suspect that an origin whose structure can be expressed as 'signifier of the signifier' conceals and erases itself in its own production. There the signified always already functions as a signifier. The secondariness that it seemed possible to ascribe to writing alone affects all signifieds in general, affects them always already, the moment they *enter the game*. There is not a single signified that escapes, even if recaptured, the play of signifying references that constitute language."[7]

Starting with this passage from Derrida's *Grammatology*, let's try to develop a reading of the *sliding of the signifier* with our purposes in mind. The hermeneutic value of this concept remains doubtful as long as all it does is sketch the simple impossibility of an interpretation that is both exhaustive and coherent. (Perhaps the simplest illustration of this is the referential structure of a dictionary, which keeps referring us on and on and on.)

Now, one might think that what is sliding here is not the signifier at all but the sense, the signified, the signified sliding along the chain of signifiers we incessantly form as we read. Why is *sliding of the signifier* nonetheless the correct expression? If we read the (metonymic) sliding of the signifier in the context of our reflections on the poetic function of language, we also recognize it as a form of metonymic negation: in the sliding of the signifier the signified changes. It is a shift of the whole that takes place, for example, when it is inserted (as a part) into a further whole or when some of its parts enter a new context. What is interesting about this for us is an othering of sense that shows how such a radical altering takes place. This othering does not dissolve the context; on the contrary, it emerges from the production of a context.

The metonymic movement of chains of signifiers always takes place; permanently, wholes large and small emerge through recursions of different magnitudes. These incessantly shift the signification of the parts they integrate. Unlike what is commonly, and falsely, assumed, the sliding of the signifier does not destroy sense. That such a sliding precludes the idea of a fixed sense easily obscures its incessant production of sense (through its shifting); indeed, there could be no sense without such sliding. Instead, it brings out the effectiveness of the potentializing function Guillaume allowed us to describe.

Metanoia and the sliding of meaning

Such a gliding of the signifier, of the chain of signifiers, and of significance generally is omnipresent. In metanoia, however, it is a comprehensive whole that, exposed to a sliding, effects the shift of all parts. As the strongest manifestation of such a sliding that takes place in all signifiers, metanoia is a powerful and fundamental procedure of instituting sense. Thus we read in Augustine: "I had no wish to read further, nor was there need. No sooner had I reached the end of the verse than the light of certainty flooded my heart and all dark shades of doubt fled away."[8]

Metanoia is certainly bound to the history of the subject, to the experience the subject has of the world and its own history. When a *whole* is shifted, the sense of all parts changes. The past is suddenly no longer that which has been. "But then, my God, my sweetness, what came before that? Was I somewhere else? Was I even someone? I have nobody to tell me: neither father nor mother could enlighten me, nor the experience of others, nor any memory of my own."[9]

A short excursus on the effect of the rhetorical *exactly*

A whole emerges once at least three elements are brought both into a contiguous as well as a recursive relation. As noted, we need at least one part, its counterpart, and a part that stands for the whole. The question whether a whole can appear to us as the illusion of unity has to be answered emphatically in the affirmative. This also shows the difference between parts that stand in relation to a whole and parts that (apparently) form a unity.

We give the name *exactly effect* to the ubiquitous phenomenon that wholes are transfigured into unities. It is characterized by the impression that all parts are given and join, as if by themselves, to form exactly one whole (e.g. "That's exactly what Derrida means..." "That's exactly what Foucault describes when he says..." "That corresponds exactly to what Deleuze calls the logic of sense.")

It is not by accident that the theoreticians usually cited in this context—Derrida's text on "Nietzsche's styles"[10] is exemplary here—have all reflected on the formative dimension of style. That they write differently is not a French spleen but a fundamental methodological imperative. Texts like Foucault's, Derrida's, Deleuze's are theories full of metanoietic appeal and potential. The reader's thought is addressed by language and enters the text's vortex: a mere reader becomes the subject of theory.

The affinity to metanoia that characterizes the texts of Foucault, Derrida, Deleuze, and other representatives of continental philosophy derives from their opening a universe of thoughts for their readers, a universe, however, that one can only enter by "thinking one's way into it." If in such a process of othering, the reader becomes a subject of theory and takes theory on *as a whole*, a misleading impression of self-evidence easily arises.

What concerns us here, however, is not a critique of such appearances (i.e. that the *exactly* is philologically inexact) but that something is accepted to be *evident*. How does this evidence come about? We believe that it is produced by the reader now referring the world to this new (new for him) whole, by his placing himself at the text's site of reference and becoming the subject of the text.

What happens here may indeed be understood as a fusion of horizons, but one in which the horizon of the work becomes the horizon of the reader. He now *experiences* his world as another world, experiences the othering characteristic of metanoia, but (only) as a fundamental change of his perspective, his perception, which has transformed and now lets him see what he has found in the world of the text—what the *exactly effect* is a symptom of. For this reader, metanoia exists (only) as a singular experience that has made him the other in which he experiences himself and the world. (But fundamentally—and we will see just how decisive this is—not much more has changed than he himself.) In short, for him, metanoia basically becomes an aesthetic experience.[11]

Three preliminary characteristics of metanoia

This very point of self-affirmation is expressed in an *exactly* that is different from the radical shifting of reference or change of the self (and the change of the world that necessarily comes with it) characteristic of metanoia. This allows us to note three characteristics of metanoia: first, the reader's thought is not just addressed by the language of a certain thought. In metanoia, you go beyond what you thought up to this point. Second, you seek a new language for this and find it where you change your own world, where you take the place of its referent. Third, you determine yourself (anew) and become an other.

Triadic logic of the sign (Peirce)

We begin with Charles Sanders Peirce's pragmatist semiotics. In the trivalent relation of the semiotic triangle he developed, object and means of signification are differentiated by an interpretant. Meaning—and this is congruent with our reflections on part-to-whole relations—always comes about in a holistic context. It emerges in a triadic relation; it cannot exist in semiotic dyads.

Semiotics provides us with a tool that makes it possible not only to articulate a poetics interested in the ontogenesis of signs but also to capture the specifically *poietic* dimensions of language and thought. Peirce's theory of the sign will help us to give a more precise account of an experimental trait at the basis of lingual attributions of meaning. Just like Peirce, we seek to guard ourselves against a practice-determined abbreviation of his semiotic pragmatism: signs are not merely determined by their everyday use. They are used daily, to be sure, but they are developed for the purpose of knowing reality. The production of signs, therefore, is not just practical but also *noietic*. A semiotically informed poetics sees the use of language as a site of knowledge.

Language situates us at the site of knowledge (i.e. in the world). Change in (and of) the world, of which we become aware as temporality, is also the precondition for our perceiving the world. (We will later examine the world-creating aspects of our constant differential matching of sense-data from the point of view of a theory of cognition.) The deictic capacity of language allows us spatially and temporally to situate ourselves (through knowledge) in the world by providing us with a semiotic agent, an interpretant. Only for that reason are we able, thanks to grammar, to deictically shift our point of view (i.e. to go beyond the here and now in thought). For example, we can only position ourselves *in* the present because tenses allow us to project a course of time and to tie it together into a whole.

The most general of semantics is continuously differentiated and concretized by syntactic structures. Summing up, Elisabeth Leiss writes "that a proposition, with the help of grammar, produces a *proper name* from a generic concept."[12] The referential structure of meaning is thus differentiated and approximates the relationships objects entertain with one another.

The primary function of signs consists in an orientation toward the world. "This is immediately obvious in the case of indication with a finger (index). The same holds for lingual signs. They simply have more and more powerful functions because they can also refer to past and future, real and contingent contexts, etc."[13] Lingual signs owe this power to their recursivity. The orientation and collaboration of the relations is crucial.

"Revolution"

We read the word "Revolution." What does it refer to? Is it a world-historical event like the French or Russian Revolution, or a Beatles song? We could also come to think of "orbit," the word's older meaning, which referred to the trajectories of stars and planets. But when we read "revolution" in the context of the *GPG "Roter Oktober" Bad Langensalza (DDR), Züchter Hermann Berger* [*Horticultural Production Cooperative "Red October" Bad Langensalza (German Democratic Republic), Hermann Berger, cultivator*], there is a shift in expectation.

We no longer expect an event or a constellation to be behind the expression: the thing to which it could refer becomes another. We now expect a plant.

The literature tells us that we are dealing with a polyantha hybrid, one of a class of roses that was immensely popular in the 1920s and 1930s.[14] We also learn that the red rose *Revolution* was cultivated in 1972. This leads us to the GPG Roter Oktober Bad Langensalza Cooperative where we can find a red rose named *Revolution*.

Semiotic relations

Our example demonstrates how, through a series of recursions, an expression becomes a sign. At each step, we have understood the expression to be part of whole semantic orders (meaning) until, with the help of spatial and temporal localizors, we came upon an object. Taken together, they form a circle that forms the basis for knowledge of the world through language.

Peirce's semiotic triad outlines a field in which it is possible to capture processes of interpretation that go far beyond language. This explains the attention his work has received in the analytic philosophy of language, which sees his semiotics as a logic of the interpretation of reality. Peircean semiotics provides a workable basis for developing the logic of a scientific analysis of languages; this throws the ballast of analyses of consciousness overboard.

Let us take a look at what relations, according to Elisabeth Leiss, linguistics finds to be in effect in the semiotic triangle:

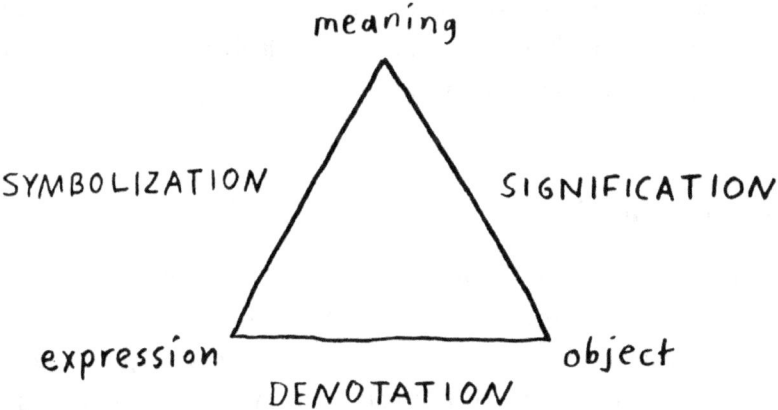

Figure 1. Semiotic triangle by Andreas Töpfer

- *Denotation*: Thanks to deixis, a lingual expression refers to objects at a spatial and temporal distance. The grammatical form of deixis establishes a relation of contiguity (i.e. a spatio-temporal localization) between expression and object.
- *Signification*: The formation of semantic classes goes from object to meaning. Semantics begins where deixis reaches its limits because the potentially infinite number of objects to be named could never be dealt with by a dyadic indexicality.[15] In the formation of semantic classes, signification shifts our focus from an indication of things to an indication of the relations between them.
- *Symbolization*: "But if human beings want to talk about more than just generic concepts, they need, in addition, a localizor that is as efficient as an index finger. This indexing function is performed by the sentence's finite elements such as, for example, the tense morphemes. They localize the object in time. Interestingly, finite elements occur only in sentences. What we can derive from this is that it is not until we are dealing with a sentence that we can speak of a complete sign.... The primary function of a sentence is to make a subject localizable and designatable."[16] Taken by itself, the expression "Revolution" is ambiguous, a sentence is needed for context: "Revolution" is a red rose cultivated by Hermann Berger in Bad Langensalza, Germany, in 1972, which can still be found there today.

Thus, for a sign's reference to become possible, semantic generic terms are formed (meaning) that are symbolized in grammar (expression) and concretized in denotation (object). No matter what semiotic element we take as our starting point for the formation of signs, it always recursively involves the other two by entering into part-to-whole relations with them.

Interpretations of reality

The vastness of the field outlined by Peirce has correlates in a wide variety of interpretations of the semiotic triangle in various discourses. Many of them even contradict each other. Nonetheless, they offer important insights into the connection of thought, language, and world that Peirce helps us understand.

In the analytic philosophy of language, Peirce's semiotics is understood as the logic of the interpretation of reality. Karl-Otto Apel describes this project as follows: "The problem into which the modern discussion has gotten us seems to lie in renewing Kant's question concerning the conditions of the possibility and validity of scientific knowledge in the form of the question of the possibility of an inter-subjective agreement [*Verständigung*] on the sense and truth of propositions or propositional systems. This would mean that the task is to transform Kant's critique of knowledge, which is an analysis of consciousness, into an analysis of signs; its 'highest point' would not be the (already attainable) objective unity of *ideas* in an allegedly intersubjective 'consciousness in general' but the unity, to be attained one day by means of a consistent interpretation of signs, of agreement in an unlimited intersubjective consensus."[17] This consensus is the end point to which the analysis of language is to lead. Peirce's triad would then be nothing more than a productive detour we'd have to take to get to the real destination, namely an explanation of the dyadic relation of the subject and the object of knowledge.

For semioticians, Umberto Eco for example, the merit of Peirce's approach lies in the fact that "the semiosis-triad is applicable to phenomena" that "do not have a sender." This, however, does not mean "in any way that semiotics is divested of conventions such that it could be considered a theory of the language of God or of Being. It only means that we describe conventions of interpretation" in other domains, "in the way in which we try to decipher natural phenomena *as if* these were signs that communicate something."[18] Here, too, the triadic semiotic relation appears as a mere key for unlocking the dyad sender–receiver.

Different readings of Peirce's semiotic triad usually take a perspective that begins with one of the semiotic elements: we recognize something to be a thing (object), a reference to a thing (expression) or to the relations between things (meaning). This results in the sign's three-dimensional power to designate.

Understanding the semiotic triad as a dimensionality of signs suggests that it is possible to develop semiotic perspectives from all three angles. We call this method *labeling*, keeping in mind that different discourses come up with different labels whose perspective on the semiotic triangle is determined by the semiotic dimension they start from.

Labelings

Let's take meaning as our first angle in the semiotic triangle. We encounter this label in discourses that are interested in "sense as such" (e.g. Igor Smirnov)[19] or in a pure semiosphere (e.g. Yuri Lotman).[20]

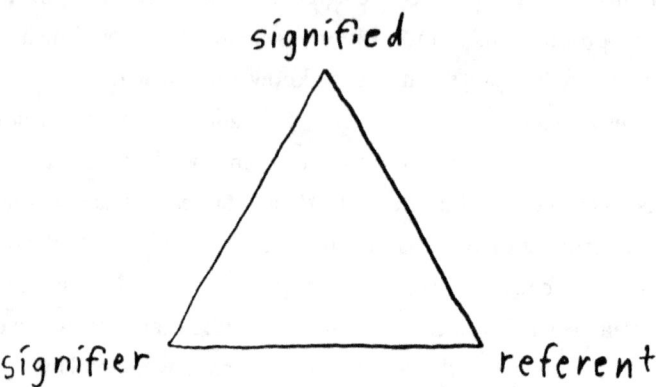

Figure 2. Semiotic triangle by Andreas Töpfer

From this perspective, all elements of the triangle are examined as to their connection with meaning. The signifier, accordingly, only signifies insofar as it is *significant* (i.e. insofar as it means the signified). As long as there is no discernible relation to a meaning, it would be questionable, from this perspective, whether, say, sound poems are lingual phenomena or whether they are mere games of the articulatory organs, whose results would have to be considered as extra-lingual things. Yet within a discourse that moves within this kind of triangle, these things only come into view insofar as they are referents (i.e. things that are referred to (by means of signs)). One example is the question of whether the hand I perceive is a part of the arm or rather of the broom it holds. It is lingually mediated meaning that tells us if we are confronted with a "whole" thing or are only dealing with partial objects. In Russian, for example, there is no separate word for "hand" besides the word for "arm" (*ruka*); only when we realize this, we might possibly notice that there is no visible limit between our hand and our arm. This way of labeling shows that the differentiation of lingual meanings determines our perception and allows us to distinguish between things.

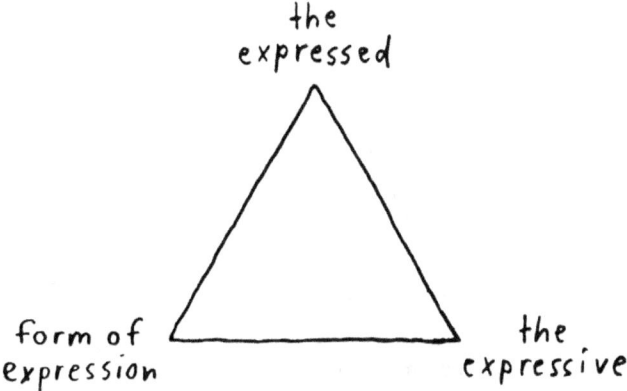

Figure 3. Semiotic triangle by Andreas Töpfer

When we start with the expression angle of the semiotic triangle, we get theories that adopt expression or expressivity as their conceptual foundation. From this perspective, every sign must be considered from the point of view of the element that is the form of expression; meaning, then, is that which is to be expressed and becomes palpable as the expressed. Form is at the center of this concept of the sign. The "thingness" of this sign confirms it to be expressive, an elementary fullness that has taken form.

Proponents of such a theory are likely to take their examples from art and extend the principle of art to all other semiotic elements. They would argue that meaning is impossible without form, the way an object without form cannot be an object. (Or, like Derrida, they would point out that every signified has always already been nothing but a signifier.) This highlights the fact that all signs share a form; without this form, there could be no signs.[21]

Finally, starting with the object in the semiotic triad, we can also conceive of a reistic triangle that allows us to distinguish between natural things, artistic artifacts, and phenomenological objects.

From this perspective, the thing is a self-sufficient whole (e.g. a stone, which takes itself to be the standard of expression and meaning). The demand addressed to expression would be—to use one of Viktor Shklovsky's famous phrases—to bring out (e.g. rhetorically) *the stoniness of the stone*— nothing more, nothing less.[22] Every theory for which the task of art is to bring out the sense-proper both of the material and of things could thus

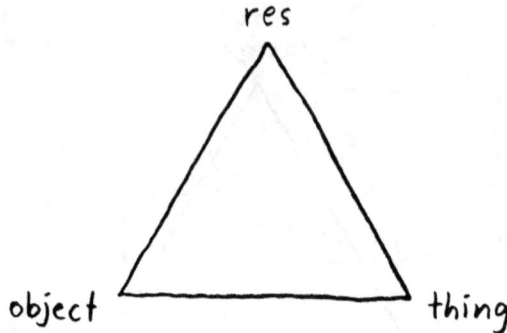

Figure 4. Semiotic triangle by Andreas Töpfer

be called a reistic theory. Unlike the theoretician of meaning who understands it to be a classification, the proponents of reistic labeling take meaning to be a singular, ideal, abstraction from a concrete thing. This places the semiotic triangle under the sign of incommensurability, the "obstinacy," the singularity of each thing.

Semiotic dimensions

The different relations within the semiotic triangle cannot be rearranged in the same way as the elements in the different perspectives just discussed. No matter how the angles are labeled, the labels do not alter the semiotic dimensions; the relations between the elements therefore remain the same. This suggests that a closer look at the semiotic dimensions will lead us to an understanding of the semiotic triangle. Peirce calls these dimensions *Firstness*, *Secondness*, and *Thirdness*. He identifies them as mono-, bi-, and trivalent semiotic relationships, to which correspond three types of signs: icon, index, and symbol.

Now, one might think that Firstness is the most originary of the semiotic dimensions, the indispensible ontic foundation of the sign-ness of signs, as it were, on which Secondness and Thirdness are built, and that icon, index, and symbols relate to each other in the same way.[23] The conspicuously inconspicuous observation that the semiotic triangle is presented as an (already) *closed* triangle, however, renders the fact that there cannot first be Firstness, then Secondness, and finally Thirdness immediately intuitive. As John K. Sheriff puts it in his outline of a semiotic theory of literature based on Peirce's insights: "No sign can be a word (written or spoken) until it has become a triad of Thirdnesses."[24]

Firstness can only be grasped once the semiotic triangle has been closed. No origin as such can be obtained—only once it has been symbolized will there have been an origin. Secondness, too, does not possess any autonomous semiotic characteristics. Bivalent signs do not constitute language because no language consists exclusively of indexical semiotic references or lexical units. No language exists without grammar. Thus, looking at the semiotic dimensions Firstness, Secondness, and Thirdness, we see that we cannot think of a sign without thinking about the closing of a semiotic triangle.

(1) In order for an *Icon* to be conceived of as such (i.e. as a *sign* that, seemingly directly and immediately, refers to something *other than* itself), it must refer to itself, which is only possible by closing a semiotic triangle.
(2) An *Index* can only ever be more than a chain of successive icons if the closure of the semiotic triangle has created an equivalence between the semiotic elements.
(3) A *Symbol* regulates or creates additional dimensions in the semiotic relations. Compared to stringing together three elements to form a chain of signs, the semiotic triangle establishes a part-to-whole relation and thereby involves a meta-relationality of semiotic elements (i.e. a relationality of relations that involves all dimensions of the sign).

Understanding the way language functions presupposes an indexical understanding of "meaning" that must have been erased. In the form of a revocation of the indexical, this already-mentioned iconoclasm internal to the sign marks the transition from Secondness to Thirdness. While Firstness is never semiotized in the present tense but always in the mode of *it will have been*, Secondness, once denied, is already part of Thirdness.

Firstness and Secondness thus exist only as mediated by Thirdness. When fetishized, Firstness is often seen as an originary whole or as something infinitely divisible; yet a part-to-whole relation only comes about thanks to Thirdness. By the same token, Secondness can only appear as an opposition within the framework of a whole, which presupposes Thirdness. When we raise the question of why the Peircean triangle is closed, we see that those moments of Firstness and Secondness that suggest that Firstness escapes semiosis (its originarity precludes the analysis of its semiotic structure) and that Secondness opposes semiosis (it is always refracted by Thirdness) only ever make sense within a closed semiotic triangle.

The *poietic* triad

We spoke of inconspicuousness when we said that the closure of the triangle is rarely thematized or even noticed. Yet once we turn our attention to it, this closure immediately becomes conspicuous and questionable. Were we, as modernists and postmodernists, not much more familiar with thinking the process of sense formation as a process that cannot come to a close? Haven't we, more often than not, become lost on the paths of sense, and do not these paths still seem a labyrinth to us? Our eyes set on the goal, we nonetheless never reach it, we do not find the definite conclusive sense, do not write the last book, and do not track down the truth once and for all. Even the philosophical adversaries discussed above, proponents of hermeneutics and of deconstruction both, agree on this point: works are as inexhaustible as the differing of *différance* is endless.

Once we understand that this movement is the production of a part-to-whole relation, once we recall that speaking actualizes a paradigm and at the same time creates a new paradigm (i.e. when we recall that both the actualizing and the potentializing function of language operate in every speech) we might be able to give a better description of the curious closedness or interruptedness of the semiotic triangle. Semiosis is the *movement* in which a new whole is produced in that an interpretant relates an element (which emerged from just such a movement) to another element (which owes its existence to just such a movement); once such a movement concluded, the answer to the question of how exactly it took place (and especially of which element was given first) entails a new movement, an interpretation. This, of course, neither implies a logical regress nor does it have to lead us to doubt that the triangle has really closed; it is simply the same principle that is known in physics as the "Heisenberg uncertainty principle."

A *différance* concerning wholes

Let's take up once more the philosophical debate that stood at the beginning of our reflections on semiotics. There, we touched on two themes for which we can now provide a semiotic explanation: first, the reproach voiced by hermeneutics that deconstruction is arbitrary; second, the charge leveled by deconstruction that hermeneutics' fixation on the unity of sense seeks to eliminate differences. From the point of view of semiotics it does, in fact, look as if Derrida and de Man describe a different semiotic movement than philosophical hermeneutics. Put in the more formal terms of a thesis: unlike traditional philosophy and hermeneutics, which is heavily invested in the perspective of *meaning*, deconstruction is more interested in the way of labeling that starts from *expression*.

This leads us to the question: Does the translation of one discourse into another create "false friends" or even "false enemies"? Each discourse looks at Peirce's semiotic triangle from a different semiotic direction. They therefore label the triangle differently as each interpretation of the semiotic movement assumes a different interruption of the triangle. Is there a misunderstanding in precisely that semiotic basis these discourses share? Do, for example, reflections on metaphors largely consist of such a misunderstanding of philosophically inflected questions in literary and cultural studies? Or is the misreading that appropriates the philosophical question of semblance for the purpose of a theory of fiction a failed reception of philosophic efforts in aesthetics and the study of art? Answering these questions can help us to understand the charges of arbitrariness or nonsensicality (charges which studies in the arts, in analytic and continental philosophy almost automatically level at one another) as semiotically conditioned discursive obstacles. They can thus help to begin removing them.

Inference makes sense

Peirce, too, understands "cognition" to be an unending process of interpreting signs in which referents are approximated. The relation of signification is never simply given; the formation of meaning is the task given to cognition. The only way this can happen is by an interpretation of *relations* in which the semiotic triangle emerges in the simultaneous addition and intervention of an interpretant. The semiotic triangle is not a constellation of three pregiven relations of equivalence to be discovered. That is impossible, if only because the elements that relate to one another belong to different semiotic dimensions. That is why the closedness of the triangle is only apparent when it is looked at from one of the possible perspectives (i.e. when it is labeled in a particular way). Only then can the various discourses begin to ask how the triangle is (or has been) able to "make sense."

Yet in every attempt to trace the closing of the triangle step by step in a *movement* starting from one of the "corners" (with the goal of thereby capturing sense as such), the incommensurability of the elements produces a drift. This makes it impossible to reconstruct the triangle as closed: the movement does not succeed in *returning* to the starting point because this point has changed in the course of the movement. This interruption, however, is not visible as long as one retains the same perspective. The triangle, after all, has not transformed into the homonymous instrument, it's just that the end point lies 'behind' or 'above' the starting point. That is why it seems to exist only as an incomplete triangle that produces infinite interpretations.

Subterfuge[25]

Winkelzüge oder nicht vermutete, aufschlussreiche Verhältnisse [*Subterfuge or Unexpected Telling Circumstances*] is the title of what poetess Elke Erb calls her "procedural discussions."[26] We would like to turn *subterfuge* into an experimental concept of speculative poetics. It allows us to trace the 'moves' by which various discourses seek to pace out the triangle. The subterfuge we thus observe in the triangle tells us a lot. It opens up the triangle by destroying its allegedly static closedness, and by actualizing new possibilities of interpretation. What is central is that in the attempt to use subterfuge to describe the recursion that establishes a whole semiotic triangle, one of the relations must remain interrupted whereas the other two seem unproblematic.

On this point, let's look at Umberto Eco's interpretation of the semiotic triangle. For him, "the damage the triangle has inflicted and continues to inflict on semiotics is that it perpetuates the view (for which mainly Frege is to be held responsible) that the meaning of an expression has something to do with the object to which the expression refers, for [on this view] the referent is the object named by the symbol."[27]

What is criticized here by Eco is nothing less than the intention of every philosophizing: the claim to truth. His description brings out a subterfuge that starts from the symbol (signifier) and proceeds via the reference (signified) to the referent (the object), where the relation of denotation is interrupted:

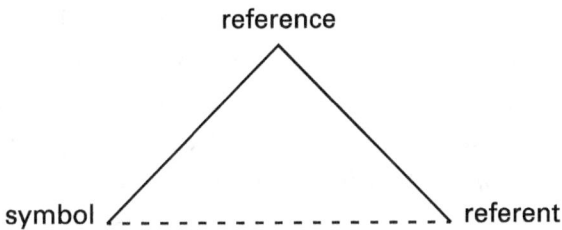

Figure 5. Eco's subterfuge

We suspect that a semiotic reading can shed light on Eco's invectives against philosophical discourse in general, just as it does on the differences between hermeneutics and deconstruction. Each discourse operates a different subterfuge because each is interested primarily in a different semiotic relation and because each believes it has to take a detour to describe this or to rewrite it in terms of two relations. We could also say: each discourse chooses to think of one side as being interrupted to get a hold on the other two relations; each discourse objectifies this choice in the concept of arbitrariness. Indeed it is possible to discern three forms of arbitrariness that correspond to the three semiotic relations.

Contingent arbitrariness

Let's take up first the relation between objects (referents/the expressive/things) and expressions (signifiers/forms of expression/objects). We all recall formulas such as the relationship between the referent and the signifier is arbitrary because the sequence of letters *apple tree* has no connection with any concrete apple tree. But, of course, every signifier—including the concrete printed *a-p-p-l-e t-r-e-e*, which you have just read in the book in your hands (and which you have thereby interpreted as the written actualization of the words *apple tree*)—entertains a certain spatiotemporal relation to any other concrete object (and thus also to the concrete thing that can be interpreted as an apple tree). What relation that is in each particular case, whether and how it can be determined, is beside the point. What is decisive is that if printed word and apple tree are concrete things, they entertain the relation that concrete things entertain with one another; this relation is neither necessary nor is it arbitrary: it is contingent. (You can move the book whatever way you like—the relation to the apple tree will be of one kind or another—but it will be what it will be, and not otherwise.) Arbitrariness has nothing to do with it.[28]

Next, let's turn to the relationship between signifier and signified, which Saussure saw as foundational of the arbitrariness of the sign. Because, so the argument goes, *pommier*, *Apfelbaum*, and *apple tree* have the same meaning—they designate a plant of the genus *malus* that belongs to the rose family (*rosaceae*)—there is no connection between the form of their signifier and their signified.

Yet all this example shows is that here, too, there is a connection that is neither arbitrary nor necessary but contingent. These signifiers have taken form within a 'space of possibility' that has continually changed as French, German, and English developed. That is also why there is no lingual expression that can be rendered completely in a different language. This is already apparent in a simple comparison of the relationship between the concepts *arbre* and *pommier* with the relationship between the concepts *tree* and *apple tree*, or of the sentence *An apple tree is a tree* with the sentence *Un pommier est un arbre*.[29] The metonymic share of all relations between signifieds and signifiers prevents sense from enjoying full liberty from its expression; that is why these relations are not arbitrary.

Third, one might think (as Eco does) that it is purely arbitrary to claim (as Frege does) that there is a connection between signified and referent. Eco cites the metaphors *Morning Star* and *Evening Star*, which, for Frege, refer to one and the same planet, Venus, and, for Eco, refer to two cultural entities. We object that it depends on the system of knowledge (i.e. the state of our knowledge of the solar system) whether the two expressions refer to one or two referents. Yet sense or the signified is nothing other than the classification that correlates with an order of knowledge, on which it is based. The example shows a sliding of the signifier, not an arbitrariness of the sign.

When we now, after these failed attempts at finding the arbitrariness of the sign on one of the sides of the triangle, return to the signifier, there suddenly seems to be an abyss between the concrete object from which we started and the word we recognize in it. The difference between the signifier and the referent, it seems, cannot be bridged.

How are we to deal with the paradox that triadic relations only produce themselves when dyadic relations are interrupted? Eco explains to us that in the case of signs, the interpretant has to enter into this relation—which is not the case for causally determined reactions to signals. There must thus be a distance for a semiotic relation to come about in the first place. Otherwise, one is presented with another thing, not with a sign: a second bean, not the sign of a bean.[30] A sign, in other words, can only emerge if there is an interpretant that differentiates two elements and places them, as part and counter-part, in a part-to-whole relation.

Daring metonymics

In Harald Weinrich's reflections we come across the idea that a daring metaphor bases itself on a more or less perceptible contradiction. The smaller the image's extension [*Bildspanne*] (i.e., the closer the two elements of the metaphor are) (Weinrich uses the example of the opening line of Paul Celan's "Death Fugue": "Black milk of dawn ..."), the more visible is the contradiction and the more daring is the metaphor. "But small extensions of the image ... are possible outside the semantic domain of nomenclature, and it is in this zone that daring metaphors thrive. This is the home of the oxymoron."[31] According to Weinrich, we forget all too easily that "our metaphors do not—as the old theories of the metaphor would have it—picture real or prefigured commonalities but ... institute their analogies, create their correspondences in the first place and thus constitute demiurgic tools."[32]

What we're fascinated by in this theory is the idea that it is difference that makes the metaphoric institution of sense possible in the first place. At the same time, a minimum of metonymic distance is required for the metaphor not to turn into perfect difference, into a simple oxymoron. While Jakobson, as we saw, considers equivalence to be the fundamental principle of metaphor, Weinrich demonstrates that this equivalence has to have been produced in the first place, that it is due to a *poiesis*. This explains how metaphors can fade when this constitutive difference becomes invisible.

From this perspective, let's take another look at lingual tropes. Metaphor and metonymy differ as to their procedures for maintaining a minimum distance. The demand for metaphoric distance on the one hand and metonymic distance on the other can be considered central to any creation of new sense and new words.

If the daring metaphor presents itself as a great contradiction in the case of a great proximity of the metaphor's elements, what would we have to think under the heading "daring metonymy"? Let's look at the relation of parts and whole on which metonymy is based and let's try an inversion similar to the one Weinrich has operated for the conception of metaphors. Just as metaphor is usually thought of on the basis of a given equivalence, so metonymy is usually understood in terms of a given whole: it either posits parts for the whole (*a fleet of thirty proud sails*) or the whole for the parts (*the hall applauded*).

What if the contribution of metonymy is that it produces a whole in the first place? This supposition becomes plausible when we base ourselves on those relations between part and whole in which an interruption and distance is inscribed. One of Oswald Egger's *quatrains* may serve as an example:

> Ich setzte
> je einen Fuß
> auf Fisch und Flossen,
> beide sinken.
>
> I placed/one foot each on/fish and fins/both sink.[33]

Who are the two that are "both" sinking? Fish and fins? Or is it both feet? Which of the feet is placed on (how many?) fins? The answer, probably: either—nor. The text leaves us to decide—but at the same time forces us to decide and hinders us—which wholenesses we want to produce in reading (and that means: what we want to see sink). And no matter what decision we take, the wholeness we form leaves a remainder.

Daring metonymies move on the edge of the indistinguishability between images and images of things. Let us recall here Deleuze's "Twenty-sixth series of language" in his *Logic of Sense*.[34] It is concerned with the minimal difference required to distinguish the referent from the material signifier (to distinguish sound as a sign from the sound produced by the mouth). Here, too, that side of the triangle (namely the relations between referent and signifier) is at the center of attention that until then had not been discussed in theories of language and could thus not be conceived of as a moment of the logic of sense.

In our view, the extreme moment of metonymy lies in a meta-moment in which the whole, thanks to the drifting relation to its parts, is exposed to a shift:

> Mit meiner vom Brüllen der Tiere besessenen Stimme.
>
> With my voice possessed by the animals' screaming.[35]

In this actualized metonymy, the voice of the lyrical I in the end belongs to the animals; we may surmise that the I has turned itself into an animal.

The linguistic turn, or the signified as predicate of the signifier

The fourth rose is the first to be red

"Rose is a rose is a rose is a rose./Loveliness extreme."[36] Gertrude Stein's famous formula (written in 1913 and published in 1922) allows us to trace how reference emerges in a metonymic movement. Some two decades later, in *Four in America*, Stein follows this up with a provocative poetological affirmation:

> Now listen! I'm no fool. I know that in daily life we don't go around saying is a ... is a ... is a ... Yes, I'm no fool; but I think that in that line the rose is red for the first time in English poetry for a hundred years.[37]

Let's try a speculative excavation of what we can learn from this formula that spins on itself. What does it tell us about the poetic function of language? Has a circle been drawn here, immanent to language, in which the first *rose* is identical with the fourth? Does this *rose* in truth return to its starting point: 1 > 2 > 3 > 1? Is the sentence an illustration of those recursive structures of which Elisabeth Leiss writes that they are only found once sentences are formed and which she cites as the reason for the claim that it is only once sentences are formed that one can speak of a *whole* sign?

If in Stein's sentence the rose really has become red for the first time in a hundred years, this would mean that Firstness emerges once the semiotic triangle has been closed. Firstness is the result of a recursive movement; only once the triad of semiotic relations has recursively established a whole and all three semiotic relations are thereby posited does the red rose emerge: Loveliness extreme.

A nominalism of roses

Let's remember that red roses have not always existed in Europe or, more precisely: the roses we find described as red roses in the literature of centuries past we would no longer call by that name today.

Today, we call the roses pictured here "purple." When this historical change took place cannot be determined with certainty. We may suppose that it began with the introduction of Chinese roses and became dominant when they were later hybridized with European varieties. The first is said to have been *Rosa chinensis Jacq.*, named by Nikolaus Joseph von Jacquin, director of the gardens at Schönbrunn.[38] Various indications support the supposition that there may have been earlier imports. Upon its arrival in Europe in 1792, however, *Rosa chinensis "semperflorens" Koehne* caused a sensation because none of the European roses displayed such a saturated red color.[39]

In 1811, this species is described as "the crimson or purple China;"[40] in England it is known by the name Slater's Crimson China.[41] The effect of this "bright-red China rose"[42] must have been extraordinary: "What a sensation the advent of these, for the most part, strong growing, free-flowering pillar roses must have created," we read in a book on roses from 1908. "Nothing like them had been seen before. No wonder they were in great demand and formed a class almost as numerous as the French rose of a preceding generation. Some few are with us still and may they long continue."[43] Slater's Crimson China does indeed still exist today, as do some others from among the original China roses. Beyond that, they served as the basis for cultivating the modern roses that bloom repeatedly.

What follows from this? Were purple or violet-red roses *erroneously* called "red" until well into the nineteenth century? Could this only be corrected once

Figure 6[44] Rosa x Centifolia "purpurea" Triomphant(e) (Netherlands, before 1790).

Figures 7[45] "Maheka" "La Belle Sultane".

there were really red roses? In reality, were there no red roses before then? Or are we to suppose, as Peter Harkness does, that "'purple' implied a more reddish tone then than it does today"?[46]

The perception of red roses has probably never been as intense as during the formation of a semantic boundary between *red* and *purple* and the ensuing

Figure 8[47] "Rosa Indica dichotoma. Le Bengale animating," Rosa Chinensis Jacq. cv.

shift of the meaning of *red*. A metaphor conventionalized since the Middle Ages (the red rose) experienced a new actualization. The roses in Romantic literature and late-Romantic music are innumerable; think, for example, of the poem "Urlicht [*Primal Light*]" from Brentano and Tieck's *Des Knaben Wunderhorn* (1805–08) with its opening line "O Röschen rot [O little red

Figure 9[48] "Rosa Indica Caryophyllea. Le Bengale Oeillet".

rose ...]," which Gustav Mahler made resound in his Symphony No. 2 of 1895.

Gertrude Stein, in turn, produces the rose's former red with purely poetic means—in a metonymic movement, her verse makes the conventionalized, faded metaphor resound. When we read the line, "Rose is a rose is a rose is a rose," we notice how the meaning shifts and how the Romantic metaphor of

Figure 10[49] "Slater's Crimson China".

the red rose actualizes itself. For the first time after 100 years of Romanticism, Stein's formulation has *poietically* created the possibility that the rose is really red. The *poietic* circle does not trace a movement from a concrete expression and back again. In the circle, all three dimensions of the sign combine: redness does not become manifest at any point along the length of the sentence. Rather, redness grows out of language, into whose paradigm the metaphor has entered. The metaphor is not a fixed or fixable correlation between its elements but a recursive *movement*. Moves in an already closed triangle can never lead to this triangle's closing—only in a circular movement does the semiotic triangle as a whole emerge.

Let's try to clarify this by way of the line from Gertrude Stein. We asked whether the sentence "Rose is a rose is a rose is a rose" returns to its starting point. We now see that it's not possible to speak of a movement "returning" to its starting point. No matter which element (or corner) of the semiotic triangle we imagine such a *movement* to start from: running through the semiotic triangle, the element does not simply return to itself—it would have to return to itself *as another* or *as another* return to itself. Recursion creates a part-to-whole relation and thus a new level of generality that did not exist before.

Linguistic realism and the iconoclasm internal to the sign

Language is poetic and has access to reality. Let's try to further justify this thesis on the ontology of language. Why does language stand in relation to reality or why does it produce reality? We have already encountered questions about the realism of language, namely in the context of a first sketch of our ideas on the iconoclasm internal to the sign. To what extent is the lingual perception of meaning more realist than sense perception? "Just as instinct communicates covert knowledge about the world, our language contains covert knowledge of the world. Hume hints at the possibility that these covert structures contain more reality than our sense perception; he thus clearly goes beyond the empiricist agenda."[50]

Elisabeth Leiss allows us to reinterpret realism (as lingual). We no longer have to believe that realism foregrounds perception as the basis of all knowledge and thus is indistinguishable from empiricism. Language already provides us with knowledge about the world. It may well be that it is a knowledge we do not recognize as such. And yet its reality content exceeds that of perception. This contains an important clue: we may relate this (as Hume did, apparently) to the fact that the referents of lingual Thirdness are to be developed in the first place. They are relations and precisely not things.

We have called "iconoclasm internal to the sign" the transition from an indexical to a symbolic sign. When we learn a language, we by no means find ever more words for ever more things. Instead, we transition to producing relations between lingual signs that then allow us to grasp ever more and, finally, infinitely many things. Perception's claim to reality seems to come up short against the lingual knowledge of relations; the idea that perception contains the *image* of the perceived falls apart. (Perhaps this is what Husserl said in his own way when he reproached perception with never having the whole thing.)

Knowledge about the relations between things is a lingual knowledge. We appropriate such a relational understanding of signs in the course of an iconoclastic appropriation of language. Thanks to this covert knowledge, language contains reality and is, in this sense, more "realistic" than perception. In the end, our perception needs tenacious training for it to be brought to the level of this knowledge of the world, a knowledge deposited in language in the course of the history of culture. The same might then be true for knowledge about a relational ontology we appropriate with language without being aware of it. Covert lingual knowledge can and must continually be exposed.

The limits of the analytic philosophy of language

When we follow the development of the analytic philosophy of language we see that it was originally much more strongly dedicated to a project of lingual realism than may seem to be the case in hindsight. Its insight into language shaping our knowledge of the world, however, increasingly tempted it to adopt the misleading assumption that our knowledge of the world could be increased by liberating it from the constraints of language (whose contingencies and apparently unordered structures are said to obstruct the attainment of a profound ontological knowledge).

Once again, let's read Elisabeth Leiss: "Analytical philosophy begins with Gottlob Frege, namely with his Leibnizian project to rid the relations between world and language of their arbitrariness. Frege did not want to give up the cognoscibility of the world. The measures he took can be called strategies for weakening nominalism:

(i) Frege's reintroduction of a differentiation between meaning (sense) and designation (reference), which is nothing but the rediscovery of the semiotic triangle, is a reintroduction of relations.
(ii) Relations are not visible but, according to Frege, they are nonetheless real in the sense that they exist independently of our ideas just like the world of real objects. Thought consists in grasping relations.

With his logical empiricism Carnap completely destroyed this project without being aware of it.[51]

One particularly telling example of how far the analytic philosophy of language moved away from such realist approaches is the criticism of language in Willard Van Orman Quine's nominalism. Quine's theory of language is built on the assumption that language above all refers to objects: "It was a lexicographer, Dr. Johnson, who demonstrated the reality of a stone by kicking it; and to begin with, at least, we have little better to go on than Johnsonian usage. The familiar material objects may not be all that is real, but they are admirable examples."[52]

Before we have even finished the sentence, a number of questions arise: Is it a coincidence that Johnson is a lexicographer, not a grammarian? Why do we have to start with things when we ask about language? Why should nouns be given precedence in language? And once we've finished the sentence, we take the liberty of asking a simple Socratic question: What evidence is there for it having been a stone whose reality was created by Dr. Johnson's foot—and not a sleeping turtle or a lithops or a piece of the fossilized sap called amber? We will return to this.

At the very beginning of Quine's *Word and Object*, there is a sense of a possible abyss in the analytic criticism of language; in the unbridgeable chasm between the physical world and the world of ideas, there is even a sense of a potential end to the analytical project as a whole. "I propose in this introductory chapter to ponder our talk of physical phenomena as a physical phenomenon, and our scientific imaginings as activities within the world that we imagine."[53] Language is thus split into two domains: on the one hand, language is an empty sound that exclusively stands in relation with physical phenomena. On the other hand, Quine situates imaginations about the world in a world that is itself imagined. It remains an open question how language is to bridge this total scissure between self-referential imaginations and a self-referential *physis*. But the analytic project is to be seen precisely as an attempt to construct such a bridge; it has proposed several solutions for explaining the relation of language—scientific, philosophical, or language generally—to objects.

In reference to Tarski's work on truth definitions, Donald Davidson, for example, writes: "The method works by enumerating the semantic properties of the items in a finite vocabulary, and on this basis recursively characterizes truth for each of the infinity of sentences. Truth is reached from the basis by the intervention of a subtle and powerful concept (satisfaction) which relates both sentences and non-sentential expressions to objects in the world."[54] This gives us a clue as to the structure of the analytic attempt at connecting language with referents by way of a theory of truth. Language here consists of a lexicon and logic, with logic replacing grammar (and syntax in particular). The signified is seen as a "semantic property" (i.e. as a predicate of the signifier), and the highly technical concept of satisfaction links sentences and referents or things.

The signified is a predicate of the signifier

From Frege to Kripke, reference seems to work like this: every semiotic relation must be subjected to the principle of identity, which lies at the basis of all logic, by 'explaining away' the difference between the sign and that which it refers to; only then can a proposition be true. We know this principle from Davidson's description. Philosophical theories connect propositions about objects with objects in the world. In the terms of a theory of reference, the thesis is that (only) the truth of a proposition about A allows for identifying the referent of the proposition, i.e. A. The proposition 'The rose is red' is true if the rose is red. If the proposition 'The rose is red' is true, we ought to be able to identify the red rose mentioned in the proposition.

But what if an event intervenes in the semantics of 'red'? Before *Rosa chinensis var. semperflorens* entered the scene, were roses red or purple? To say that there were no red roses before there were red roses (but only purple ones) seems not only logical but also trivial. But the same trivial logical compels us to say that for centuries there were no red roses; we even have to be careful not to call any rose red—perhaps we're wrong and it is not really red.

Red: color synonyms and the system of colors

Let's take another look at red roses and read what the most important German cultivator of roses in the first half of the twentieth century has to say about our problem:

> Every rose lover who has ever opened a mail-order catalog and read through the color descriptions will admit it to be simply impossible to visualize the real color of a given variety. The names in our catalogs are often very arbitrary or not very well defined. Most of us have an idea of what "coral" might mean although nobody denies that corals can be of various shades of red. "Salmon" is already more tricky. But once we get to descriptions like "tango," nobody who has not had a chance to consult the color table from which the description has been taken will know what color that is supposed to be. It was about time to make fundamental changes and to create a color table with descriptions fixed once and for all. Under the leadership of Prof. Dr. Krüger, the German Color Laboratories have already concluded the theoretical work in this field. They have constructed machines that allow any desired color at any time to be measured and reproduced. For his color tables, Krüger has had to draw on the numbers and letters employed on Ostwald's scale because our vocabulary is insufficient by far to designate the many possible gradations.[55]

We can see how the meaning of "red" shifts or, rather, how it dissolves to make place for an ever-denser description to finally be replaced by a measurable property. Since the development of modern optics, not just the synonyms and variants of "red" (such as crimson, copper, scarlet, vermilion, burgundy, or ruby), *all* colors are affected by the question of their existence. What has changed, of course, is the type of sign at issue. We are now dealing with symbolic designations instead of indexical ones, with symbolic designations that obtain their meaning within the framework of a theory that then allows us to test them as to their truth. Ever since roses have been given names in trade and cultivation, regular tests of the referent have become necessary.

Since the first systematic cultivations in the early nineteenth century, thousands of cultivated roses have disappeared. This we know from rose gardens, nurseries, and trade catalogs, from cultivators' indexes and nomenclatures. These list a large number of names to which no roses in any of the great rose collections in the world correspond (anymore). There are also many cases of duplications and mix-ups. In 1963, for example, Graham Stuart Thomas thought he had solved the riddle of the musk rose when he found (or so he believed) an old musk rose in an English garden. He accordingly set about revising all roses and ideas of roses which had come down to us under the name 'musk' and claimed that the "old" musk-rose mentioned in Shakespeare, Keats, and Bacon, is not a musk-rose at all but a *rosa arvensis*.[56]

There are also a number of names to which several roses are attributed. In these cases, plantings are organized for comparison, and the signified (i.e. the description of a rose as to its size, foliage, florescence, infructescence, etc.) serves as the basis for a judgment about what referent the signifier refers to. Today, there are an ever-increasing number of projects concerned with the history of roses. This has been completely confused in barely 200 years of cultivation, due to genetic databases. It is questionable whether these efforts will be crowned by success, especially since it is to be feared that in the short run, the conventional ordering of roses in species and classes is going to collapse.

The pathos of a theory of language in which language assumes the place of the transcendental subject of knowledge consists of the utopian conception that a perfect language, cleansed of all contingency, would designate all things and also allow each and every particular thing to be identified on the basis of its description or name. Such a language, however, would be robbed of its productive, *poietic* function. It would have no claim to be an ideal language (or the ideal of language)—indeed, it would not be a language at all. To put it differently: the more a language approximates the ideal of an ideal language, the further it moves away from the things to which it owes its reality until, finally, it lets things be things and does its own thing—itself, that is.

We will continue to pursue the question to what extent the *poietic* formation of concepts guarantees a relation to referents. How can we justify the claim that signifiers create more than just signifieds? At this stage, our thesis is that significant partition creates referents because partitioning continuously specifies a part-to-whole relation.

The disciplined subterfuges of analytic philosophy

The project of analytic philosophy can thus be described as follows: its subterfuge outlines (i.e. circumscribes and goes around) the relation of referent and signified and places it under the criteria of truth. Expression, accordingly, only comes into view within the perspective of its concordance with or deviance from logical principles; its task is limited to living up to the criteria of truth and thereby guaranteeing reference. This is also the origin of the tendencies toward standardization that every interpretation of language as a (deficient) logical system entails: the goal of attaining referents with a theory of truth presupposes an absolute discipline of language. To the extent that signifieds or signifiers avoid the correct predication, the success of the truth-loving subterfuge that leads from meaning via expression to the referent is also endangered.

Metaphor and semblance

This is also the place to look for an explanation of the themes of aesthetic semblance and poetic metaphor central to the philosophy of language. Is it not the case that metaphor and semblance—*a* appears as/to be *A*—attract such attention precisely because they seem to make it impossible to identify signified and signifier? We already know what's at stake—namely the (lingual) access to referents—when a theory of metaphor or fiction is unable to re-establish the adequation of sound and world by means of a correct logic of transformation. If the bridge between sign and world is not to be mere metaphorical semblance, a function has to be found, something, an *X*, that can be held responsible for the deviation: *X* makes *a* seem like *A*.

Metaphor and semblance are a problem for the analytic philosophy of language because they undermine the tacit assumption that the signified is the predicate of the signifier. In the case of semblance, the signifier would have to claim to be the signifier of the signified when it is not. In the case of metaphor, the signified would have to claim incorrectly to be the signified of the signifier.

What analytic philosophy discusses with such great effort and with many detours is something that might, in principle, be quite simple: it is nothing but the difference between signifier and signified. The philosophical focus on the semiotic relation of signification (between signified and referent) leads to a symptomatic reemergence of the relation of symbolization (between signified and signifier). This last relation appears to philosophical discourse as a problem specific to poetic language and as an existential threat wherever philosophy itself threatens to drift off into literature. Here, we also find an explanation of the symptomatic defense reactions against continental philosophy's alleged undisciplined veering off into the gray area between philosophy and literature.

At this point, we can see what is at stake in the attempt of the philosophy of language to circumvent in a subterfuge the difference between signified and referent such that it is no longer important: language is to receive non-arbitrary access to the world. From this point of view, however, language is true only on the condition that it excludes all its *poietic* moments. The philosophy of language seeks to draw a clear boundary between literature and philosophy, to regulate phenomena of fiction with clear rules, and to ban, completely if possible, phenomena of semblance.

S *means* X *by* Y (Kripke, Meillassoux, Harman)

Paraphrasing Descartes, we could characterize the enthusiasm that drives analytic philosophy as follows: "I think things truthfully, therefore they are. If, then, I translate my thinking into propositions that follow the rules of logic, I can identify things." But within the project of analytic philosophy, the capacity to identify things by propositions is lost time and again. Even though a theory of truth is developed as a theory of meaning, time and again it loses its relation to the things of the world or, as linguistics calls them, "the referents."

We've already seen how in Quine an unbridgeable abyss opens up between meaning and referent. We come across a similar scenario in Davidson's reflections on the status of translation manuals, in which sentences lose the function of referring to referents and only refer to sentences in (another) language: "For a translation manual is only a method of going from sentences of one language to sentences of another, and we can infer from it nothing about the relations between words and objects. Of course we know, or think we know, what the words in our own language refer to, but this is information no translation manual contains. Translation is a purely syntactic notion. Questions of reference do not arise in syntax, much less get settled."[57] Despite (or precisely because of) the reduction of syntax to a logical calculus or the transformation of the signified into a predicate, the relation to the referent dissolves time and again into a mystery.

"There can be no fact as to what I mean by 'plus', or any other word at any time."[58] What keywords for a metaphysics of meaning does this thesis of

Kripke's provide us with? It obviously gets at a central point of the philosophy of language. That there is no fact that I mean by X can be put as "Meaning is never the referent." In other words, the linguistic turn did not provide analytic philosophy with a solution for its core problem, and we once more find ourselves at the breaking point between meaning and referent. Kripke systematically gives examples that present analytic philosophers with the choice of either giving up their belief in facts or forgoing the assumption that it has to be able to articulate them without contradiction. "Recall Wittgenstein's skeptical conclusion: no facts, no truth conditions, correspond to statements such as 'Jones means addition by '+'.' (The present remarks about meaning and use do not in themselves provide such truth conditions)."[59] Let's continue these reflections of Kripke's by way of an example from the secondary literature: "'Odd means redness by '*'.' For instance, it might be thought that what makes the case that Odd means redness by '*' is some special mental state that he instantiates when and only when he grasps the concept of redness.... But there is nothing in Odd's mind or brain that shows that he meant redness rather than some closely related property such as scarlet or crimson."[60]

Let's also recall a remark by Wittgenstein in which we encounter an as if hermeneutic-semiotic view: "What is the criterion for our understanding the word 'red'? That we pick out a red object from others on demand, or that we can give the ostensive definition of the word 'red'? We regard both things as signs of understanding."[61] We could also put it like this: there is no fact that makes true the sentence "By 'this red rose,' Odd means this red rose."

A sentence such as "By 'this red rose,' Odd means this red rose" can thus not only be understood as a true or false statement by Odd (about the redness of this rose) but also as an attribution of an opinion to Odd. "S means X by Y" thus becomes a statement about S instead of stating a condition for the identity of X and Y. This turnover point from a use-theory of meaning (Odd uses the expression 'this red rose' and means this red rose by it) to an attribution of an opinion to Odd (the possibly historical character of Odd's perception of red) is made plausible once more by Peirce ("the mind is a sign developing according to the laws of inference"[62]) because Odd now appears as the interpretant of the redness of the rose; he thus stands in for the redness of the rose.

The subject of semiosis

Philosophy thus provides us with another invaluable find. In its theory of meaning, it brings out the subject. Originally, this was due only to the effort to salvage the existence of things that contain mutually exclusive determinations (e.g. Marcel Duchamps' marble sugar or Méret Oppenheim's fur cup) without having to release them from the dependence of this existence on a theory of truth. Although, then, the subject was merely supposed to play the role of a scapegoat or one of support for the contradiction, it quickly becomes clear that the idea that semiosis has a subject has far-reaching consequences.

We asked what indications we have for it being a stone that was kicked by Dr. Johnson. The question is an easy one to answer: the indication is that this is what Quine tells us. Put differently: Quine (as the subject of semiosis) stands for it being a stone—and it does not matter here whether it is an (invented) anecdote or whether Dr. Johnson really at some point kicked something that may, in fact, have been a piece of amber or a lithops.

The very possibility of Quine bringing up this example to illustrate his thesis that there is an unbridgeable gap between reality and language refutes his conception and confirms ours: namely that the subject must stand for the truth it creates (poetically). We admit, we accept the evidence thus adduced by Dr. Johnson. We could not have understood the evidence if we had not interpreted 'stone' as a word that refers to a real object that can be kicked.

Quine's example, of course, at the same time demonstrates that the reality demonstrated by Dr. Johnson is a reality that can only be demonstrated by language in the first place—not because the kickable object was created by language but because language makes a *stone* of this thing, a *stone* whose reality Dr. Johnson can demonstrate by kicking it. As language contains the knowledge that a stone is a real thing, kicking it can serve as a demonstration of reality. "The familiar material objects may not be all that is real, but they are admirable examples."

Yet aren't these reflections the ultimate expression of a correlationist theory of language? What does this imply for the question of the contingency or causality of facts and for the access we, as subjects, have to facts? Does it not amount to the old, familiar supposition that all the knowledge we can have of reality is limited by our perspective?

We think that, on the contrary, these reflections provide us with the means to disprove the (implicit or explicit) suspicion entertained by the new speculative philosophers, namely that it is impossible for the approach of the philosophy of language to avoid correlationalism. One good starting point is Graham Harman's attempt to free Bruno Latour's reflections of their correlationist dimensions: "Latour's main point is that reality is made of *propositions*, in Whitehead's sense of the term—defined not as verbal statements by conscious humans, but mutual relations in which two things articulate each other ever more fully. Pasteur brings microbes into focus from the dubious grey matter and various symptoms through which they are announced; in turn, microbes bring Pasteur into focus as a genius and national hero."[63] This forges an alliance between speculative realists and historians of science in their common struggle against the nominalism of the philosophy of language that defines the limits of the analytic project and that we, too, seek to overcome.

Using our example sentence "S means X by Y," the speculative thesis according to which the relation between the subject of knowledge and its object is not different from relations between things, can be put as follows: by S we are not to understand a person but a thing ('mare means a female horse'). In Latour, this speculative thought is clad in the following thesis about the connection between cultivator and rose or botanist and plant: "The botanist learns new things ... the plants are transformed also. From this point of view there is no difference between observation and experience."[64] Latour, too, connects such reflections with a criticism of habits adopted in the analytic philosophy of language: "The philosophy of language makes it seem as if there exist two disjointed spheres separated by a unique and radical gap that must be reduced through the search for correspondence, for reference, between words and the world ... Knowledge, it seems, does not reside in the face-to-face confrontation of a mind with an object, any more than reference designates a thing by means of a sentence verified by that thing. On the contrary, at every stage we have recognized a common operator, which belongs to matter at one end, to form at the other, and which is separated from the stage that follows it by a gap that no resemblance could fill. The operators are linked in a series that *passes across* the difference between things and words, and that redistributes these two obsolete fixtures of the philosophy of language: the earth becomes a cardboard cube, words become paper, colors become numbers and so forth. . . .

The word 'reference' designates the quality of the chain in its entirety, and no longer *adequatio rei et intellectus*."[65]

We have to take this thought further and try to get to the point at which we can articulate reference metonymically, that is, via part-to-whole relations. The reference to red cannot be obtained via relations between classes or the adequation or equivalence of rose and redness. This is where the distinction between singular and plural, which Guillaume had described as the most fundamental lingual difference, becomes relevant. Could it serve as the basic distinction to characterize something as a sign? Rephrased in the terms of our example: semiotic relations develop from the relationship between rose and roses. We will see later that abduction as a procedure of inferring concrete things will greatly advance our reflections.

To Kripke we owe the idea of a reference to be thought in chains and to which the question of transmitting reference is central.[66] It is to preserve the relation of referent and signified from the dissolution that threatens it in an ever-more-precise differentiation because interrupting it would undermine the realist potential of language. Truth that refers to this relation (*adequatio rei et intellectus*) cannot be had as a semiotic relation. Yet it drives the discourse and leads to a continuous differentiation of this relation and thus also to what we know as an ever-closer description of the referent.

Do theories that promise us an ever-more-precise differentiation really show us a way out or do they, if we use them instead of traditional (i.e. adequation) theories of truth, simply enshrine the interruption of the semiotic triangle? We hope that here, too, part-to-whole relations will allow us to advance. In the cases described by Latour, then, we find neither a relation of unity and opposition nor a relation of identity and difference: in operations of partitioning and the recursive formation of a whole, reality and thereby reference is created. The metonymic character of this operation allows for distance to emerge but never difference, a whole but never unity.

Contingency creates reference

We saw that what we may call the logical contradictoriness of things[67] cannot be circumvented by any subterfuge. The speculative realist Quentin Meillassoux confronts this problem by assuming a contradictory factiality with which he replaces the demand for coherent facticity: "Accordingly, the principle of facticity can be stated as follows: *only facticity is not factual.*"[68] The situation of the referent then presents itself in the following terms: facts do not follow from natural laws but are contingent.

"Why can't physicists demonstrate the necessary determination of a law by reason alone? Because these are *facts*, not necessities . . . I call 'facticity' the lack of reason for any reality; that is, the impossibility of giving an ultimate ground to the existence of any being." Meillassoux thus shows us a way out of the aporia that the analytic philosophers of language have articulated. As long as we believe that we have to declare the principle of causality to be a necessary principle, the ambiguous identification of referents dissolves the capacity of language for creating references. When we recognize, however, that *in* reality there *can* be no necessity but that there must necessarily be contingency, then the possible consequences of the logical contradictions of our propositions appear in a new light.

The contradiction: red and not-red

"Imagine or rather try to conceive what a being able to support any contradiction would be: it has the property a, and at the same time, and in exactly the same conditions, it has the property not-a. The object is only red, and not only red but also not-red. And it is the same for any property you can conceive: b and not-b, c and not-c, etc. Now, try to conceive that this entity has to change—to become something it is not—would it be conceivable? Of course not, it is already everything and its contrary."[69] There can be no such object. And not because it contains a logical contradiction but because such an object would have attained factual necessity, which is factually impossible: it could not be a fact because it would lack contingency.

Let's take this thought experiment of Meillassoux's as a starting point for raising once more the question of the redness of the rose. We saw that its disturbing redness and simultaneous non-redness derive from its changeability, from the fact that the color of roses has shifted thanks to a hybridization with Chinese rose varieties. This changeability already distinguishes every concrete rose (and every other real thing) from the hypothetical object described by Meillassoux, which cannot exist because it would not be able to change.

Let's shift our focus and look, not at the objects (roses) to which the expression *red* can be referred, but at the expression itself, that is, at the signifier (the expression *red*). What are the consequences of the history of red roses for the signifier? As we saw, the word *red* can also refer to the not-red red we today call *purple*. But not just that: it can also refer to political movements (as in "the Reds"), it is a synonym of extreme anger ("he saw red") or, in connection with traffic lights, for example, it simply means "Stop!" What actually keeps us from using *red* as code for anything possible, for any object, any idea, any fact, or anything whatsoever? If *red* can refer both to a red and a not-red (purple) and factually can refer to anything possible, is not the signifier, in opposition to what we thought, arbitrary after all?

Let us imagine a sign that would, in fact, refer to anything possible. It would refer to an object with the property *a* and, at the same time, to an object with the property *not-a*; to an object that is red and, at the same time, to an object that is not red. Furthermore, it would refer to an object with the property *b* and, at the same time, to an object with property *not-b*, to an object with the property *c* and, at the same time, to an object with property *not-c*, etc. In short: there would be no connection between the sign and any of the objects to which it would refer, and thus also no connection between the sign and any other object that would, in turn, refer as a sign to another object. Can we imagine such a sign? Of course not: precisely because it could refer to anything, there would be nothing to which it would refer. Such a sign could not exist—and if only because such a sign, in fact arbitrary, would have no connection to any object; it would lack contiguity.

We may relate these reflections to what Quentin Meillassoux says about the *signe depourvu du sens* (a sign devoid of sense). An "empty sign possesses an immaterial property of identical reproduction. But since it is arbitrary, no concept can capture its essence—it is infinitely variable in principle with regard to its form, and this form has no necessity in itself. And since I can posit distinct types of empty sign, its iterable identity is no longer that of the general concept of the meaningless sign."[70]

The "empty sign" conceived by Meillassoux is the foil, as it were, against which we can outline the necessary properties of any concrete sign. The concrete sign derives its semioticity from its diverging, in a significant manner, from the determinations of the empty sign: its arbitrariness, its iterability, and its variability are limited already by the requirement that it must at the same time be a real thing. Every concrete sign, in other words, can only be a sign because it differs from the empty sign—if only because as a real thing, it entertains a certain (but contingent) relation with other real things. We could also say that the gliding of signifiers, which we saw was a necessary property of any (real) sign, presupposes real changeability, a precondition fulfilled by every (real) sign—insofar as it is (at the same time) a concrete thing.

This leads us to a simple answer to the (apparently rhetorical) question we asked earlier: What keeps us from using *red* as code for anything possible? Well, the simple fact that we cannot mean "anything possible." As real beings (and thus as contingent material things) we are subject to the factuality of reality and cannot know everything that is possible. We cannot, in any case, imagine a real thing that would have access to information about everything that is possible. For the existence of information presupposes that other possibilities of information have been excluded. This is the flip side, as it were, of a correlationism that would have us believe that the signs we use are arbitrary because we can assign contingent meanings to them.

Contingency and history

When we conceive of red and not-red as a contradiction, to remain consistent, we have to declare any proposition about the color of a rose or about red roses in general to be arbitrary—as such propositions would be propositions about a self-contradictory, and therefore non-existent, object. The history of roses, however, should teach us that this contradiction does not have to end up in our doubting the existence of an object or the possibilities of language. Contradictions can just as well be resolved in a history. Put succinctly: contradiction has an event as its referent. By this we mean that contradictions in this history (of roses) do not refer to a contradictory thing ('a red and simultaneously not-red rose') or even doubt its existence ('there really aren't any red roses'), but instead shift reference: the referent is now the historical event itself—in our case the spread of Chinese roses. The contradiction also refers to the emergence of a semantic difference between red and purple and allows us to recognize a change of perception ("violet-red was perceived as more reddish").

Catherine Malabou, working on Hegel, has temporalized correlate ideas about "contradiction."⁷¹ As temporal process of the momentum proper to contradictions, history can guarantee the existence of even those referents that are not things identical to themselves. Our interest in metanoia is precisely an interest in that *poiesis* in which things change, an opening up of truth in which something happens.

Truth is opened up by means of a creation and (at this stage) a connection with *poietic* practice and production. It contradicts a preceding truth and negates it. Of course it is not negation alone that opens up something. In Guillaume's sense, sketched earlier, the contingency, inappropriateness, and negativity of a sign come out at the moment at which it is called upon to designate something new; the potentiality of language leads to a poetic project.

Lingual things and the ontology of individuals (Strawson)

Predicates can also be subjects

We've already come across the possibility of interpreting as a subject what Peirce's semiotics calls "the Interpretant." Since such a conception brings out the ontological dimension of semiotics, it is only coherent for Umberto Eco to warn us about the consequences of this interpretation: "It's not for nothing that the concept of the Interpretant has scared off many a scholar. They were quick to banish it because they misunderstood it (Interpretant = interpreter or receiver of the message). Yet the idea of the Interpretant turns semiotics into a rigorous science of cultural phenomena because it frees semiotics from the metaphysics of the referent."⁷²

We, too, consider semiotics to be a rigorous science—not because it could demonstrate that language has nothing to do with reality but, on the contrary, because it helps us to better understand why language could not be thought without such a reference. Let us take seriously, therefore, Eco's warning about a truth that might be hidden here and go down the path Eco seeks to block.

Peter Strawson has added a grammatical and explicitly metaphysical dimension to the analytic approaches discussed here. This dimension opens onto a new crossroads, namely the question whether a thing can be captured by language in its uniqueness or whether this requires a complete description of the world in its entirety.

Such a description, even if a divine ego could provide it, would still require a deictic moment, an abstract index finger. According to Strawson, "the theoretical indispensability of a demonstrative element in identifying thought about particulars is not just a peculiarity of this or that conceptual scheme which allows for particulars, but a necessary feature of any conceptual scheme, of any ontology, in which particulars occur."[73] This is true both for identifying the object and for identifying the subject. Strawson's "aim is to establish and explain the connexion between the idea of a particular in general and that of an object of reference or logical subject."[74]

Strawson, semiotically

What is particularly relevant to our problem is Strawson's attempt to present the reciprocal relationships between things and subjects in semiotic relationships in such a way that both equally appear as individuals. An essential step of the argument consists in asserting that individuals are not to be situated at the end of the semiotic chain of interpretations but occur among the things about which we make statements. Individuals or, more generally, persons or, in the widest sense, individual consciousness, belong to the primary referents of our relation to the world.

The epistemological consequence is that reference is dependent on experience and tied into a movement, first, from the thing to the subject and, second, from perception to a metaphysical reference. Against the background of Strawson's ontology, we obtain the following reading of the semiotic triad from the point of view of a metaphysics of the sign: the individual is a matter of thinking; individuals cannot simply be perceived, we can only refer to them when we think of them, not when we merely perceive them. Reference to individuals is necessarily based on thought (and, as a general tendency, this is true of every thing).[75] What does this mean? It's obviously not enough to understand the interpretant merely as a *user* of signs, nor does it suffice to understand the interpretant as an interpreter in the sense in which a sociologically oriented semiology would employ the term.

We came across something similar in our discussion of the formula "*S* means *X* by *Y*." Reference cannot be separated from experience and remains bound to a subject. In the formula, "means" allows us to trace a shift, a shift of *S* as a subject ("*S* [=Gertrude Stein] means roses are red") and of *S* as a signifier ("*S* [=mare] means a female horse"). We explained that the turnover consists in the ascription to *S* of an opinion that characterizes *S*. To understand the person as a concept to be characterized, as Strawson does, leads to a reflection about whether individuals can also be looked at as predicates and not just—as has been done up to now—as logical subjects of predication.

In the final analysis, the conclusion we draw from Strawson's approach is that the individual is also a signified. As signifieds, individuals are not objects of perception nor are they agents of an intersubjective consensus. Proving that the subject is essential for all elements of meaning dismisses *aisthesis* as the foremost form of access to meaning and ranges thought among the originary acts of referring. Individuals are first and foremost *recognized*, not *perceived*. Our access to the world is above all mediated by thoughts and language. For us, Strawson's commitment to metaphysics is an insistence on a relation to the world that takes place primarily in thought.

The thesis according to which the world first and foremost consists of intelligible individuals requires further analysis. This shift in the relationship of thought and perception seems significant to us, especially when we once more turn our attention to a crucial question raised by every metanoia: the relationship between *poiesis*, *aisthesis*, and *noiesis*.

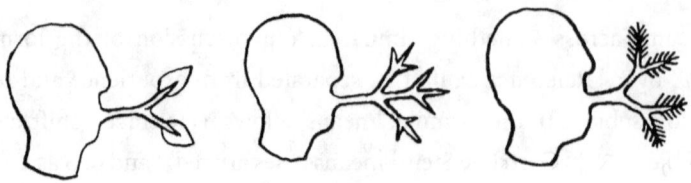

To express a new thought is always also to invent a new language game for this thought.

Language is not arbitrary   it is the differentiation   of thought and world.

 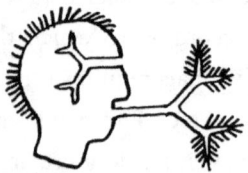

Language unfolds our understanding of the world to the extent to which it develops itself.

possible new understanding

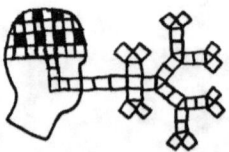 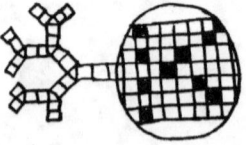

finding and inventing a new language

through reading, the world has become a different world

III

Speculation

Aspects of a Poetics of Thought

What philosophers say about actuality is often just as disappointing as it is when one reads on a sign in a secondhand shop: Pressing Done Here. If a person were to bring his clothes to be pressed, he would be duped, for the sign is merely for sale.

Søren Kierkegaard

Violation of hermeneutic rules

"One of the methodological principles that I constantly follow in my investigations is to identify in the texts and contexts on which I work what Feuerbach used to call the philosophical element, that is to say, the point of their *Entwicklungsfähigkeit* (literally, capacity to be developed) the locus and the moment wherein they are susceptible to a development. Nevertheless, whenever we interpret and develop the text of an author in this way, there comes a moment when we are aware of our inability to proceed any further without contravening the most elementary rules of hermeneutics. This means that the development of the text in question has reached a point of undecidability where it becomes impossible to distinguish between the author and the interpreter. Although this is a particularly happy moment for the interpreter, he knows that now is the time to abandon the text that he is analyzing and to proceed on his own."[1]

What is the violation of the most elementary rules of hermeneutics Giorgio Agamben speaks of here? Can we relate his doubts about the legitimacy of his own procedure to our reading of the hermeneutic circle? Or, rather, to what extent do these doubts apply to the movement by means of which we interpreted the circle as a tool for the production of a meaningful whole? Philosophical readers—i.e. readers who actualize the philosophical element of a text—have to give up the illusion that, in reading, they have brought all parts into a coherent whole, that they have *discovered* its unity. Why does sense not close to form a perfect sign, and why does the installation of the semiotic triangle always take place with an eye on the parts?

Among the relations of the semiotic triangle, there is always one that is interrupted and accessible only indirectly, by means of a subterfuge. But why is it that the ideal path to the whole always appears to be a further partitioning of the semiotic relation already interrupted? Why is it that, time and again, the belief arises that clearing up a misunderstanding, resolving an equivocation, or bringing in new details could amount to producing a whole? Or, asked differently, why is it that we hope that all these operations could restore a whole? Subterfuge follows on subterfuge but no triangle is ever closing.

When we look at it, it seems as if it were already closed although we know and can even prove that its being closed is just an illusion. But we can't stop there: we can become aware of why the closedness we seek cannot be found with the categories of intuitiveness (i.e. of aesthetics) and why it cannot but appear as semblance when we represent it to ourselves (as a triangle). The more often this partition is repeated, the more often the interrupted relation is partitioned, and the more often the interrupted relation is differentiated—without, however, being reconstructed as a closed relation.

Instead of criticizing it as a reduction, we would like to note that this process appears as a straightforward inverted recursion. It is important to see that, instead of forming a whole from the parts, recursion to the whole always produces difference. Instead of lamenting the failure to attain the fullness of semiotic sense, we would like to retain two effects of this movement of partition: first, a work interpreted this way is inexhaustible precisely because the interrupted semiotic relation can be partitioned further and further; second, an infinite differentiation of signs (of semiotic relations) always comes with an ever-denser description. (This is what, in the previous chapter, we discerned to be the insight shared by hermeneutics and deconstruction.)

Agamben proposes yet another reading. He marks a boundary at which the hermeneutic rules are violated. In reading, we always reach a point at which it becomes impossible to discern the difference between the interpreter and the author. Kripke's reading of Wittgenstein comes to mind as an example of such a reading, in which the subjects of the text are difficult to distinguish. For that reason, the author of the thoughts developed in Kripke's *Wittgenstein on Rules and Private Language* is often referred to by the name "Kripkenstein." The moment at which the distinction between author and reader dissolves is also the moment at which the interpreter exits the work. He changes from being the work's interpreter to being its interpretant; he brings the work's parts into a new constellation instead of constantly re-arranging the parts with a view to its wholeness.

There is one more aspect at the margins of hermeneutics we should mention here, one which remains implicit in Agamben's description. It concerns the technique of hermeneutical reading itself: a very specific technique shaped above all by nineteenth-century literature. The indistinguishability of author and reader (or the merging of their horizons) is prefigured by the literary technique of focalization perfected in the nineteenth century. The formation, by the text, of a perspective from which we can read it is a recursive strategy central to the effectiveness of the classical novel and of the hermeneutic circle. For the reader of these texts to be able to assume this perspective, there needs to be an othering. Hermeneutics is interested less in the shift of standpoint thus taking place (i.e. it focuses less on the *movement* or the *moveability* that make it possible) than in the question of how one finds the standpoint from which "one enters into the text" to be able to unlock the fullness of meaning it contains.

In contrast, Agamben describes a fundamentally different kind of reading whose noietic immersion in the text and adoption of the text's perspective no longer just leads into an unfathomable text; instead it advances to a breaking point at which something new opens up from within the text, something that had not already been inscribed *in it* as its timeless inexhaustibility. The issue, in other words, is to go beyond the work into whose horizon we have entered thanks to an othering and to make the work—in the name of its capacity for development (which Agamben calls "philosophical element")—undergo an othering.

Predicative and speculative reading

Drawing on our earlier reflections, we can provide a linguistic interpretation of this rule-breaking. Let's recall that language is also a noietic tool, which implies a potentializing function. The potentializing of a paradigmatic element takes place in speaking because speaking *qua poiesis* uses an old expression for a new noietic momentum.[2] In this respect, every reading and every writing is formative of paradigms.

Let's take a look back at the problem of philosophical reading and ask specifically about the relationship between truth-loving reader and philosophical text. Can the reader identify with the text at all? What would such an identification look like? Would it be an appropriation of an absolute knowledge through and about the text (as well as its referents)? Or is there a reason for the compulsion to rewrite or overwrite it? Taking up Hegel, Catherine Malabou presents this as a demand for speculative reading: "Similarly, a statement, even if already written, is only speculative in the true sense when it cannot be read without being rewritten."[3] Put this way, the question concerning philosophical reading is a question concerning writing.

Hegel writes in the Preface of the *Phenomenology of Spirit*:

> One difficulty which should be avoided comes from mixing up the speculative with the ratiocinative methods, so that what is said of the Subject at one time signifies its Notion, at another time merely its Predicate or accidental property. The one method interferes with the other, and only a philosophical exposition that rigidly excludes the usual way of relating the parts of a proposition could achieve the goal of plasticity.[4]

Malabou takes these reflections on speculative reading and interpreting further:

> Now this "exclusion" explicitly requires the proposition's *reading subject*. For Hegel pursues his analysis of the speculative proposition by placing himself in the perspective of its addressee, namely the reader. Indeed it is the latter who experiences the conflict between the form and the content of the proposition. It is the reader who has the responsibility of "setting forth (*darstellen*)" the "return of the concept into itself (*das Zurückgehen des Begriffs in sich*)". Consequently, the plasticity of meaning is inseparable from a plasticity of reading, a reading which gives form to the utterance it receives.

> The philosophical decision finds itself in a new modality determined by the transition from the predicative to the speculative. This is the freedom and the responsibility of *interpretation*.[5]

Hegel understands spirit's "coming-to-itself" as a reflexive moment governed by the relations of opposition and unity. Unity produces itself as synthesis; it is already contained in the opposition and sublates this opposition completely in itself. In contrast, the recursive movement of parts and whole (which we consider to take place in speculative reading as well), the new that emerges, is contingent. Spirit unfolds because of a recursion that can be described linguistically; it is not driven by an absolute concept that would come into its own by means of reflection or have a dialectically unfolding teleology inscribed in it.

Before spirit can be understood, the speculative proposition forces it to a new stage. What does the predicative structure of the speculative proposition look like? Hegel thinks of it as a loop: "This movement which constitutes what formerly the proof was supposed to accomplish, is the dialectical movement of the proposition itself. This alone is the speculative *in act*, and only the expression of this movement is a speculative exposition. ... The *proposition* should express *what* the True is; but essentially the True is Subject. As such it is merely the dialectical movement, this course that generates itself, going forth from, and returning to, itself."[6] Reading thus begins with the subject of the proposition—but the predicate turns out not to be a predicate but a substance. The subject can no longer transcend a predicate that turns out to be a substance. In consequence, the subject of the proposition collapses and the proposition turns dialectically on itself.

When thought thus attacks itself, knowledge can be saved only if absolute knowledge takes the place of the proposition's original subject. In this replacement, however, the concept becomes more than a noun: it acquires a recursive propositional structure. In the predicative structure of the proposition, the concept—i.e. the logical subject of the proposition—determines itself. The expansion from noun to proposition is a movement of generalization. In Hegel, this generalization manifests itself as a dialectical movement from a concept to a more general concept. In the dialectical movement of a proposition, its original subject is negated by a predicate that turns out to be a substance. "Thus the content is, in fact, no longer a Predicate of the Subject, but is the Substance, the essence and the Notion of what is under discussion . . . Starting from the Subject as though this were a permanent ground, it finds that, since the Predicate is really the Substance, the Subject has passed over into the Predicate, and, by this very fact, has been sublated."[7]

In this movement, the unity of oppositions is to transition to a higher unity. Yet this sublation can only take place thanks to the proposition's recursion to its subject: a part-to-whole relation emerges within the proposition itself. That is why, for Hegel, the whole of knowledge can for a moment light up as the subject of the proposition. It is also the part-to-whole relation that is responsible for the higher degree of generality that distinguishes the concept qua proposition from the concept qua noun.

The signifier of predication

Is it possible to see, at this stage, why Hegel calls for an account of the speculative proposition? From a linguistic perspective, this is where one could apply the difference between lexical and syntactic reading. In lexical reading, we semantically relate the subject and the predicate of a proposition or we establish a logical relationship between them. In a lexical reading of the proposition "*Mare* is *a female horse*," we assign a given semantic meaning to a given expression; the proposition "A female horse is called a mare," in that case, only appears as a more cumbersome, unnecessarily complicated (if only because of the use of the passive voice), less precise formulation of what is meant. In syntactic reading, in contrast, we follow the recursive structure of a proposition or the gliding of the signifiers. The differences between our two example sentences now become quite clear. In the first proposition, we first read the expression *mare* and (by means of recursion) assign to it the meaning *female horse*. In the second proposition, we start with the meaning *female horse* and (recursively) relate it to the concept *mare*. In a syntactic reading, that is, we establish a part-to-whole relation, whereas in lexical reading, we presuppose this relation and merely derive information from the proposition concerning the relationships of predication between the parts.[8]

We will hardly recognize the signifier that takes place in a syntactic reading of the proposition "*Mare* is *a female horse*" as a sliding because we are well acquainted with the whole we thereby produce. It is quite the contrary in the case of the Oswald Egger *quatrain*, "Mit meiner/vom Brüllen/der Tiere/besessenen Stimme [With my voice possessed by the animals' screaming],"[9] where we already noticed the drift we get ourselves into when we read it. We cannot grasp the wholeness we produce in reading, cannot even grasp why it is whole at all. It is impossible for us to say with certainty to whom the voice we hear in the poem belongs. And yet we do hear a voice, heard the screaming and how the screaming became the screaming of the voice. How could we hear it when we do not know whose screaming voice it is? At the beginning, it is "my" voice, but then it belongs to the screaming; this screaming, in turn, seems to belong to the animals. But the animals do not belong to "me."

The quatrain identifies the screaming of the I with an animal. To this end, the order of subject and predicate must be reversed, and it must be reversed as we follow the syntactic movement. This can be pinpointed in the switchover of the meaning of "possessed"—with the voice possessed by the animals, the subject no longer possesses its voice in the same way (i.e. the voice is no longer the predicate of the subject). On the contrary, the subject has become the prey of the animals, possessed by an "animality" previously not its own. We are caught up in a metonymic shift—in reading, we come dangerously close to our animal other.

Does this interpretation not overlook something crucial, though? "With my voice possessed by the animals' screaming" is not a sentence—it lacks a predicate. But that, precisely, allows the quatrain to illustrate the principle of the speculative proposition. More than that: the speculative turns out to be *in* reading the quatrain; *in* reading, we can experience how language goes beyond itself. For the speculative proposition, too, must be driven beyond itself, must, in all senses of the term, overstep its limits. The speculative proposition must not only leave behind its semantic content, its syntactic structure, but also its factual being-tied-in with a textual context, even its factual being-tied-in with a virtual intertextuality, even, in a sense, its being-tied-in with the given system of language, its virtual paradigm—only this leaving behind opens up a new possibility of thought.

The transfer from a lexical to a syntactic understanding requires such a separate presentation because every lexical understanding is preceded by a syntactical understanding that, once it has taken place, seems to be absorbed in the lexical. In Guillaume's terms, the potential paradigm (which is formed in every speaking, thinking, or reading) tends to become invisible because it differs only infinitesimally from the actual paradigm. Hegel calls this a plastic exposition and demands that it exclude the usual relationships of the parts of the proposition. It is, as we now realize, not the transition from the reasoning to the speculative proposition that calls for an exposition: the speculative proposition itself calls for an exposition.

Every proposition must be pronounced because the signified could not exist without a signifier. But for a proposition to be a speculative proposition, it is not enough for it to actualize the predicative structure of a signified. A speculative proposition is not simply the signifier of an already existent signified; it has yet to *become significant*, become a signifier. In the speculative proposition, the potentializing function of language has to come into its own. This potentializing function is not limited to actualizing possibilities that are already there in language.

Absolute predictions

"To illustrate what has been said: in the proposition 'God is being,' the Predicate is 'being'; it has the significance of something substantial in which the Subject is dissolved. 'Being' is here meant to be not a Predicate, but rather the essence; it seems, consequently, that God ceases to be what he is from his position in the proposition, viz. a fixed Subject. Here thinking, instead of making progress in the transition from Subject to Predicate, in reality feels itself checked by the loss of the Subject, and, missing it, is thrown back on to the thought of the Subject. Or, since the Predicate itself has been expressed as a Subject, as *the* being or *essence* which exhausts the nature of the Subject, thinking finds the Subject immediately in the Predicate; and now, having returned into itself in the Predicate, instead of being in a position where it has freedom for argument, it is still absorbed in the content, or at least is faced with the demand that it should be."[10]

Hegel's example is telling. The question of predication in general arises in confronting the ultimate or most impossible of all predicates: *Being*. And by way of the example of the absolute subject, *God*, the question of the subject in general arises.[11] We do not want to repeat the steps of this dialectical argument (let us just note the installation of the great Other—God—on the throne of knowledge) for that would only conceal the decisive difference between Hegel's reading of the movement of explication and the movement of exposition we consider to be decisive. Hegel is concerned with presenting the logical-semantic content of a speculative proposition. In this respect, the movement with which Hegel develops the content does not differ from a mathematical proof and could also be described in the language of formal logic. Hegel seeks to develop from out of the speculative proposition the truth it already contains. His demand for presentation [*Darstellung*] is philosophical idealism, not experimental writing; his philosophical starting point is the signified that is to receive a signifier.

We are more interested in operations in which something new emerges thanks to an othering of signifying structures, something not already virtually contained in these structures. For us, language is not a development tool, as it is for Hegel, a tool the World Spirit uses to bring itself into appearance by developing itself. In our conception, the "tool being" of language (Graham Harman) is a *contingent* potentiality, an actual capacity for development in which the future development is strictly unforeseeable. This is not the least of reasons for which we hold on to the necessity of writing, which we also see as a necessity for philosophy. This means: yes, we can become Hegelians or Deleuzians or Strawsonians by reading Hegel or Deleuze or Strawson; we then see the world with new eyes because the inexhaustible sense contained in their works changes our thinking, our perception and thereby our image of the world. In reading we merely actualize the (as we said, inexhaustible) possibilities that lie in these works (i.e. what the "exactly" effect is a symptom of). When, however, we write *about* Hegel, *about* Deleuze, *about* Strawson, in short: *about* the texts we read, we can realize the contingent potential that lies in them. This potential does not exhaust itself in the merely potentialized virtual inexhaustibility of all existing texts.

Speculation gets a movement going that is to be conceived of as a generalization of thought. When in this movement something general emerges, it presents itself to the subject of thinking as new wholeness: what we call metanoia. It is not just the subject that emerges from the process of metanoia as a changed subject, the object must also have been transformed. In mereological terms: in the newly emerging part-to-whole relation, the subject finds itself as one of the parts.

There is no telling in advance what direction this movement will take. For its goal is not set by a great Other, nor does the movement come to a halt when some kind of "unity" has been reached. Instead, it is engaged in an active othering, which can productively refer both to the subject and to the object. The othering of the parts is interested in the parts of a whole both to manipulate them and to experiment with them. This othering, in our conception, is not a deviation from the imperative to know but instead the imperative to expand our possibilities of knowing.

Triadic epistemic situation

Let's recall once more Karl-Otto Apel's reflections that helped us to recognize how semiotics sees itself as the successor of transcendental philosophy and takes up the claim to explain the intersubjective validity of knowledge. Semiotics translates the critique of knowledge (as an analysis of consciousness) into a critique of sense (as an analysis of signs). Yet, as we can see now, the knowledge gained by a semiotic critique of sense can be translated into a new triadic epistemic situation.

The epistemic situation of philosophy is not sufficiently understood if it is conceived of as dyadic. It would be interpreted incorrectly even if we articulated the need for extending the engagement of a (reading) subject with a (text) object by a third pole (the other). In reading, we often approach the texts with the claim that we are less (unrestrainedly) subjective than they are. One example of this is Roman Jakobson and Claude Lévi-Strauss's reading of Baudelaire's *Les chats*, which has drawn criticism for its ruthless objectivism.[12]

What is normal for writing in literary criticism is also possible in everyday novel reading; indeed, it is all the more likely the more subjective or personal a text's approach to us is (think of Ingeborg Bachmann's *Malina* or Cesare Pavese's diaries). The text only achieves significance for the reader when it goes out to meet him as subject and the reader can only understand a book when, at the end, he returns to himself as changed (which does not, in itself, constitute a metanoia). There is no interpretant of a text without such othering.

The interpretant is to be understood as a semiotic dimension of referents *and* of signifiers and finally of signifieds. That is why we do not read the passage from Agamben cited above as postulating a dyadic relationship of subjective reader and objective text (or an opposition reader–text). We interpret Agamben's insight into reading to be speculative: to read is to encounter both the subjectivity and the objectivity of a text; the danger of losing their own subjectivity forces readers to operate an othering of the text.

A linguistic ontology of language

Our interest in a speculative ontology of language makes it necessary to revise Agamben's boundary between language as the object of linguistics and the interest philosophy has in language: "If the object of linguistics is language (understood as shorthand for the *factum linguae*, the *factum linguarum*, and the *factum grammaticae*), philosophy is instead concerned with the *factum loquendi*, which linguistics must simply presuppose. Philosophy is the attempt to *expose* this presupposition, to become conscious of the meaning of the fact that human beings speak. It is possible to see how it is the *factum grammaticae* that marks the difference between philosophy and linguistics: philosophy is concerned with the pure existence of language, independent of its real properties (transcendental properties, which belong to philosophical reflection, do not go beyond the field of pure existence), while linguistics is concerned with language insofar as it is describable in terms of real properties, insofar as it has (or, rather, is) a grammar.... The pure existence (without any properties other than transcendental ones) that constitutes the sole object of philosophy is something to which philosophy has no access other than through reflection on the *factum loquendi* and the construction of an experience in which this *factum* is thematically at issue. Only the *experience of the pure existence of language allows thought to consider the pure existence of the world*."[13]

This characterization situates the speculative moment of language on the side of philosophy and the interest in facts on the side of linguistics. So strict a division, however, is not necessary. Neither meaning nor grammar are given as facticities of language. Since such a separation of interests does not apply, we insist so emphatically on the potentiality of language anchored in speech we read about in Gustave Guillaume. Let us therefore question Agamben's distribution or division of jurisdictions and fields of inquiry. Let's try to further develop what Guillaume allowed us to show earlier: namely that paradigms are created in speech.

Agamben's delimitation is of great heuristic value because it marks the differences between philosophy and applied, or descriptive, linguistics. Yet the distinction cannot be employed in Guillaume's speculative linguistics—in what Elisabeth Leiss describes as the project of a "philosophy of language"—as doing so would destroy these theories' cognitive potential.

Our emphasis, inspired by Guillaume, on the relationship between language and speech sheds new light on another philosophical aspect, namely an ontological dimension of the *langage spéculative* [speculative speech] hardly noticed in Derrida's deconstructive approach. A linguistically informed philosophy of language can conceive of itself as an ontology to the extent that it understands how language provides us with epistemic tools with which we experience the world and which can change our experience of the world. It is this moment of changing the world that we call metanoia. Just as "plastic reading" is connected to Malabou's concept of a *plasticité noétique* [noetic plasticity], so speculative reading probably correlates with what Derrida calls *langage spéculative*.[14] Our thesis is that speculation is not just a matter of meaning but equally affects signifiers and their grammatical-syntactic order. Without the moment of the world's changing that can thereby emerge, metanoia cannot be thought.

First, we developed our speculative ontology of language out of a linguistic tradition. We are now looking for an area in which the *poiesis* of language creates space for itself in reading and writing. When we go beyond the pathos of Agamben's italicized sentence—"Only the *experience of the pure existence of language allows thought to consider the pure existence of the world*"[15]—we can take up his thoughts and take them further, we can ask what the philosophical and the linguistic approach to language have in common.[16]

Agamben speaks of philosophy's interest in the existentiales of language and juxtaposes it to the interest in the facts of language he ascribes to linguistics. Let's recall that what Heidegger called "existentiales" were those objects intuition gives to itself (as we mentioned, Heidegger's existential analysis is rooted in a transcendental aesthetic). It is by no means necessary to view the existentiales from the perspective of *aiesthesis*. Since we are here dealing with an intuition that gives its objects to itself (and with speech that creates its objects for itself) we can also focus on *poiesis* (the giving or creating of objects) and that means regarding existentiales as the core of a transcendental poetics.

The emphasis on the *poietic* moment of philosophy and the interpretation of the existential character of language cannot, therefore, be separated.

The speculative triad

Semiotic realism

In the previous chapter, we established the semiotic character of the part-to-whole relations to which every sign owes its reality content. Our indication of the part-to-whole relation in which the elements that constitute the semiotic triangle stand to one another revises a late-structuralist understanding of semiotics that theorizes the formation of meaning in terms of dyadic oppositions and differences. No matter how differentiated, interrupted and opposed the components of meaning might be, it always emerges because the semiotic triad brings them into a part-to-whole relation.

The institution of meaning in a triad of part-to-whole relations shifted our focus to the discourse of hermeneutics. Our question was to what extent the meaning that has emerged (or emerges) in a text qua *poiesis* opens up truth and how readers make this truth explicit by means of the hermeneutic circle. The creation of part-to-whole relations obviously also has an epistemic function here, if only because the whole is more abstract than its parts. In coming back to its starting point, the recursive structure of the circle creates a new generality. In a corresponding speculative reading, the movement of thought thus takes lingual shape.

On the basis of these findings, our concern now is to develop a language-ontological speculation, a speculative ontology of language. We want to determine the way in which language relates our thought and our perception of the world. The interface of semiotic and language-ontological speculation could be articulated in terms of a realism of language: every attempt to play the reality content of knowledge arising from the perception of things (i.e. from *aisthesis*) off against the reality content of knowledge instituted by semiotic part-to-whole relations (i.e. by *poiesis*) aims for a self-dissolution of thinking (*noiesis*). If, however, thinking does not want to destroy itself it must, so to speak, divert the nihilistic impulse of such attempts by declaring either *poiesis* or *aisthesis* to be invisible.

Dimensions of language-realist poetics

Our speculative poetics has to be able to give an account of how the products of lingual *poiesis* participate in the institution of knowledge and how *aisthesis* and *noiesis* cooperate in this process. More precisely, the question is how the institution of signifieds, the creation of signifiers, and the production of referents are not only connected but necessarily indistinguishable—in the end, this is what we also call reading or writing. How does this create *signifiers*, *referents*, and *signifieds*? Intuitively, we might suspect that *poiesis* only creates the signifier while we refer to referents through *aisthesis*, and meaning is a matter of *noiesis* alone. That they are all equally the product of a *poiesis* might seem doubtful, especially in the case of referents of which we might want to say that they exist before language and are perceptible and knowable without language as well.

We believe that *aisthesis*, *poiesis* and *noiesis* are all equally involved in language-realist semiosis. By looking at these, we hope to come to a more precise definition of the relation between the realist and the semiotic moments of our poetics.

(1) *Aisthesis*: Sensibility allows us to perceive differences. By making distinctions, it creates from the matter that surrounds us the material without which there could be no semiosis. In terms of our earlier example, this means, initially, nothing more and nothing less than this: without our sensory apparatus, we could not even distinguish between the written *apple tree* and an apple tree, because we could not distinguish between any given signifier and any given referent. From a semiotic perspective, the relationship between *apple tree* and apple tree would indeed be arbitrary (as every relationship between any signifier whatsoever and any referent whatsoever). Looked at this way, it is sensibility that makes it such that the relation of denotation is not arbitrary but contingent.

But sensibility makes another indispensable contribution to semiosis, because it is differentiated (i.e. assembled from different faculties) and puts these differences at the disposal of the formation of meaning qua semiosis, without which we could not perceive any things, signifiers, or referents. We thus conceive of *aisthesis* cross-modally:

meanings never contain single sensate (e.g. optic or acoustic) moments, but always a synthesis of sensate (e.g. optic *and* acoustic) ideas. In allowing us to distinguish between things, space, and time, the combination of sensate moments makes our perception of world possible.
(2) *Noiesis*: To understand what role cognition or truth is assigned from a poetological perspective, we have drawn above all on the analytic philosophy of language.

Most relevant for our purposes is the analytic claim of bringing about a theory of truth to render lingual signs non-arbitrary.

Every logic (i.e. every reference of signifiers to signifieds strictly regulated by identity) aims for the identifiability of referents. We saw that aesthetic semblance and poetic metaphor are two sets of problems central to the analytic approach because they undermine this principle of identity. We will have to explain in more detail why every attempt to cut the Gordian knot by imposing the principle of identity on language turns against the ability of language to produce reference (and thus turns against the productivity of *noiesis*).
(3) *Poiesis* is the central function of our semiotic poetics. This much we learned from Gustave Guillaume: signs are created; every natural language includes a language-creating function. In the poetic function as described by Roman Jakobson, language reflexively relates to its own paradigms by means of similarity and equivalence; in the (*poietic-*)poetic function of language we outline, language recursively produces its own paradigms through mereological procedures. As becomes increasingly clear, however, this recursion movement cannot be thought purely as immanent to language but presupposes the combination of language and reality.

This constitutes a methodical opposition to two abstractions. We argue, on the one hand, against positivist literary criticism, which presupposes that there is meaning beyond its own activity and thereby abstracts from the language-creating qualities of reading; and, on the other hand, against a literary aesthetics that ignores these qualities by focusing on allegedly more general philosophical problems.

Aesthetic and poetic *noiesis*

A speculative poetics is interested in the relationship between *poiesis* and *noiesis*. Aesthetics, in contrast, is characterized by understanding *noiesis* with a view to *aisthesis*: its vanishing point is "sensible thought," not metanoia. This, however, ignores the dimension of *poiesis*—the possibility that something new emerges has to remain inexplicable, it becomes a mystery. The history of aesthetics can be described as an attempt to find an explanation for this mystery. For it is precisely the genuine object of aesthetics—art—that cannot, in our view, be conceived of as anything other than the result of *poiesis*.

One of the prime examples of aesthetics, the "ready-made," seems to us to be particularly eloquent on this disappearance of the genesis of the work. Aesthetics assures us that the ready-made is a kind of non-made work, an industrial product that cannot be the object of a poetics because it is centrally determined by a concept of making (which is understood pragmatically). But why not argue the other way around and say that the discourse and practices of language around the ready-made can be understood as the *poiesis* of a concept of art and that it is through this concept that the industrial product *becomes* a work of art? At the same time, we oppose the usual philosophical conceptions of experience that cleanse experience of its *poietic* moments. Since it is an (as we'll see, constitutive) discipline of philosophy, this opposition also applies to aesthetics: aesthetics must, so to speak, be blind to the effectiveness of *poiesis*.

Diacritics

How are we to characterize *noiesis* in the context of our poetics? What, in other words, are the poetic specifics of semiotic reason? The answers to these questions must not fall behind critical thought. Günther Wohlfahrt, for instance, outlines it from a Kantian perspective with a view to Hegel: "Usually, the business of critique is diacritical. Thus Kant, for example, operates the 'classical' distinction between analytical and synthetic judgments, between the mere *concept of an object* and the *object of a concept* that can only be given in experience. He does so, ultimately, to show that it is impossible to try to 'collect' the *existence of an object* from the *concept of that object*. According to Hegel, speculative thought consists in bringing together these two 'diacritical' ideas.

In reflecting on what we do when we reflect diacritically, doesn't in this case the 'bringing together' of ideas lead to the insight that all we possess of that object of the concept is only our *concept of that object of the concept*? Does this not lead us further, to the question whether the 'dialectics' of this 'diacritics' does not consist in the fact that the extra-conceptuality of that object's existence is in turn 'collected' from the concept, to the question, that is, whether it is only 'within' the concept that we can be 'outside' the concept, whether it is only 'within' language that we can be 'outside' of language?"[17]

Let's try to take the last question of this train of thought as seriously and in as full a sense as possible. One of the goals of our method is to find precisely those forms of movement within language that open up something new, a new Outside of language. We have already said how we think of this: in every movement of speculative thought that creates a plasticity of concepts, the greatest triumph of thought consists in a switch to a more general level. The most famous articulation of this point is once again found in Hegel's *Phenomenology*: "The True is thus the Bacchanalian revel in which no member is not drunk; yet because each member collapses as soon as he drops out, the revel is just as much transparent and simple repose."[18]

In the interest of a speculative poetics, we follow the speculating intoxication of thought that liquefies concepts. But we want to go beyond the dialectic movement of thought by which it spirals upward to ever-greater generalities. We want to make this movement turn around once more and focus on the point at which the members or parts reappear and turn out to have been completely changed. It is this *poietic* going-beyond-thinking that we call metanoia. In short: philosophical speculation gets high on the whole; metanoia gets high on the parts.

Subject—object—other: our methodical constellation

Poiesis as othering

We are suspicious of all attempts to describe *aisthesis* and *noiesis* dyadically, which, as we have seen, also happens in aesthetics. From the perspective of aesthetics, it must seem as if *aisthesis* could be sufficiently determined by the relationship of a subject to an object. The same holds for the view that *noiesis* only takes place between the senses and the understanding and that the question is merely whether reality is to be attributed to the products of the understanding. Metanoia, however, makes us understand that *poiesis*, too, stands in relation to *aisthesis* and *noiesis* (and in different relations than those described by aesthetics). As soon as we begin with such a three-dimensional view, we see that *poiesis* maps onto the two other relations in the form of an othering.

Attempts at fashioning a different, a non-aesthetic tradition of art range from the early Romantic idea of the work of art as a medial reflective connection (perhaps even better described as a recursive connection) via Walter Benjamin's romantic practice of art criticism to Howard Caygill's speculative interpretation of Benjamin. Inspired less by an emphatic concept of the work of art than by a critical concept of literature, these attempts are not directed only at hermeneutic analyses of single works but also at literature's potential for speculative criticism. Work and experience expose one another to critical change. Caygill writes about Benjamin's analysis of Friedrich Schlegel's and Novalis's insights into what we call othering: "Immanent critique is speculative in acknowledging that both it and the work or object being judged are transformed by their encounter."[19]

Every perspective deviates from the object at which it is directed: this is the insight we would like to render more productive than it is able to be within the framework of theories of interpreting or analyzing literary texts that believe the goal of interpreting activity to lie in doing justice to the work. Our discussion of the British metaphysician Strawson showed how the subject is present in the semiotic triangle as a whole. What Peirce calls the interpretant is a dimension of sense to be found in all semiotic elements. There is no facticity independently determined by a subject. This does not mean, however, that the difference between subject and object no longer existed. Instead, it demands, on our view, a commitment to the unavoidable subjectivity of our access to the object, a subjectivity we seek to endow with critical relevance instead of seeing in it merely an inevitable residue.

Every work, understood as an original creation, has always already deviated from a status quo of good form. To take the significance of the literary work for a subject into account, we do not see any alternative other than to ask about reading. Readers change with the works they read. We become Tolstoyans, we become biographers of Sylvia Plath, and we see ourselves and the world through the eyes of Marx or Spengler, Weininger or Butler, Lacan or Bourdieu. If our goal is to develop reading as an experimental technique, we must not avert our eyes from the othering of the text that comes with every reading. We do not wish to leave it at the arbitrariness of this othering or leave this othering to such arbitrariness, but instead clarify the conditions to which it is subjected.

Juranville reads Lacan

To further motivate our methodical triad, especially the aspect of an othering of object and subject, we can go back to some reflections by Alain Juranville, who has subjected Lacanian psychoanalysis to a radical philosophical systematization. In Juranville's exposition (which also exemplifies what we called speculative reading) Lacan's psychoanalysis is a philosophy insofar as it depicts a genuine epistemic situation, a situation in which, for us, the emphasis is less on the concept of the unconscious than on the constellation of subject, object, and other that institutes both meaning and knowledge.

We should note here that the three logical "moments of the signifier" identified by Lacan are "those of the dialectical process as Hegel describes it" and "are, very generally, the necessary consequences of a philosophical consideration of language, of the logos." The first moment is "that of the immediate relationship with the object, the second that of the subject positing the object—more precisely, we discover that the object is what it is only for the subject, that it is *posited* by the subject. The third [moment], finally, is that of the dialectical identity of subject and object, the moment in which the subject posits itself as object but also the moment in which the object appears in its effective reality, which consists in being a subject—a moment we can characterize as the moment of the positing of positing itself."[20]

The problem of the analytic approach turned out to be that language loses its access to things, its referents, as soon as it is no longer possible to articulate a theory of absolute truth. Lacan's philosophy, in contrast, makes do with a partial truth and, despite the indelibility of the Big Other, articulates a logic of the signifier that thematizes the contact with the thing. A subject can entertain relations (of knowledge) with an object that can lead it to knowledge of a truth.

Lacan writes: "I stressed the division that I make by opposing, in relation to the entrance of the unconscious, the two fields of the subject and the Other. The Other is the locus in which is situated the chain of the signifier that governs whatever may be made present of the subject—it is the field of that living being in which the subject has to appear."[21] A subject of knowledge is not simply given as an ego *prior* to the cognitive process. The signifier does not address a pre-existing subject of thought. The more we realize that the subject only constitutes itself in the relation to an other in the first place—"The signifier, producing itself in the field of the Other, makes manifest the subject of its signification"[22]—the more the question of the relation of such a subject to the object of knowledge becomes acute.

If we limited ourselves to a dialectic auto-constitution (of a subject or an object), our theory would not advance beyond articulating a paradox: a subject that cannot become identical to itself does not get any closer to the truth than it does in the proposition, "I'm lying." This "central defect" results from the "dialectic" articulated by Lacan, according to which "the subject depends on the signifier and … the signifier is first of all in the field of the Other."[23]

Yet according to Hegel, as Slavoj Žižek has pointed out, the object itself can never be identical with its concept: "Apropos of the notion of truth, Hegel accomplished his famous reversal: truth does not consist in the correspondence of our thought (proposition, notion) with an object, but in the correspondence of the object itself to its notion; as is well known, Heidegger retorted that this reversal remains within the confines of the same metaphysical notion of truth as correspondence. What, however, eludes this Heideggerian reproach is the radically *asymmetric* character of the Hegelian reversal: with Hegel, we have *three* and not two elements—the dual relationship of 'knowledge' between 'thought' and its 'object' is replaced with the triangle of (subjective) thought, the object and its notion *which in no way coincides with thought*. For this reason, the encounter of the object with its notion (with the notion in the strict dialectical sense and not with the abstract-general Platonic idea) is necessarily a *failed* encounter."[24]

Over against readings of Hegel guided by deconstruction and negative dialectics, which criticize Hegel as the thinker of an absolute from which what is other about the negative escapes, Žižek emphasizes that the demonstration of the impossibility of "absolute knowledge" must also at the same time highlight a subversive dimension of this "absolute knowledge." Since from the perspective of an "absolute knowledge" every possible (concrete) knowledge necessarily appears as arbitrary and insufficient, "absolute knowledge" can in the end not allow for any knowledge at all. Thinking the absolute here is "critical" of knowledge, and it is an instrument for transforming any knowledge into a critical knowledge, for emphasizing its critical status. It is crucial for us that this critical moment (a general moment applicable to every knowledge) not be lost to some kind of agnosticism.

In reference to the subject, the first question to ask is: how does one become anything like a Wertherian or a Houellebecqian anyway? If metanoia takes place in the encounter with a literary work, then the work is assigned absolute knowledge. Yet (from the perspective of the work) the work cannot but fail to attain its concept because as object, it cannot, as we saw, encounter *its* concept. This, of course, is not a question about the justification of different interpretations or the popular and familiar (familiar since modernism, since 1800, since forever) idea that literary texts "understand themselves."

These questions can be cleared up by looking at the third position in this dialectic movement: the concept itself triggers an othering. We read Žižek's determination of the paradoxical, failing encounter of subject and other as a determination of speculative reading, as a description of the experience of the subject we conceive of as metanoia: the whole all of a sudden becomes another. "The re-cognition of the subject in the alienated substance does not aim for an 'appropriation' of the content of the substance, for recognizing it as resulting from its own activity; on the contrary, it comes to know its defectiveness as the effect of a hole, of a lack in the Other, it comes to know its being separate from substance the effect of a diremption, a split in the innermost of substance itself."[25]

We have already traced a similar argument in the context of the production of part-to-whole relations and in our discussion of the debate between hermeneutics and deconstruction. For the understanding from which hermeneutics draws its ontology is possible only in a triadic whole, not in a fusing of horizons, not in a *unio mystica* of work and reader. And only in a triadic whole, not thanks to mere relations of opposition, does the delirium of the senses arise that so fascinates late structuralism and deconstruction. This also includes, as Lorenzo Chiesa has shown, the position of the subject: "the

Lacanian subject is a *subjectivized* lack, *not a lacking* subject."[26] An element acquires its meaning in relation to another element whose effect can only unfold in a recursive movement, a movement that creates a whole by means of a third element. Only in a whole does one of the elements appear as an absolute and another element as its negation.

Linguistic turntable

"[T]here is no such thing as metalanguage (an assertion made so as to situate all of logical positivism), no language able to say the truth about truth, since truth is grounded in the fact that truth speaks, and that it has no other means by which to become grounded."[27] It is this criticism of Lacan's of a metalanguage that has inspired us to methodically recall the triadic epistemic situation of psychoanalysis (consisting of subject, object, and other).

From this point of view, let's try once again to situate our method in relation to the two discourses of philosophy and contemporary linguistics, namely against the background of analytic philosophy's attempts at making epistemology progress in the form of lingual analysis. At the end of this paradigm, the image of language was so distorted that it provoked massive objections from both the theory of language and from philosophy itself.

"What is needed is a confrontation with the proponents of the 'linguistic turn;' what is needed, too, is a return to linguistics, i.e. to an engagement with language that is based on sound knowledge."[28] Elisabeth Leiss's accusation against philosophy as it developed in the wake of the so-called linguistic turn is substantial. In generalized form, her reproach is that the philosophy of language lacks insight into the way language functions and is therefore incapable of knowing anything about the world or of developing an ontology; it argues without knowing anything about its objects or isn't, in the end, interested in them at all. Various currents of contemporary philosophy—from Badiou's mathematical ontology to Latour's theory of science—develop a complementary criticism: they reproach the philosophies shaped by the linguistic turn of language with having lost its genuinely philosophical dimension.

Are these just superficial agreements? Or do they conceal fundamental commonalities that overlap with our project of a realist theory of language?

From this perspective, we can name at least four commonalities relevant to an ontological understanding of language: first, the anti-causality of language; second, its relationism; third, its realism; and fourth, its circularity.

First we can see a general anti-causal argument shared by Elisabeth Leiss and philosophical anti-nominalisms. "The main difference between a rationalist universal grammar and a semiotically conceived one is that the latter does not admit causal explanations."[29] The two discourses have very different reasons for rejecting causality; but they share the insight that thought and language are not causally linked to their objects. Meillassoux focuses on the concept of the facticity of facts, Leiss on the non-arbitrariness of language. We saw how they condition each other.

Second, there is a point of connection or an interface between recent linguistic realism and Speculative Realism in what we call an ontology of relations or relational ontology. Its essential insight is that language communicates to its speakers a relational knowledge. With this knowledge, we know the world—a world that consists of relations between things, to which we, too, belong. (Let's recall that we already found this leveling of the difference between things and objects, both considered to be "individuals," in Strawson's metaphysics.)

Third, we do not think it is a coincidence that both discourses are anti-nominalist. We believe that the insights emerging in both cannot be translated into any nominalism—just as our ontological reflections have led us to a theory of language and our linguistic reflections impose a corresponding realism. The occasion for our discussion of this realism is the central myth of modern linguistics: the arbitrariness of the sign. Often, this just refers to the difference between the semiotic elements. That just means that referents, signifiers, and signifieds are distinct—it already counts as reason for the arbitrariness of the sign that they cannot be directly projected one onto the other.

We countered this misunderstanding with the insight from semiotics that the negation of an indexical relationship between referents and signifiers in language is a precondition for establishing symbolic semiotic relations: Thirdness or signs that are the expression of a meta-relationality emerge in the negation of indexical relations (i.e. from Secondness). The myth of the arbitrariness of language unilaterally declares this moment of the genesis of Thirdness (i.e. of lingual relationality) to be absolute.

Fourth, the circularity of language makes it possible to discern the procedure by which part-to-whole relations emerge. They emerge through recursion, whose procedural specifics we described as contiguous. We must not, in this context, overlook the fundamental difference between two relations in language: the distinction between part-to-whole relations and equivalence (as positive or negative identity in reference to a characteristic) makes all the difference.

The usual reservations against circular structures in language stem mainly from the incompatibility of part-to-whole relations and negative relations of equivalence as well as from the fact that, when they cross, they produce paradoxes ("I'm lying"). This often-criticized figure emerges when negation and self-reflexivity come together. In part-to-whole relations that arise from recursion, however, negativity in the form of Secondness is not only not problematic, it is also even constitutive; it only turns into a paradox when it is interpreted as Firstness. Yet we saw that Firstness only emerges in running through the semiotic triangle (i.e. it already contains a difference). When part-to-whole relations are recursively introduced into one another, no such contradictions arise. What's more, within triadic part-to-whole relations, we can refer paradoxes to Firstnesses and perceive them as aesthetic.

In recursive structures, the structure itself "simply" becomes ever-more complex. The form of lingual recursion thus heightens the realism of language and increases its possibilities of reference. We encounter a process that unfolds completely differently from what is described in those deadlocked avantgardistic concepts of self-reflexivity that take equivalence as their basic relation. Self-reflexivity based on equivalence may obscure reference—but recursivity, which is based on metonymic part-to-whole relations, certainly does not.

Our criticism of the generalization of relations of equivalence and its effects is congruent with the philosophical criticism of a correlationist understanding of language articulated by speculative materialist Quentin Meillassoux: "Correlationism takes many contemporary forms, but particularly those of transcendental philosophy, the varieties of phenomenology, and post-modernism. But although these currents are all extraordinarily varied in themselves, they all share, according to me, a more or less explicit decision: that there are no objects, no events, no laws, no beings which are not always-already correlated with a point of view, with a subjective access. Anyone maintaining the contrary—i.e. that it is possible to attain something like a reality in itself, existing absolutely independently of his viewpoint, or his categories, or his epoch, or his culture, or his language, etc.—this person would be exemplarily naïve, or if you prefer: a realist, a metaphysician, a quaintly dogmatic Philosopher."[30]

We can see clearly now that correlationism, which Meillassoux makes out to be the antagonist of any realism or materialism, presupposes a specific theory of language. If we were linguists, we'd call such a theory a relationism of equivalences. In such a relationism of equivalences or correlationist theory of language, the paradoxes, mirror effects, and equi-univocities produced in circles by relations of equivalence necessarily turn against realism.

Abduction as a *poietic* procedure

We're looking for models that allow us to describe how metanoia institutes knowledge. To be able to distinguish the *poietic* moment of thought from "mere speculation," we have to determine the logic it obeys. Without such an element, in turn, thinking would be indistinguishable from mere logistics.

Individual theoretical idioms have helped us in highlighting various aspects of metanoia. First, we attempted to outline and revise the theoretical discourse of poetics about the figure of metonymy. In this context, we also suggested a different definition of the lingual function of poetry. Instead of equivalence, we've championed contiguity as the principle of the lingual function. Taking an intermediary step via linguistics, we came upon the significance of recursive structures. The particular focus of our analyses was on part-to-whole relations, which also provide the basis for the fundamentally synecdochal moment of metonymies. Part-to-whole relations not only describe the formation of each and every whole, they also—as we saw with reference to the analytic philosophy of language—raise the question of the referentiality of language.

Next, we were concerned with why this question cannot be answered outside the domain of an ontology of language. We marked ourselves off from a conception of metalanguage based on the principle of equivalence and from a methodology that makes identity its principle; instead, we emphasized the meta-moment that language, because of its recursivity, contains. Finally, we described a corresponding methodological setting that introduces—besides, first, the subject and, second, the object of knowledge—third, an other.

Our methodical othering shows that not every difference that results from a subject's perspective onto the object of its description can be "explained" by a fundamental arbitrariness or singularity. We may here follow Hölderlin's emphatic definition: "Judgment: is in the highest and strictest sense the original sundering of Subject and Object most intimately united in intellectual intuition, the very sundering which first makes Object and Subject possible, the *Ur-Theilung*. In the concept of division [*Theilung*] there lies already the concept of the reciprocal relation [*Beziehung*] of Object and Subject to one another, and the necessary presupposition of a whole of which Object and Subject are the parts."[31] If we did not systematically trace this insight in a logic of judgment, we would in the end be forced to create a methodological illusion: subject and object could only be identified, and adequate knowledge would only be possible in a kind of aesthetic semblance.

To answer this question, let's look at a parallel dilemma that arises between object and concept on the one hand and their projected adequation on the other: between the two, only induction and deduction initially seem conceivable. Yet perhaps a third procedure of inference, the procedure of abduction, provides a solution. Instead of partial identification, it first introduces a temporalization: abduction presents hypotheses and concepts of which it cannot be determined in the moment of abduction whether objects correspond to them.

We can see what makes abduction so valuable for us when we contrast it with other inference procedures. In a deduction, we conclude a particular case from a law and a context. In an induction, we conclude a law from a particular case and a context. In an abduction, however, we do not reflect or determine what is the law and what an individual case; instead, we hypothetically infer a context from an individual case *and* a rule.

Once again it was Peirce who first recognized the potential of abduction, which intrigues us for three main reasons. First, abduction connects logic and hermeneutics insofar as it mediates between understanding and explanation or, rather, bases explanation on an understanding. Second, in abduction the paradox of innovation and rule, which represents a core paradox of poetics both in theory and in practice, dissolves. And third, abduction understood as a scientific procedure justifies, as we'll see, the programmatic character and preliminary nature of methods of investigation.

Four forms of abduction

A more precise understanding of abduction, we hope, will thus specify further our understanding of how a philosophical and literary hermeneutics proceeds. For—according to Umberto Eco—"the text is an object that the interpretation builds up in the course of the circular effort of validating itself on the basis of what it makes up as its result. I am not shamed to admit that I am so defining the old and still valid 'hermeneutic circle.' The logic of interpretation is the Peircean logic of abduction."[32] Eco's semiotic differentiation between four forms of abduction will support our reflections.

(1) "*Hypothesis or overcoded abduction*. The law is given automatically or semi-automatically. Let us call this kind of law a *coded* law. It is very important to assume that even interpreting through codes presupposes an abductional effort, however minimal."[33]

    To clarify this point, let's take an example. A graduate student in literature reads Beckett and Updike, and in his attempt to give a phenomenological description of his literary experience, he comes upon the novels' surprising use of tense. All facts collected in the secondary literature suggest something that is nonetheless not accounted for by any theory, namely that all these novels written (mostly) in the present tense are emphatic novels of the present. The topic of the master's thesis, arrived at abductively, is: the present tense is responsible for the effect of presentness and momentaneity often mentioned in the secondary literature. (Let's note, only for the sake of our argument here, that his thesis receives an A: it is not obviously wrong, it is well-researched, and provides a new thesis to plausibly synthesize the available literature.)

(2) "*Undercoded abduction*. The rule must be selected from a series of equiprobable rules put at our disposal by the current world knowledge (or semiotic encyclopedia).... Since the rule is selected as the more plausible among many, but it is not certain whether it is the 'correct' one or not, the explanation is only *entertained*, waiting for further tests."[34]

Let's imagine that our student has not immediately lost interest in the present tense; instead, a peculiar lack of explanation has bothered him, he has not stopped reading novels written in the present tense, and he decides to submit a dissertation proposal on the basis of an expanded corpus of material. The thesis that is to secure the necessary funding is that in the twentieth century, an autonomous literary phenomenon develops: the present tense novel. He contrasts his thesis with the received opinion of conservative literary criticism, which condemns the present tense novel as a superficial fad and a renunciation of the complex narrative possibilities of the nineteenth century, in which a highly artificial tense technique, the epic past tense with its ability to presentify the past, had been perfected.

Our PhD student, first, closes gaps in the material (central chapters are dedicated to the novels of Hubert Fichte, Claude Simon, and Thomas Pynchon) and, second, takes a close look at the nineteenth century as well. And, what do you know, he finds countless passages written in the present tense in classical novels, too—his findings concern the abundant use of the present tense in texts about madness, dreams, and hallucinations by E. T. A. Hoffmann, Gogol, and Strindberg—that come in to support his thesis, which until now has remained rather implausible: the present tense novel, he will now claim, generalizes a present tense that, although traditionally marginalized as "historical present tense," has always existed in the novel and raises it to the level of the normative tense. (Although, once again, it does not yet really matter, let's mention the following: the, in his advisors' view, thorough study of his material has earned our exemplary student a *summa cum laude*—for years, our newly minted PhD will erroneously believe he owes this distinction to the discovery of a genuine phenomenon—and although dangerous doubts about his method crop up in his mind as early as at his defense, he does not digress, does not contradict himself, and graduates with the highest honor.)

(3) "*Creative abduction.* The law must be *invented ex novo*. To invent a law is not so difficult, provided our mind is 'creative' enough.... [T]his creativity involves also aesthetic aspects. In any case this kind of invention obliges one to make (more than in cases of over-coded or

under-coded abductions) a meta-abduction. Examples of creative abductions are found in these 'revolutionary' discoveries that change an established scientific paradigm...."[35]

Fortunately for our narrative, it only takes a short while after his graduation ceremony until our student is offered a very-well-paid position at an immensely-well-endowed research institution. The catch: he has only one week to come up with a high-impact thesis that is as innovative as it is well-founded and will produce results that can be securely predicted. He remembers his readings on how the hermeneutic circle functions and—repeat offender that he is—he immediately comes up with a working title for his second book: "The Reinvention of the Novel in the Second Half of the Twentieth Century." He still believes it possible to translate his hypothesis concerning the existence of a phenomenon called "present tense novel" into a valid inference, and he believes that all that material cannot but allow for an induction. The reflection on method he now resolves to undertake is also meant to help him regain the deductive path to his material.

He looks for certain criteria for the transition from the classical novel in the past tense to the novel in the present tense; in the attempt, however, he finds that they both slip through his fingers. When he looks back at his material from the point of view of the as it were 'mature' present tense novel, the present tense novel is always already there, and he can't find an example of a past tense novel even among those texts written largely in the past tense. When, inversely, he takes the point of view forward, as it were, from the classical novel, he can't discern a fully actualized present tense novel. All the way up to the present, every novel appears as a botched farewell to the past tense—none seems to succeed, none really to be written in the present tense but none wholly to be written in the past tense either. "Perhaps," he thinks time and again over the years, "perhaps they were right from the beginning, those linguists who thought that tense has no temporal meaning, and with them the narratologists who think tense performs no function in the structure of the novel."

Headstrong (postdoctoral) fellow that he is, our hero sees no way of resolving the massive problems of referentialization he is facing other than inventing a rule thanks to which present and past tense appear, in the novel (in *every* novel), as two perspectives of tense that only obtain sense in their interaction. He has to give up the claim to have found his theory in the material. Instead, he proposes to subject the material to rewritings that will produce specimens for analysis. (Even though he hints at these self-doubts, he was smart enough to have established sufficient standing among the mostly male members of the commission: he is tenured.)

(4) "*Meta-abduction*. It consists in deciding as to whether the possible universe outlined by our first-level abductions is the same as the universe of our experience. In over- and under-coded abductions, this meta-level of inference is not compulsory, since we get the law from a storage of already checked actual world experience. In other words, we are entitled by common world knowledge to think that, provided the law is the suitable one, it already holds in the world of our experience. In creative abductions we do not have this kind of certainty. We are making a complete 'fair guess' not only about the nature of the result (its cause) but also about the nature of the encyclopedia (so that, if the new law results in being verified, our discovery leads to a change of paradigm)."[36]

Ignoring sound advice from friends and colleagues, our freshly appointed faculty member decides to thoroughly revise his thesis. He does not shrink from his still-youthful desire for absolute knowledge and immerses himself in the analytic philosophy of time and in speculative linguistics. Indeed, he develops a new tense-philosophical approach that enables him to give an account of the fundamental temporal bipolarity of all fictional narration.

In months and months of focused rumination and reading, he realizes the real reason for his doubts. His most important hypotheses go back to inventions that he owes to the poetics of the present tense novels, a poetics whose existence he long doubted. It must have happened like this: without his becoming aware of it, the novels have taught him a new way of reading. (Although readers will certainly want to know more, we are not in a position to provide any further information about what fate has in store for our hero. We are alarmed, however, by a vague sense that the loss of his academic reputation might be imminent.)

What is the central discrepancy we're dealing with in all forms of abductive inference, be it a translation, a diagnosis, an action, or the oft-cited criminal investigation? Abductive inference reacts to a discrepancy between a particular case (or fact) and a law (or rule). It is precisely because no valid inference can be made that there is a need for interpretation. A connection between fact and rule has to be *produced*. Because it is not clear what rule explains the fact, this logical problem can be reformulated as a semiotic situation or as an act of interpretation.

In over-coded abduction, the fact that there could be a problem with the rule does not yet become apparent. The interpreter usually only relates parts to a whole without being aware that in his so doing, the poetic function of language is operative. The principle of *poiesis* is to *invent* a rule; in over-coded abduction, the interpreter then finds this rule once more in the system of knowledge he is in. Since he has successfully applied it in interpreting the work, it has proven itself productive to him and its validity is confirmed.

In the second type of abductive inference, which Eco has called "under-coded abduction," reflection takes place on the level of rules: a choice has to be made between several equally possible rules that could serve as foundation for the context in question. As in the case of the inconspicuous circle of over-coded abduction, this comes with a reflection on the rule. Abduction transforms associations into abstractions that imply references: if something in a text seems familiar to us, for example, or reminds us of something, we can, on the one hand, search our memory for an explanation; on the other hand, however, we can infer a regularity and find the rule that implies the fact we have found— and in this way create reference.

In these first two types, abduction does not yet show what distinguishes it from induction and deduction. One could still suppose that it's just a deduction, albeit one that relies not on a law but on a hypothesis. It could also be the case that one is dealing with an induction that is lacking just one fact, the tiniest of leads in an uninterrupted chain, like a murder weapon whose existence is undoubted and that only needs to be found.

The form of abduction Eco calls "creative" leads us to the two forms of inference relevant to our question. They foreground the futural or modal moment of a *poiesis* of world or, in the words of Peirce: "Deduction proves that something *must* be; Induction shows that something *actually is* operative;

Abduction merely suggests that something *may be*."[37] The *poietic* productivity of abductions is due to the fact that its results are of a modal nature.

Eco, too, emphasizes the modal aspect of abduction, and he highlights its textuality, its linguicity, its semioticity. "Undercoded abductions not to speak of the creative ones are world-creating devices."[38] But for Eco, the connection of language and world (or of possible and real lingual worlds) is based solely on convention, even if the equivalence produced by dense codes might suggest such a connection. This, precisely, is what we consider semiotic idealism. Language is not arbitrary but contingent and metonymic; it is structured recursively and is part of the reality to which it refers. The world projected thus does not belong to some possible universe; in reality it is the (presumed) whole into which a detail is to be integrated as a new or future part. Instead of relocating contingency, without which no abductions are possible, outside of the world and shifting it to a universe of possible worlds, we consider it possible to include it in the history of the world's development.

Abductively produced worlds strain against the *present* world or the world presently acknowledged as real. And whenever meta-abductions reach the proportions of paradigm shifts (however small these may be) the problem arises that there is no expression yet in language for what has been created as a possibility in abduction. Language reveals a developmental lag; it contains no expression for what has been abductively created and thus does not fulfill its function as an interpretant. Treating this discrepancy of the historical level of knowledge as a question of social consensus (of the language of the sciences) overlooks the contingency of knowledge, which Meillassoux's speculative materialism has so forcefully introduced to current philosophical and artistic debates.

Eco, whose descriptions of language structures always favor figures of equivalence over figures of contiguity, sees the stakes of creative abductions—not to speak of meta-abductions—to lie in the equivalence of abductions and facts (or of signs and referents).

What, then, is the fundamental difference between the various types of abductions? In creative abductions, there is a fact. But there is no rule that could explain it. Nor, more importantly, is there a context that could tell us that we can apply the (sought-after) rule to the fact at hand. The situation, compared with under-coded abductions, has become more acute. Two contexts have to be established. The fact has to be linked to a rule and a second fact, since this context has yet not come in as a result of an interpretation. In the process, abduction breaks out of its hermeneutic enclosure, which already forces it into finding knowledge or insight, and begins to invent.

To be sure, (self-)reflections in the theory of science do occasionally remark that invented rules should follow aesthetic parameters (i.e. they should be "beautiful," "simple," or "elegant.") But reducing these rules to obeying a preexisting metarule obscures the moment of invention and ultimately marginalizes it. In creative abduction as we conceive of it, the semiotic subject begins to make bets and occasionally makes bets, against all odds, on highly surprising solutions—even if there is no way of knowing whether a beautiful or elegant rule will develop or not. We speculatively enter the game of tentative pro-positions and con-jectures, are simultaneously guided by the evidence of newly-found vocabularies and surprised by the temporality of suddenness with which they appear. But what is this about? Are these just figments to trap a Cartesian subject or are facts in play as well?

Two consequences result from such a speculative abduction. The first, "objective" consequence concerns the development of an appropriate methodology, which we seek to develop in this book. What interests us specifically at this point, however, is the "subjective" question of whether speculation can trigger a meta-abduction.

The inferential procedure Eco calls "meta-abduction" suggests that the facts thus created are accepted by someone: the references implied call for a testing that simultaneously includes an appeal to the subject itself. At the point these references emerge, both the facts and the rule by which they could be confirmed are missing (as in the case of speculative abduction). The one making the inferences bears the procedure's entire weight. Such is the structure of scientific paradigm shifts (e.g. as it is of "precursorship" or "avant-garde," perhaps of every authorship).

To understand what is happening here, we can use the same example we brought in above to describe the principle of part-to-whole relations. Let's imagine we lived in a world in which it would be unproblematic, on the one hand, to refer *moth* to the wholeness *animals* and *tree* to the wholeness *plants* but in which, on the other hand, no one would claim that plants had anything in common that would distinguish them from other, inanimate objects (e.g.

stones). There would be no rule to tell us what such a difference or such a commonality would consist in; indeed, we would not even know what concept to use. Bionism? Living stuff?

Were we to try to find such a concept and establish such a rule, our fellow organisms might (rightly, to a certain extent) consider this to be unwarranted speculations to which no facts correspond. Perhaps we had such stupid ideas because we saw a moth start flying that had been sitting on a tree and at first appeared to us as a piece of bark. Or perhaps, we might be told, we were misguided by the imprecision of everyday language: although one speaks of trees living and dying, that, of course, is only a metaphor, as everyone knows— the way one also speaks of volcanoes, rivers, or other natural phenomena as being dead or capable of coming to life, whereas that is true, strictly speaking, only of human beings and animals. Of course there are commonalities between moth and tree, it might be said—both, for example, are material objects, and the moth wings' color and pattern resemble tree bark. But one mustn't be confused by such coincidental similarities. The very fact that the moth—unlike the tree—can move on its own would clearly show the fundamental difference between the plant, tree, and the animal, moth. It is childish, we might be told, to want to deny it with some arbitrary invented concept. In short, the "living being" (as one might ironically call it to ridicule us) or whatever name one might give this figment, exists only in our heads.

To the phenomenology of meta-abduction corresponds the surprising inference from fact to fact. A fact stands at the beginning and at the end of the procedure.[39] In Eco's terms, the second fact is the exemplar of a second world from which we take the rule for interpreting the fact of our first world. That is why he calls this procedure meta-abduction. A world in the world is at play.

Instead of constructing a second world and raising it above our own as an (exemplary) meta- or super-world, the procedure can also be interpreted as a continual recursion. The real achievement of abductive inference is that it produces reference. Whenever a creative element participates in an abduction (e.g. when a fact falls under a particular rule) it transforms details into parts of a new wholeness, and the belonging thus instituted creates a referent.

Meta-abduction confronts the one who makes inferences with the question whether he would like to acknowledge the comprehensive whole and turn it into the rule of his own experience: meta-abduction concerns and affects the worldview of the one who infers. Unlike Eco, we do not describe meta-abduction as feigning another world but as a *poietic* change of the (one) world. The one who makes meta-abductive inferences takes responsibility for a referentialization, or for seeking one. This is what accounts for the fundamental wavering triggered by the meta-abductive procedures typical of metanoia.

What does it mean that assuming a new point of view amounts to assuming a changed word, that the new world and its subject cannot (can no longer) be separated? The equivocalness of the term *assume* may be an indication of a hypothesis becoming an ethical act, of a *logos* becoming an *ēthos*. But we must not forget that assumption demands or implies a change of position, indeed, that the subject only ever achieves a position of its own in this change in the first place.

This is where we find the boundary between speculative nominalism and speculative realism. Either we stop at the rule invented and assert that no referents in the world correspond to it, just as there is no fact that Jones can mean by "+". Or we take the step into a realism and recognize that in our favorite formula "S means X by Y," an attribution takes place, the attribution of reference to the subject as the position of the subject. If the subject S operates a meta-abduction, its property will henceforth be to argue that X is identifiable by Y. S not only identifies X by Y; from now on, S is someone/something identifying an X by Y.

Speculative abductions do not provide certainty. "Probably the true difference between abductions from fact to laws and abduction from facts to facts," Eco writes, "lies in the meta-abductional flexibility, that is, in the courage of challenging without further tests the basic fallibilism that governs human knowledge."[40] The fallibility or infallibility of knowledge or absolute knowledge and its critique thus constitute a succession of methodical positions. Discovering these forms of abduction as they build on one another demands that we accept a not knowing, an inability to know, and a new or renewed search for knowledge. The particular knowledge possible at every stage is upset in favor of assuming an absolute knowledge: we maintain the relation to truth on the condition of an othering. To reject such an unconditional theorizing, one would have to be ready to accept such not knowing already at the stage of over-coded abduction and switch to a positive history of science without ever again looking for possible new rules and different regularities.

Poeticizing philosophy

(Anti-aesthetics as) an ethics of abduction

For our literary scholar-protagonist, the ethical component concerns first of all what we could call the consequences of his metanoietic research habits. A progress in knowledge through abduction leads consequentially from the overcoded forms of abductive reference to creative abduction and, sooner or later, confronts researchers with the choice opened up by every meta-abduction: to become a nominalist or a speculative philosopher.

Our protagonist has not become a nominalist. He has, in the emphatic sense, taken responsibility for the rules he has found and has not let the sense he has created become meaningless. This is also the point where the transition from research to authorship takes place because the rule has been invented by the researcher as an author. New rules can only find their reason through us: the difference between the facts we produce and ourselves as their interpretants, then, is minimal. The role of abduction thus concerns both the referentializing of meaning and an othering of the subject. The risk that comes with this is not negligible.

Aesthetic perception

In thinking about an "ethics of abduction," we cannot help but think about whether aesthetics, too, might not play a different role. This concerns, in concrete terms, an aisthetic dimension: more precisely, an abductive dimension of *aisthesis*. For it is not the case, as the aesthetic tradition holds, that sensibility precedes judgment. Abductive inference is an inference *in* perception.

To clarify this point, let us join Peirce, who was not only a major theoretician of abduction but also situated it in perception, and look at this drawing (Figure 11). "The first time it is shown to us, it seems as completely beyond the control of rational criticism as any percept is; but after many repetitions of the now familiar experiment, the illusion wears off, becoming first less decided, and ultimately ceasing completely. This shows that these phenomena are true connecting links between abductions and perceptions."[41] The quote tells us two things. We do not start with induction and then invent a rule to deductively

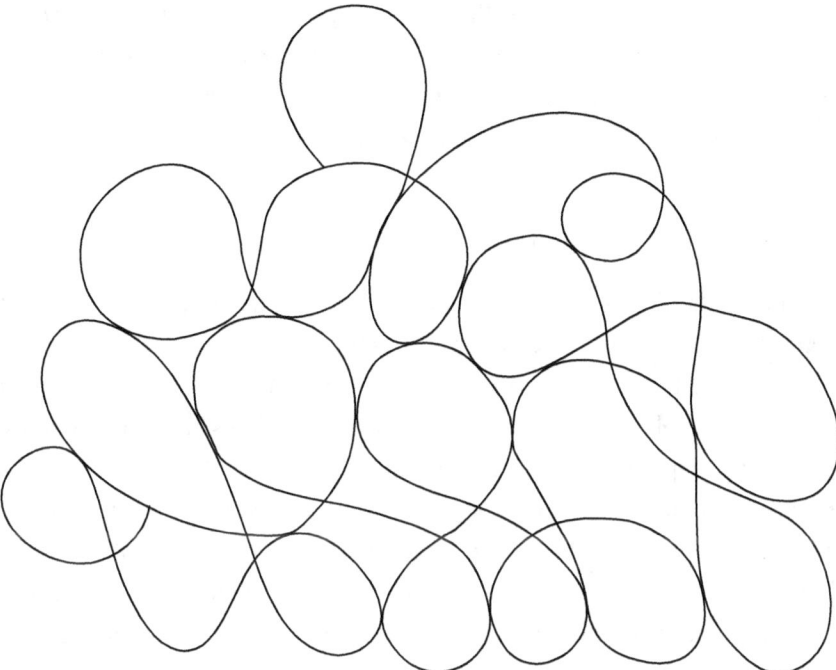

Figure 11[42] Abduction in perception

return to the facts. Instead, as we can see now, abduction is already contained in perception, which would not even be possible otherwise.

Even in a (purely) aesthetic experience of this figure, our thought is at play from the beginning; the recursive circles, in which thought follows its own movement, ultimately produce a sensible experience. In aesthetic experience, therefore, it is not at all the case that we slowly ascend from the lower cognitive faculties of sensible perception to a perfect knowledge. Abductive inference creates a specific form of sensibility, namely a surprising, sudden, flash-like and overwhelming form, which leads the subject into a wavering of its sense of reality.

Aesthetic theory provides us with corresponding descriptions of our sensible experience but—since Leibniz and Wolff and in explicitly "aesthetic" terms since Baumgarten—qualifies this experience as the darkness of the lower faculties. And yet it isn't a problem of the darkness of knowledge, for Peircean abduction is neither dark nor irrational. For Peirce, abduction is that kind of argument that starts with a surprising experience, which contradicts an active or passive conviction. Abduction takes the form of a judgment of perception or of a proposition referring to such a judgment. To generalize the surprising experience thus necessitates a new form of conviction.[43]

Peirce's definition of aesthetic pleasure

The dizziness of perception thus goes back to the necessity of a change of conviction in the sense of a switch in positions. Without a factual cognitive theory of the I—for which we'll turn to Thomas Metzinger—we are not yet able to fully explain the extent to which our sense organs are also productive organs. The hypothesis, in any case, is that the phenomenality of the world is produced by our sense organs. If our senses are overtaxed in an aesthetic experience, that is not because the knowledge at work in them is dark or because they lack rationality. The switch in the position of the ego instead demands a renewed production of the phenomenal world for the ego. We could also say the effects described are the result of a reprogramming.

We know that traditional definitions of *aesthetic experience* focus on the level of the senses and stick to their aesthetic capacities. When we take an interest in a *poietic experience*, we do so with a view to the *poietic* dimension necessarily overlooked by aesthetic philosophy. Our question concerns the productive dimension of our senses. Their productive task does not come to the fore only as long as the cognitive model with which they operate remains stable. If, however, there is a switch of positions (induced, for example, by art), if, in the most radical case, there is a metanoia, the sense organs, which carry out the new phenomenal world view according to the newly found rule, do not fully function until the cognitive model and the sense organs have been recursively synchronized—that is what we mean when we say "we see the world with new eyes."

Philosophy as aesthetics

Aesthetics comes up with its own history, in which it goes back to a revolution of philosophy and effects a revision of the theory of the Fine or Liberal Arts. "This formula gave a name to the strategic concept of the new philosophical discipline, aesthetics: aesthetics was the theory of the arts in so far as it undertook to double poetics and rhetoric with a second layer of explanations, explanations taken from the reservoir of what, following Leibniz and Wolff, was called sense perceptions."[44] Rüdiger Campe's description shows that from that point forward, this history has two sides. On the one hand, aesthetics replaces poetics and rhetoric as *the* theory of the arts. On the other hand, there is a change within philosophy that belongs to the history of how aesthetics became *the* philosophical discipline.

In a recent book, Christoph Menke "revisit[s] the role played by aesthetics by way of a retelling, that is a retelling of the 'birth' of aesthetics in the eighteenth century, in the period between Baumgarten's *Aesthetics* and Kant's *Critique of Judgment*. We will see that aesthetics did not expand the range of the legitimate objects of philosophical inquiry. All of these objects existed before aesthetics. Rather, by introducing the category of 'the aesthetic,' aesthetics fundamentally redefined these objects. Most important, this account of the historical genesis of aesthetics will show that the introduction of the category of the 'aesthetic' required nothing less than a transformation of the fundamental terms of philosophy. The beginning of aesthetics is, in fact, the beginning of modern philosophy."[45]

Aesthetic experience reloaded

In our argument for a new and speculative poetics, we read these two histories together. That is why our criticism is not only a criticism of aesthetics as a theory of the arts but also of its role within philosophy. Let's take seriously the claim that in the history of philosophy, the discipline of aesthetics is the foundational discipline of modern philosophy; let's hold it to that standard.

One central moment of philosophy-become-aesthetics concerns the concept of experience. Kant's critique of knowledge—in which, by the way, the concept "aesthetic experience" is nowhere to be found—turned the level of our experience into the last level of certainty about the world and declared (naive) access to things in themselves and any immediate ontology to be forever impossible. All of modernity's aestheticizing philosophy stands in this correlationist tradition. But does it not thereby overlook essential insights of modern critiques of experience?

Since Benjamin, at the latest, we have known that an ineradicable moment of estrangement inscribes itself in modern experience. This crisis of experience cannot find an explanation within the Kantian circularity of an experience continually drawing on our faculties (which means, in the end, on itself). From the circle of experience, no moment of estrangement can emerge. Epistemology can limit the domain of our experience, but it cannot explain why experience enters into a crisis of self-estrangement, a crisis so profound that experience loses all ability to generate history and tradition. But the overtaxing of experience by the culture industry and its crippling on the scenes of war and terror in the twentieth century has deeply unsettled experience in its self-referential and self-assured humanism.

The speculative and critical poetics practiced by Benjamin rests on the practices of modernity. And it can provide a better explanation of the deformations of experience than the aesthetics of shock and breakage that like so emphatically to invoke Benjamin. From these deformations of experience, Benjamin derives an argument for the immanence of an absolute in every experience and thereby disputes not the findings but the conclusions drawn in Kant's critique of knowledge.

Benjamin agrees with Kant that our experience never provides us with anything other than an image of the things in themselves, an image preformed, and thus deformed, by our faculties. But that the absolute does show itself in our experience only as deformed is what Benjamin turns into the program of a speculative access to the absolute made possible by a critique of experience. That is the task of the poetic. "The 'Poetic' is a speculative concept which synthetically unites the absolute ('spiritual order') with spatiotemporal experience ('intuitive order')."[46] And because spatio-temporal experience only ever provides us with a deformed image of the absolute, we need a critical poetics.

The usual post-revolutionary dwelling on the aesthetic beginnings of modern philosophy also ignores crucial achievements of twentieth-century analytic philosophy of language. In Menke's description of the object and aim of Baumgarten's aesthetics, "the 'internal principle' of sensible activity presents itself as a *faculty*, the faculty of engendering sensible cognitions that are as indeterminable as they are adequate."[47] The objection of the analytic philosophy of language is an objection both to such an inner principle of sensibility independent of language and to an independence of knowledge from language. In contrast, we have emphasized that neither *aisthesis* nor *noiesis* can be had independently of *poiesis*. That is also the reason why a theory of language cannot do without a *poetics* of thought. If, then, we want to further develop the critical momentum of the analytic philosophy of language against the aesthetization of philosophy, we also have to develop a new poetics of philosophy. In other words, we advocate a poeticization of philosophy not least because it would allow for criticizing the restrictive effects of the ongoing aestheticization of philosophy.[48]

Poetics and aesthetics in Baumgarten

The clearly circumscribed domain of classical poetics is apparent in the explicit references to poetics and poetry we find in Baumgarten: "By *poem* we mean a perfect sensate discourse, by *poetics* the body of rules to which a poem conforms, by *philosophical poetics* the science of poetics, by *poetry* the state of composing a poem, and by *poet* the man who enjoys that state."[49]

Baumgarten's explicit statements justify a reading according to which aesthetics is also to be understood as abolishing the classical discipline of poetics. This, however, we regard as symptomatic, above all, of an insufficient consideration of language. Or, put differently: Baumgarten's conception of poetry establishes aesthetic categories in the domain of the poetic. Literary language is said to be able to clarify by enriching characteristics or by ensuring differentiated expression in the dissection of ideas into their parts. "Therefore, for things to be determined as far as possible when they are to be represented in a poem is poetic."[50]

Insofar as we find in Baumgarten's definitions of the poem or of poetic language those characterizations he had discerned in sensible knowledge, the historical qualification that aesthetics abolishes and integrates classical poetics is justified. Yet there is also Baumgarten's concept of "presentation" (which cannot make do without an element of *poiesis*), which is something like an unofficial poetics (clouded, however, by a kind of reentry of aesthetics into all elements of his system). This is evident in the third chapter of the *Metaphysics*, the "Psychology," in which we find a series of definitions of aesthetics that can be assigned to poetics differently conceived. Just to give a few examples: "The science of knowing and presenting with regard to the senses is *aesthetics* (the logic of the inferior cognitive faculty, the philosophy of graces and muses, inferior gnoseology, the art of thinking beautifully, the art of the analogue of reason)."[51]—"The science of thinking by imagining and presenting of what is thus thought is the *aesthetics of the imagination*."[52]—"The *aesthetics of perspicaciousness* is the part of aesthetics concerned with thinking and presenting with wit and acumen." [53]—"The *aesthetics of the mythical* is the part of aesthetics that devises and presents fictions [*Erdichtungen*]."[54]

Undercover poetics

The figure used in the historiography of philosophy of a revolution of philosophy under the auspices of sensible knowledge is most emphatically confirmed in the definitions we find in the ninth section of Baumgarten's *Metaphysics*: "Hence the art of forming taste, or the art concerning judging sensitively and presenting its judgment, is *aesthetic criticism*."[55] In Baumgarten's text, however, there are two more sections, concerned with "anticipatory sensations" or anticipations as "the object of the aesthetic mantic art" and with the "aesthetics of characterization"[56]: "The science of sensitive knowledge that is concerned with signs, and the science of this sort of presentation, is the *aesthetics of characterization*, and it is both heuristics and hermeneutics." [57]

We are particularly interested in the last two sections because we think that the "aesthetic mantic art" discussed there may harbor a speculative dimension of poetics and that the art of characterization prefigures a semiotic poetics and hermeneutics. In our description of metanoia in a poetic register, we are not least of all concerned with transferring "experience" from an aesthetic to a poetic paradigm and thereby also with emphasizing the prevalence of *poiesis* over *aisthesis*. We are interested in Baumgarten precisely because we do not think metanoia comes down to a phenomenon (however drastic) of aesthetic experience (which is at best a symptom of metanoia, where it does not slow down its dynamics): we read in his aesthetic reflections an undercover poetics. Our definition of the relationship of poetics and aesthetics aims at underscoring, thanks to the concept of metanoia, all those *poietic* aspects that are discernible in experience, sometimes more clearly, sometimes less.

An aesthetic model of language

Is it possible to discern something like an aesthetic model of language to correlate with the philosophical model of language? In his discussion of Baumgarten's aesthetics, Klaus Weimar voices fundamental doubts: "The short-circuiting and blending of reader and poet as well as the equivocation of the term 'sensible knowledge' that unwittingly testifies to it are durably preserved in the name 'aesthetics' (*scientia sensitivae cognitionis*) and can no longer be removed from either the name or its deployment. Baumgarten clung to this equivocation and this blending and, for the sake of a new philosophical discipline, he accepted all the swopping and deceiving that becomes necessary and unavoidable when one thinks this approach through to the end. What follows from it is the theoretical annihilation of everything that lies 'between' the poet's thought and the reader's knowledge, that is, the annihilation of writing, of the text, and of reading."[58]

In aesthetics, therefore, the entire layer of mediation by language between the poet's and the reader's thought is cancelled out. There's more: not only is there no medium of transmission between author and reader, it is lacking already in their thought. Sensibility and thought are not mediated by language. This also obscures all *poietic* possibilities of language (as well as of the speculative poetics of reading and writing).

What, now, does language look like when it becomes the object of aesthetics? What deformations does it have to be subjected to in order to be understood as a manifestation or model of sensible knowledge? Such an aestheticized language tends toward reflexivity on the one hand and a void of sense on the other. While the first property results from its cognitive character, the second derives from its sensibility. The sensibility of language obscures its meaning and its self-reflexivity obscures its reference.

Let's recall once more what we said about the two readings of the poetic function of language. Jakobson only sees the reflexivity of the poetic function and thus turns out to be a peculiar aestheticist of language. In his conception, the poetic function reflects itself, thereby producing a specific economy of attention. The function's *poietic* element is replaced by an aesthetic one and is limited to having created the object of a reflexive perception. We can generalize this moment of (self-)reflection and we can discern in it an aesthetic model of language.

On this point, most aesthetics of language go even further than Jakobson, in whose conception the referential function of language is obscured by its poetic function. What strikes us here is the connection between a theory of reflection and a theory of a language without reference. A literary language that refers to itself—especially the language of classical modernism—is thus not only reflexive; in closing in on itself, it also cuts itself off from its reference to the world. The correlate of reflexivity is referencelessness, both on the level of a theory of language and on the level of a theory of literature (where referencelessness is usually designated a sublime "void of meaning").

In Romantic and modernist theory, music constitutes the vanishing point of aesthetic language. The extent to which sensibility and reflexivity are thought together here is evident in the fact that music is seen not only as the embodiment of a maximum of sensibility (of language) but also stands for the maximization of the abstract and reflexive moments of sensibility: "In the dissociation from the presence of the object, repeatability opens up the sphere of mental images, and in continued abstraction and repetition, a fixation of certain complexes of sound, image and movement can emerge. At the same time, the increase in possible re-combinations of abstract ideational images also paves the way for grammaticizing signs and thus, in the end, for language in the full sense of the term.... This hypothesis has far-reaching consequences. They imply that human modes of symbolic presentation, in the form of a language of the body, of movements, tones, forms and colors, precede cognitive language and abstract concepts in the strict sense.... Language in the strict sense would then no longer form the basis of the symbolic register but simply drive it to new cognitive shores."[59]

We are able to amend Winfried Menninghaus's hypotheses about the theory of evolution to the extent that in an aesthetic conception of language, music not only precedes cognitive language, it also succeeds it and goes beyond it insofar as cognition is concerned. As a theory of the arts, aesthetic theory is also more accommodating of the fine arts than it is of literature. In their sensible and abstract moments, images are much more plausibly understood as sensible knowledge than literature can be. At first sight, a literary text makes an extraordinarily non-sensible impression and at the same time rejects the logical form of knowledge, with which it nonetheless shares one and the same medium, language. From this we infer that sensibility and knowledge have to be connected in a way that differs from what happens in aesthetic theory. For us, literary metanoia exemplifies the sensibility that results from the recursivity of language. That is why we understand abductive judgments to be poetic a priori syntheses. We conceive of them, on the one hand, as synthetic judgments because they are not analytically inductive and, on the other, as a priori judgments because they are not tied to experience. They do indeed emerge *in* perception, but they do not emerge *from* perception.[60]

The opposition between a model of language based on relations of equivalence (and their reflexivity) and a model in which language consists of recursive part-to-whole relations can thus also be understood as the difference between a poetic and an aesthetic model of language. On one side, we have a correlationist theory of language and a corresponding aesthetics of literature, which wants to trace the event character of the literary back to a reference withdrawn from the subject. The work does not appear as the result of a *poiesis* but only of a practice in which it has been produced for a reflexive *aisthesis*. On the other side, our model of language allows for an understanding of the productive, *poietic* dimensions of metanoia.

Experimental invention of concepts

We understand language to be an instrument for optimizing cognition constructed from metonymic part-to-whole relations. Such an understanding is, of course, not encumbered by the alleged non-sensibility and relationality of language—quite the contrary.

In investigating metanoia, we have come across different *poietic* aspects of the concept. The understanding of the concept that comes closest to ours is that developed by Deleuze and Guattari in *What is Philosophy?* "What defines thought in its three great forms—art, science, and philosophy—is always confronting chaos, laying out a plane, throwing a plane over chaos. But philosophy wants to save the infinite by giving it consistency: it lays out a plane of immanence that, through the action of conceptual personae, takes events or consistent concepts to infinity. Science, on the other hand, relinquishes the infinite in order to gain reference: it lays out a plane of simply undefined coordinates that each time, through the action of partial observers, defines states of affairs, functions, or referential propositions. Art wants to create the finite that restores the infinite: it lays out a plane of composition that, in turn, through the action of aesthetic figures bears monuments or composite sensations."[61]

But why not, as we suggest, connect the elements of the three great discourses philosophy, science, and art to introduce the *poietic* moment of thought into the concept of thought? Philosophical "concept" (in the service of the infinite), scientific "function" (in the service of reference), and aesthetic "percepts and affects" (in the service of sensation) are all aspects of *poietic* language. Metanoia is that kind of conceptual thinking that literature practices in the service of reference. In order to understand metanoia, we therefore have to think all three aspects together.

For us, the concept, the creation of the concept, and the experiment as the path that leads there are to be understood as directives: we want to connect the experimental invention of concepts, a literature that does not think of itself as the messenger of sensation, and a science that situates its experimental spirit beyond positivism. In particular, we distinguish the experimental invention of concepts [*Begriffserfindung*] from a form of conceptualization [*Begriffsfindung*] that would best be called conceptual contextualism and is widely applied in literary studies. It is exemplified by the way in which philosophers read Walter Benjamin, film theorists read Stanley Cavell, or literary scholars read Mikhail Bakhtin in order to shape the concepts they use in their descriptions of the material at hand. In this process, the abductive moment of the invention of concepts is often quite simply overlooked, and later, is hidden away with a bad conscience or even consciously suppressed until it disappears from the practice of literary studies.

On the one hand, we're looking for a different understanding of cognition that brings out the *poietic* aspects of thought. On the other hand, we're looking for concepts that clarify the relationship between cognition and language in order to lend support to our theses from the perspective of a theory of cognition as well. For us, a poetics of thought is necessarily tied in with a theory of language. The question then becomes how both language and thought develop and, even more so, how they change. In this sense, our claim to salvage a critical moment of analytic philosophy also presupposes a new poetics of philosophy.

Our criticism of aesthetic philosophy implies that we ask the question of genesis not in terms of a genealogy, not as a retrospective on becoming, but in terms of the cognitive shift we call metanoia. Metanoia, accordingly, is the attempt to get to an experience of becoming by simply "resetting" everything—here and now. That is not difficult. It breaks with what has become—the more radically, the better—and starts all over again. It is a repetition (in the sense of the third form of repetition described by Deleuze). It does not begin with anything dark, unknown, sensible. The starting point of metanoietic becoming is the rigid, educated, trained, cultivated, rational subject. To break with the *ergon*, no force is needed. A drift is enough, decay suffices, nothing but an othering is necessary.

No force is able to produce a subject; it takes an other, an othering.

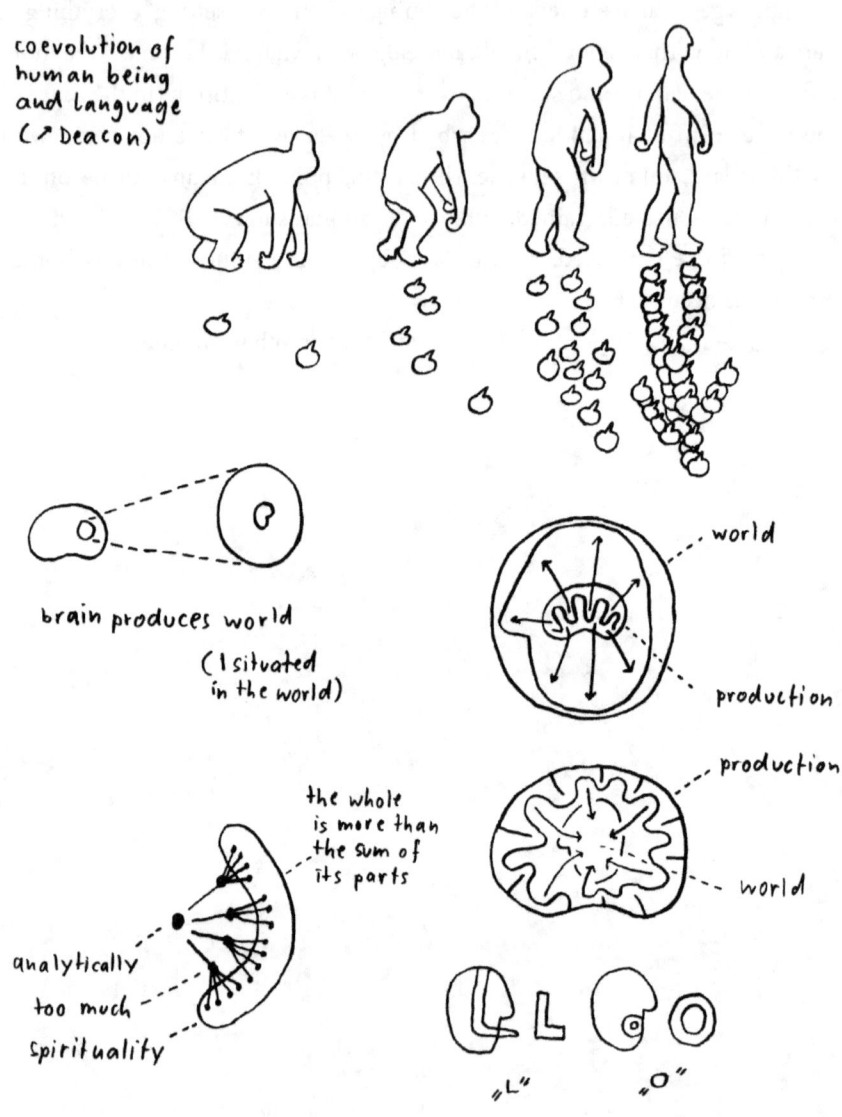

IV

Cognition

Metanoia is an Anagram of Anatomie[1]

The brain is a work, and we do not know it. We are its subjects—authors and products at once—and we do not know it. "Humans make their own history, but they do not know that they make it," says Marx, intending thereby to awaken a consciousness of historicity. In a certain way, such words apply precisely to our context and object: "Humans make their own brain, but they do not know that they make it."

Catherine Malabou

The labor of the brain

Catherine Malabou opens her philosophical critique of the neurosciences with the words used here as our epigraph. They exemplify the global significance we, too, attribute to research in the cognitive sciences. We are particularly interested in the irreducibly dialectical, perhaps even circular, relationship between authorship and its products. We draw on contributions from the cognitive and neurosciences to define additional dimensions of the relationship between practice and *poiesis* in the context of a history of thought.

This chapter was one of the first we planned for this book, with a mixture of ignorance and the thrill of discovery. We wanted to draw the picture of thought that we saw in metanoia, the thought that is being experienced in metanoia and is, at the same time, produced by it. How does metanoia blow up our thought, this machinery that is so carefully retooled as a theater?

Our interest was and is focused on what Malabou calls plasticity, a dimension of thought that both gives and experiences form. We were well aware of having entered a circle, which did not trouble us too much since the methodology of the humanities had familiarized us with circular instruments. It seemed possible to us to rely on advocates of the circle like Heidegger and to draw on hermeneutical descriptions to follow a circular path, to make an estimate of what might typically be found along such a winding road, and in the process to reach at least some kind of phenomenology, whose circles are narrower.

The regulative state of exception in thinking

On many points, our interests were accommodated by Thomas Metzinger's approach to describing thought. Metzinger considers those phenomena that are taboo for logical thought: out-of-body experiences, hallucinations, meditation, or Cotard syndrome, in which patients believe they do not exist. Looking at forms of thought usually ignored promised insight into how thought was not just to be conceived of but plastically produced, and how it can, in the emphatic poietic sense, open up a truth.

In the states of exception of thought—and metanoia is one of them—the nature of the entire apparatus becomes apparent. Metzinger is no longer guided by a conception of an ideal or absolute consciousness; he describes the functioning of a meta-machine whose dysfunctions and liminal phenomena reveal what determines its normalcy.

This approach allows for describing consciousness as the product of the circles created by thought. We see this very globally as a figure that describes a meta-level (a qualitative shift or renewal), employing terms of contiguity and recursion, not of equivalence or reflection. We want to continue this approach with a view to considering the capacity of language to exceed its given possibilities. This belongs to a different conception of language than that of structural linguistics, which is built on equivalence and difference.

In Metzinger, thought is an activity he seeks to understand starting from the materiality of the brain. What is the standard product of this brain activity? And what, in the best of cases, does the brain produce? The job of the brain is not only to produce "I" and "world." Above all, its function consists in the production of a circle that situates an ego in its world and is responsible for the arrangement of I and world.

Thought and I (Kant)

Going out from "thought" as brain activity, there are thus two directions; one goes from thought to world, the other ties thought to an I. To discuss the latter constellation, let's take a quick look at Kant's famous transcendental or "original apperception." It is an original apperception "since it is that self-consciousness which, because it produces the representation *I think*, must be able to accompany all others and which in all consciousness is one and the same, and cannot be accompanied by any further representation. I also call its unity the *transcendental* unity of self-consciousness in order to designate the possibility of *a priori* cognition from it."[2]

In Kant, the function of consciousness is to guarantee the reproduction of ideas in a series or succession. Without consciousness, the manifolds we perceive could never be transformed into a whole. The unchangeable identity of self-consciousness thus guarantees the unity of the manifold of intuition just as concepts guarantee the unity of objects. Kant conceives a complex logic of successive stages of synthesis to provide an account of the subject's capacity for knowledge or a priori possibility of experience: the synthesis of apprehension (in intuition), synthesis of reproduction (in the imagination), and synthesis of recognition (in the concept). They work hand in hand; we may suspect that for Kant, recognition also serves as the teleological guarantor of the earlier syntheses.

Metzinger, beginning with a quote from contemporary philosopher Diana Raffmann, presents a wholly different picture. "'We are much better at discriminating perceptual values (i.e. making same/different judgments) than we are at identifying or recognizing them.' Technically, this means we do not possess *introspective identity criteria* for man of the simplest states of consciousness. Our perceptual memory is extremely limited."[3]

This is illustrated by the fact that on the spectrum of wavelengths from 430 to 650 nanometers, we can differentiate between 150 shades of color but can only identify 15 of them. If we combined this finding with the reflection that meaning is not created by referring to (or identifying) referents, we'd assume the position of the analytic philosophy of language criticized above. This would correspond to a world in which, in 135 out of 150 cases, we could neither identify nor express the red of a rose variety; we would only have access to the various reds by means of differential description of the entire color spectrum (as was suggested by Wilhelm Kordes and other rose cultivators).

Reflecting on semiotic reason, we discussed Kripke's statement—there is no fact that any word in language could mean—as the unavoidable dead end of the paradigm of the analytic philosophy of language. Cognitivist experiments on the question of identifying what is meant, perceived, or thought conform to this analytic insight by stating an "ineffability" of qualities. In Kantian terms, only consciousness is able to transform each given individual perceived into an element of a whole (or into a unity within the manifold), which is why Kant is not interested in the determination of how such individuals could be determined. He is interested in how to determine the limits of thought.[4] What in Kant becomes a critique of thought in Kripke becomes a critique of language.

Thought and world (Descartes)

Descartes' *cogito ergo sum* might well serve to illustrate the movement that leads from thought to the I. We would like to use this formula to spell out the second movement, the movement that leads from thought to the world. While the dictum at first only seems to designate a solipsistic connection of thought and the I, the *Meditations* are well aware of the "world" as an external guarantor of thought. In fact, it is not that difficult to rearticulate Descartes's dyad into a triad and for the second direction to become visible.

Let's begin our rearticulation by describing a few aspects that are centrally important for metanoia as well. There is always, in Descartes, a connection of thought, ego, and world. Let's expand his formula: "I think, therefore I am in the world." The first I in this phrase is the subject of thought, the second the subject of being. The question has to remain open for now whether self-consciousness is able to create an identity within this difference—its formula would be "I am conscious of thought as my way of existing." In any case, our formula can be rearticulated from the perspective of the neurosciences as "As long as my brain is in the world, thinking, I am."

Contemporary medicine makes the same point by considering the end of being in the world to be marked by brain death. This material interpretation can be supplemented by a productive or recursive one: *ergo* it is my brain that thinks me and necessarily situates me in the world.

The circular structure of consciousness as depicted by Metzinger is metanoietic. When we think about the change of our thought that we become aware of as metanoia, we realize that thinking always begins with a recursion. We never reflect on a single point of departure, as a Kantian reading of Metzinger would suggest. This insight allows us to see that consciousness is that form of circular thought that creates an *I-here-now-origo* and situates us in a milieu. We now see a completely different relationship of thought and world come up: the world emerges in an externalization of the differences that result from the permanent matching of deictic information. This is what above we called "reprogramming." The permanent circle of personal, temporal, and spatial difference emits, in recursive loops, information (information on me & you, now & then, and here & there), and thereby lets an image of and a perspective on the world emerge.

If our perspective on the world does not emerge until deictic differences arise, metanoia could also be called, with only a slight exaggeration, a kind of revenge of deixis. For metanoia is the principle of those deictic expressions whose spatial, temporal, and personal determinations remain open in order to guarantee the imperceptible adaptation of language to the world of (contingent) facts. In this respect, they are the point of entry for a complete and whole lingual turn (of space, time, and ego).

Three forms of con-scientia

"Consciousness is what binds things together into a comprehensive, simultaneous whole. If we have this whole, then a world appears to us. If the information flow from your sensory organs is unified, you experience the world.... The unity of consciousness... is the not-so-simple phenomenological fact that all the contents of your current experience are seamlessly correlated, forming a coherent whole, the world in which you live your life."[5]

As soon as we think about the triad of thought, ego, and world not from the perspective of sense experience, of *aisthesis*, but from the perspective of *poiesis*, it appears in a new constellation. Our suggestion is to no longer start from an ego that, reflecting (and metareflecting) on itself, develops a self-consciousness, realizes that its relation to the world is due to its limited sensibility alone and comes to know its boundaries to then correct its image of the world by realizing that this image is a semblance. Instead, thought (probably in league with our sense organs) creates a phenomenal world (with shapes and colors, sounds and smells); it also creates an ego as its content, an ego that it situates in a phenomenal world as its product.

Let's recapitulate by running through three steps, three different models of consciousness. The first conception is of pre-Cartesian beauty. *Con-scientia* formed an unfathomable inner space, a transcendental area of contact with an ideal other, with a divine subject. "Consciousness was an inner space providing a point of contact between the real human being and the ideal one inside, the only space in which you could be together with God even before death."[6] *Con-scientia* is an immersion in contemplation and meditative dialog that allows for Being even prior to death. Consciousness thus conceived always already means a co-knowledge, a divine con-sciousness, with which a subject constitutes its truth.

Despite the bravado of fashioning a world for the subject out of thought, Descartes' second epochal conception of consciousness does not forget that it owes its existence to a dialogue. For all its modern furor, it still needs a divine guarantee of the world as a whole, even if the divine other has largely lost his function *in* the world. The ambiguity of the world as offspring of the mind remains: a deceptive God could, after all, have put us in a vat. A benevolent Other is necessary to guarantee the existence of the world and of the subject.

This disposition, third, is the basis for Metzinger's non-schizophrenic division or doubling of the self. "Our evolved type of conscious self-model is unique to the human brain, in that by representing the process of representation itself, we can catch ourselves ... in the act of knowing. We mentally represent ourselves *as* representational systems, in phenomenological real time."[7]

This means: "I" is the content of my thought, the result of a circular operation. Conscious thought or thinking in dialog with a consciousness does not have to be understood as self-consciousness. Thinking consciously can also mean thinking with an *other* consciousness and by no means implies being conscious of one*self*. It may well be the consciousness of an other, an anonymous other, a general or an ideal consciousness with which one thinks.

This allows us to formulate the triad I–thought–world even more precisely, as follows: it (the brain) thinks me (the ego as content of thought) into a world (which is a product of the brain). This formulation, however, raises the question of what enables my brain to situate me in the world in such circular fashion. It must, it seems, be the case that the brain is as physical as the world. How else would it perform the task of permanently localizing our *physis* in the world and providing us with a permanent consciousness of this? What is the role of language here?

The recursive structure of cognition (Metzinger and Malabou)

I think the book in my hand

We have come across this point several times: recursivity, which is based on part-to-whole relations, is an instrument for forming a delicate, flexible, dialectic tectonic. Recursion is thus a precision instrument for the production of ordered complexity. The question now becomes how coherent these complex constructs are. Let's take as the guide for our reflection an example familiar to every reader, which Thomas Metzinger uses to exemplify central aspects of his theory.

"We want a large-scale coherence spanning many areas of the brain and flexibly binding many different contents into a conscious hierarchy: the letters into the page, the page into the book, the hand holding the book into your bodily self, and the self sitting in a chair in the room and understanding the words."[8] Coherence emerges from the continual insertion of parts into wholes. Self-representation unfolds recursively: higher levels of wholes of information are permanently projected onto lower levels and thereby form their own context and their own filtering mechanism.

"Imagine you could suddenly apprehend the whole world, your own body, the book in your hands, and all of your current surroundings as a 'mental model.' Would this still be conscious experience?"[9] At these outer limits of consciousness, it veers into what Metzinger calls its "altered states." It is on this outer face of consciousness that it becomes clear that consciousness needs both a world and an ego. This, however, implies the formation of an immanent limit in the ever more highly hierarchized insertions of data into a mental model. On every level of integration and coherence formation, there is also a simultaneous externalization of the mental model that is integrated. This allows us to see what the recursive movement of a gain in knowledge or consciousness consists in: it is about putting the cognitive circle—according to which a certain figure always depicts a mental model—into relation with a new external fact.

"In a certain sense, we must perceive the perceiving while it happens. If this idea is true, the brain state creating your conscious perception of the book in your hand right now must have two logical parts: one portraying the book and one continuously representing the state itself. One part points at the world, and one at itself. Conscious states could be exactly those states that 'metarepresent' themselves while representing something else."[10] The temporality of this parallel operation, however, is not easy to understand, even when the question of how the self appears in consciousness has been answered. Why is the recursive hierarchization of levels of consciousness not just spatially embedded in a Here, why does it also generate a Now?

We've already said that one of the central properties of consciousness consists in situating us in the world. "When you wake up in the morning, you experience yourself as existing at a specific time, at a single location, and embedded in a scene: A single and integrated *Situation* emerges."[11] Why does a spatial coordination with its delicate hierarchy of embeddings (the book embedded in our hand, the hand as part of our body, our body in the armchair, the armchair in the room, the room in the house, the house in the street, etc.) require integration into a Now? Why doesn't it suffice that space is infinitely divisible and that infinitely many levels of embeddings into a wholeness can be thought up? Why does a singular Now appear? Why does time appear?

It is obviously "a network of neurons representing a single object—the book—for you *at a particular moment*. Holding it all together is coherence *in time*."[12] In the dialectic of an embedding and an externalization of part-to-whole relations, a (temporal) moment must be involved. But the fact that a now-moment is constructed in recursive processes and in the hierarchizations of part-to-whole relations also needs an explanation. One interpretation proffered by Metzinger is that the speed of cognitive processing procedures is a filtering mechanism and performs the function of establishing, among the multitude of possible levels, an unambiguous zero level.

"If the first-order process—the process creating the seen object, the book in your hands—integrates its information in a smaller time-window than the second-order process (namely, the attention you're directing at this new inner model), then the integration process on the first-order level will itself become transparent, in the sense that you cannot consciously experience it. By necessity, you are now blind to the fundamental construction process."[13] The fastest processing procedures are those most easily automated and transformed into foundational levels and available contexts. This makes duration a factor of hierarchization: the fastest processes provide the foundations for the slower ones. Those processes that are situated on the highest level of the Now take place so slowly that we can follow them and perceive them as changes.

In short, the fundamental spatial and temporal aspects of the world produced by our brain emerge from the characteristics of the processing mechanisms themselves. The difference between time and space exists because (one) state is permanently projected onto another. The simultaneity of two states (in one state) constitutes space, the divergence of states (from one another) creates time.

Let's try and spell this out: when it does not make a difference, the projection of one state onto another makes up space. When it does make a difference, this is between the state now and the previous state. Space is in time because the production of context takes place from out of recursion and because the projection of one state in the other, therefore, forms a part-to-whole relation. This means that space is in time as a part is in the whole. In this way, neurophilosophy provides reasons for the often dismissed everyday concept of time according to which we live *in* time and only its present moment is real to us.

Naive realism

Running parallel to this rearrangement of ego, world, and thought we can see a redistribution of the relations between facts, appearances, and productions. Developing a "naive" realism is a necessary task but by no means a simple one; indeed, it is rather complex. Although it is not an "originary" metanoia, it constitutes the very ground without which metanoia would not even be thinkable. The idea that the world can change has to be preceded by the idea that the world is that which is given to us (in sensibility). Naïve realism is thus correlationist through and through, it appears as empiricism—*world* here is equivalent to *world for the subject*. Only when there is this naïve realism can thought reflect on it and thereby come up against the boundaries we exemplified with Kant and Kripke's critiques.

Metzinger explains the complexity of realism by way of hallucinations and dreams, which, in principle, satisfy all the demands made of consciousness and, even more so, self-consciousness: they situate an ego in the world. However, in them, we become conscious of something else, namely that the world appears to our consciousness and that it never confronts us in any other mode than that of appearance. The aesthetic character of 'our world' comes out in all liminal states of consciousness, but in the case of dreaming and of conscious dreaming, this knowledge cannot be avoided.

This points to an opposition between the two positions we have named that draw on the neurosciences, the philosophy of mind on the one hand, which Metzinger takes in the direction of an aesthetics, and Catherine Malabou's critical dialectics on the other, which brings out a poietic dimension. Metzinger's model itself constitutes something like a methodological overcoming of naive realism, an overcoming that consists in our becoming aware of the actual relationships in terms of which we think the world: in circles. Since in this overcoming, we become conscious that we think the world, the world in its entirety becomes an aesthetic world. To a consciousness that becomes conscious of how it thinks the world, the world in its entirety *appears* as an aesthetic world, appears in its quality of appearance.

To what extent does Malabou's way of drawing on neuroscientific studies differ from this? What we see coming to the fore in the cognitive revolution of the theory of consciousness on which Malabou focuses is the poietic dimension of every change of consciousness. This dimension takes the preliminary form of astonishment or wonder: we recognize in the world as it appears to us a product of the activity of our mind, but we are astonished that our mind does not persist in a tautological aestheticism. Malabou makes our brain the object of a historical–materialist labor ethics and investigates the conditions under which it performs its labor.

We believe that it also takes a poetics (that takes the poietic dimension of language into account) to existentialize the productions of our brain. As soon as we ask ourselves this question, it is no longer enough to say that the labor of the brain has a world appear to us. Let us, therefore, shift the emphasis and underscore the poietic potential: metanoia is the principle by which the brain exercises its function of creating a phenomenal world for us and at the same time prompts us to actively participate in this process of production and thereby to open up a truth.

Yet let's continue with Metzinger for a moment. One consequence of his approach is that sense organs appear as productive organs. They create and organize the interface on which the differences interpreted by our brain are exposed. Thus, for example, it is our eyes that produce variations of red from certain frequencies of light. The cross-modal connection of different sense data we discussed gives rise to lingual object that have visual, haptic ('purple is a velvety red'), and perhaps also acoustical characteristics.

Let's look at the possibility of a differentiating sense (e.g. seeing with two eyes). The basic constellation of our perception of space is a synthesis of seeing (the binocularity of two eyes), hearing, and touching. The difference between the individual sense impressions that we synthesize does not dissolve things but leads to our perceiving them as different things in space. Similarly, the difference between hearing and seeing does not entail a loss of spatial coherence or the splitting of things in perception; instead, both are 'situated' in time. We even suspect that the asynchrony of the senses is the only material and sensate basis of the perception of time. There are thus different forms of cross-modal organization of the senses at work in the distinction of things (unified cross-modality), space (synthetic cross-modality), and time (differential cross-modality).

Language integrates seeing by relating parts and wholes, creating extended free spaces between individual sense data. The collaboration of the senses is usually thought in terms of equivalences. Our interest in part-to-whole relations, however, also leads us to see an asymmetry, one often encountered in works of art. We find an example in the attempt of silent films to produce a hearing within seeing, or in the attempts of language to give rise to a seeing as its own "inner form." In both cases, one sense is contained within another, as a part of a whole. This mereological form of organizing the senses effects the sense organs themselves.

Even grammatical competence relates to the primary cognitive representations of our body schema.[14] An ontology that takes these connections into account does not simply contain individual things to which we ascribe sense qualities and to which we refer by means of language. Nor do our senses collaborate arbitrarily; they do so in very specific ways to produce lingual objects. The connection of sense impressions, for example of seeing and hearing, leads to a whole, usually to a thing.

Yet significant as the plasticity of sense organs may be: *aisthesis* could never by itself produce the recursive structures on which the development of language is based. This may or may not be a reason for the relative aisthetic poverty of language. It is, however, certain that language is a very precise instrument for materializing productions of thought (e.g., giving us red roses to see).

Language thus brings into our purview how much *noiesis* participates in *poiesis*. To pick up the example developed by Metzinger about the book you are now holding in your hands: it is one thing to feel its weight; it is another to read and to understand it. What you read appears in the letters before your eyes. Yet you can only understand if you also think what you read. Stating that you are dealing with a text in English already operates the first abduction. Until you have an understanding of the text, you will follow up with many more.

The language of thought

At some points, Metzinger discusses an apophasis, an ineffability of certain qualities that is difficult to grasp (as we saw above in the example of the red of the "Revolution" rose). This suggests that he has built his theory from a position contrary to that of the analytic philosophy of language. That there is no language module in his model of the brain is probably also the reason why Metzinger discusses a neuroscientific aesthetic of the mind but not a poetics of the mind. In other words, we still don't know enough about the extent to which language or, more precisely, reading and writing participate in the labor of the brain and the formation of consciousness.

"One question which has rather fruitlessly preoccupied philosophers," we read in Gustave Guillaume, "is that of the close tie between language and thought. Some have identified thought and language, making one inseparable from the other. But the true situation is quite different.... In *tongue*—considered in and for itself—the careful observer discovers the very mechanisms thought uses to prehend itself. These mechanisms belong to a systematics, the study of which constitutes a new branch of linguistics which I call the *psycho-systematics of language*."[15]

According to Guillaume, these psycho-systematic mechanisms do not belong to the performativity of language (i.e. they do not improve either the immediate capacity for thought or the capacity for expression as such). He situates them on a level of lingual paradigms. "It should be noted that these mechanisms, which lie deep beneath the surface, are inaccessible to observation except in tongue, the mind's sole monument to its own activity. Granted, the whole of literature bears witness to man's power of thought, but literary works reflect the exercising of that power, not the power itself."[16]

The paradigm of language, which Guillaume calls *la langue*, not only lies behind language, it also lies ahead of language. It thereby allows for the comprehensive cognitive anchoring and stabilization of structures that experimental or speculative speech creates as possible paradigms. Recursive procedures that constitute *la langue*, such as metonymy or syntactic recursion, are the foundation of the human brain's effectiveness. It is the function of *la langue* to let thought return to itself and grasp itself in its activity.

Integrating a consciousness of language as one more level of consciousness into Metzinger's theory is thus less problematic than we first thought. The wording is quite similar to some of Guillaume's descriptions of the psycho-mechanisms of language: "In its totality, tongue is a vast construct, built according to a general law: the coherence of the parts within the whole. And, as experience tells us, this extensive, coherently-built construct (a system, thanks to its coherence), can be divided into several partial, interiorly coherent constructs, which are integrated systems within the overall integrating system. Like any system, these partial, integrated systems integrate their own constituent parts; they have their own unity, which makes each one a distinctly analyzable whole."[17]

This is a description of a lingual function tasked with establishing higher cognitive levels. Language fixates recursive states on the next-higher level of wholeness/totality. It is a speculative tool for thinking the world.

The coevolution of language and the brain

Language acquisition

Metanoia seems to be a radicalization of the poietic function of language, a radicalization of the tool that pushes the development of language by language forward. It also seems to combine the development of thought with the development of language. How, then, are the evolutions of language and thought connected?

We are particularly interested in answering two of these questions (these are also of methodological relevance). First, the attempt to forge a theoretical link between evolutionary and self-organizing processes. This is a result of the assumption, in Terrence Deacon's terms, that "many structural features of language are derived from sources of 'information' other than nature or nurture. The demands of symbol learning can ultimately be construed as selection pressures over and above those that are contributed by genetic, neural, social, or ecological sources."[18]

Second, and as a consequence of the integral capacities of auto-*poietic* organizational forces, we are interested in the phylo- and ontogenetic interplay between language and the brain, because, as Charles N. Li and Jean-Marie Hombert write, "[w]hat is innate ... is the architectural and chronotopic development of the human brain in ontogeny, which channels the human infant's attention to the linguistic and social interaction of his/her environment and enables the human infant to learn a complex symbolic behavior requiring, among other things, a prodigious memory. The acquisition of language is, then, a complex interplay between this innate predisposition and the language environment."[19]

That biological change is much more inflexible and slower than lingual shifts, that the lingual capacities of a child change in a few years to an extent for which the brain needs millennia—this immense difference in evolutionary mobility suggests that the so-far dominant focus on changes in the brain alone puts the question in terms that are much too narrow. How does language itself change, and can this change be gathered from the effects of or interaction with bodily changes?

In his by now classic study *The Symbolic Species*, Deacon captures this change in the formula of a "co-evolutionary dynamic between language and its host."[20] Language, on this reading, is a parasitic organism switching between activity and passivity, simultaneously dependent *on* and constitutive *of* bodily changes (bipedality, larynx, etc.). Let's follow Deacon's exposition.

"It would not be too much of a simplification to say that the size and shape of my hand and the types of cells that compose it were mostly determined by processes that took place in my hand during its development."[21] This is true, and especially so, for brain cells, whose "complex interplay of local and distant cell interactions is capable of producing far more cellular heterogeneity, and therefore far more potential for functional differentiation, than is possible in any other organ system. Neurons born in distant regions and following very different developmental trajectories can directly and specifically communicate with each other." This makes the development of the brain a "particularly complicated and counterintuitive"[22] process, in which the nervous system actively participates in its own construction.

Auto-*poietic* accounts of language

An essential insight of recent research is a certain auto-*poietic* component. Let's begin, once again, with Terrence Deacon, specifically with his supposition "that universal rules or implicit axioms of grammar aren't really stored or located anywhere," that "they are not *determined* at all" but instead "have emerged spontaneously and independently in each evolving language." Structural similarities between the languages of different cultures are due to "forces of selection" (the human capacity for learning, remembering, and perceiving, anatomical constraints on forming vowels and the ability to hear, etc.). Such "forces of selection should be most intense at the level of the logical structure of a language (grammar and syntax)."[23] Deacon connects this biological evolutionary thesis with a brain-anatomical deterritorialization according to which specific lingual functions are not housed in individual areas, domains, or spheres but are always co-processed by the entire brain.

From the point of view of a theory of language, such a holistic understanding of auto-*poietic* processes also has the advantage of a dynamic understanding of the vividness immanent to the development of language. In a manner analog to the familiar schema of linguistic evolution, lingual structures reveal themselves on all levels to be "products of powerful multilevel evolutionary processes, to which innate mental tendencies contribute only one subtle source of the Darwinian selection biases." That is why we, unlike followers of a Chomskyan universal grammar, do not have to assume an innate lingual capacity or an originary language instinct. "Languages have adapted to human brains and human brains have adapted to languages, but the rate of language change is hundreds or thousand times more rapid than biological change. . . . The brain has co-evolved with respect to language, but languages have done most of the adapting."[24]

The thesis of a reciprocal material recursivity between language and the brain also suggests a revision of models of evolution that concern the development of our language or our brain. James Mark Baldwin's model of an evolutionary self-referentiality seems to be attractive in this respect. His monistic model of evolution allows the question of how "learning and behavioral flexibility can play a role in amplifying and biasing natural selection" to be answered. They do so by enabling individuals to change their cultural and also their evolutionary context.[25] Without having to assume, as Lamarck did, a direct transmission of individual behavior patterns to the next generation, Baldwin's theory offers an approach for an explanation of how trained behaviors can affect evolutionary changes.

We may assume that such generative transmissions take place by way of a storage medium into which what has been learned is entered such that it can be retrieved. Like Gustave Guillaume, we presume that language fixes a form that sets a lingual level as a cognitive minimum level for a language community. When universal grammar looks for structures shared by cognition and language, this should not be understood (in a relativistic, some would say 'postmodern' sense) to imply that individual languages fix different views of the world.[26] Instead, it is to be understood to imply that speech, thought, and the formation of a perspective onto world recursively refer to one another. The potential of a universal grammar would then be to define this reciprocal referentiality.

The reciprocal relationship between language and thought is hardly ever described either in terms of causality or in terms of influence, as Whorf still tried to do; more frequently, it is described using concepts such as "correlation" or, within a historical perspective, "coevolution." Philip Lieberman has suggested an explanation in which human linguistic capacities derive from the same neurological mechanisms that structure both our cognitive behavior and that of animals as well as from "a limited set of language-specific mechanisms that differentiate the particular manner in which we transmit information" and "the anatomical and neural input-output mechanisms for the production of speech and some of the neural mechanisms that structure rule-governed syntax."[27]

However essential a role auto-*poietic* processes may play, the evolution of the brain can be described as a self-organizing but not an automatic process. The *poietic* and experimental moment of the evolution of our brain has to be taken into account. This leads to a crossing (or reciprocal re-entry) of neurosciences and neuroethics. Just as meaning emerges from semiotic experiments and language games (a process that provides instruments for the perception of the world and in which the brain, which processes language, develops itself) so the brain, too, develops by experimenting on the meta-reflexive levels, thereby recursively changing itself.

Aspects of universal grammar (Chomsky v Leiss): generative, extra-linguistic, cognitive

In the course of the so-called "second cognitive revolution," which began with Noam Chomsky in the 1950s, the perspective of linguistics shifted away from an older, universally familiar thesis of Whorf and Sapir's about the influence of individual languages on the thoughts of their respective community. Attention was now focused less on particular (metaphorical) homologies between lingual and cognitive figures than on the cognitive nature of human linguality. For linguistics, this meant a shift of the horizon of inquiry from individual languages and comparative grammar to a universal grammar.

This came with a significant rapprochement with the analytic philosophy of language, which connected Chomsky's cognitive theses (even if today they are considered to have been refuted) with epistemological questions. Karl-Otto Apel notes that "Chomsky's theory of generative transformational grammar is inconceivable without the background of modern analytical philosophy and its logico-mathematical aids. It is precisely this close contact that had made it possible for his theory of language to have a revolutionary effect, as an epistemologically and perhaps even meta-logically relevant theory of mind, upon analytical philosophy itself."[28]

Chomsky assumes a human "language faculty" that enables us to acquire and use language. Universal grammar, then, is the theory of the originary state of the lingual capacity, an expression of our genes. This is linked with what we may call a new kind of "ontology of language." "In this perspective, language is a natural object, a component of the human mind, physically represented in the brain and part of the biological endowment of the species."[29]

Generative grammar

The assumption of a language faculty in our cognitive apparatus, which would produce our speech, led to a reconstruction of grammar itself. Grammar now includes, first, a generative moment (which concerns the way in which lingual structures are performed thanks to cognitive competence); second, a transformative moment (since cognitive structures are transformed into lingual structures); and this implies, third, covert structures that are of a cognitive nature and form the core of a deep grammar.

Chomsky writes: "Within the new approach, Universal Grammar is not just a grammatical metatheory, and becomes an integral component of particular grammars. In particular, UG is a system of universal principles, some of which contain parameters, choice points which can be fixed in one of a limited number of ways. A particular grammar then is immediately derived from UG by fixing the parameters in a certain way: Italian, French, Chinese, etc. are direct expressions of UG under particular, and distinct, sets of parametric values. No language-specific rule system is postulated: structures are directly computed by UG principles, under particular parametric choices. At the same time, the notion of a construction-specific rule dissolves. Take for instance the passive, in a sense the prototypical case of a construction-specific rule."[30]

For Elisabeth Leiss, however, the renewal of the format of a universal grammar is tied to assigning a central role to the concept of function within universal grammar. Since language, as we saw in part thanks to Leiss's analyses, consists almost exclusively of part-to-whole relations, universal grammar must draw on the logic of part-to-whole relations (mereology) as one of its tools. The primary function of signs consists in guiding our attention to a detail of the world that surrounds us.[31]

Extralinguistic grammar

To understand universal grammar as a global grammar of all languages is still to undervalue it; nor does understanding it as a grammatical metatheory account for the fascination it exerts. Let's imagine instead that all existing languages are merely the visible surface of an additional dimension of language that goes beyond the dimensions of language known so far. Could we not, with a view to thought, describe an increase of levels in grammar? Let's call the grammar that thereby becomes conceivable an extralinguistic grammar. The task of universal grammar would then be the explanation, in linguistics and beyond, of the interdependencies language maintains with thought on the one hand and world on the other. Leiss, as we just saw, has emphasized the function universal grammar plays as an argument for a language-ontological realism. We would like to underscore the impulses universal grammar provides to theories of cognition. An extralinguistic grammar as it arises from the connection of linguistics and neuroscience generates a new horizon of inquiry. From within this horizon, the "intralinguistic" aims and methodological achievements of Chomskyan universal grammar would have to be criticized.

Cognitive grammar

Universal grammar, conceived of as an "extralinguistic" grammar, acquires a function in human ontogenesis. Universal grammar, Chomsky tells us, "expresses the universal properties of natural languages; in terms of the adopted cognitive perspective, Universal Grammar expresses the biologically necessary universals, the properties that are universal because they are determined by our in-born language faculty, a component of the biological endowment of the species."[32]

From the cognitive perspective, however, it is another thesis from universal grammar that appears in a new light. "The critical formal contribution of early generative grammar was to show that the regularity and unboundedness of natural language syntax were expressible by precise grammatical models endowed with recursive procedures. Knowing a language amounts to tacitly possessing a recursive generative procedure."[33] To our mind, the greatest achievement of a universal grammar understood to be extralinguistic is the new sense that finding syntactic recursive structures acquires. The fact that language returns to itself evinces its speculative function, which we have described as the dialectical development of language and thought.

Recursive structures in syntax are not the mere play of language in which it mirrors itself. "It seems that it is the genetically determined lingual organ that is responsible for the production of recursivity."[34] The next step on the path to a realist ontology of language has been reached in the insight that language does not merely form the world or create world-pictures but furthermore optimizes human cognition by means of recursive structures. Language (in referring) relates to the object to be known by recursively forming the matter of knowledge. To this extent, language makes "specifically human cognition possible in the first place," writes Leiss in reference to Derek Bickerton. "According to this approach, language is the interface between the world and a material brain, which otherwise isn't very exciting. Language thus optimizes a primate's brain and produces cognition that is specifically human."[35]

Semiotics of the brain (Deacon)

Forgetting and unlearning

How, then, can the co-evolution of thought and speech be conceived of if not in terms of reciprocal influence or reciprocal advancement? Deacon describes a systematic mutual "displacement" of language and thought, which we read as a "shift" and a "dislocation." Does the thesis, counterintuitive at first sight, that the co-evolution of language and thought comes with an amplification of differences—the evolution of language and thought would thus be something like an armament race—contain a first hint at the function of metanoia? Is metanoia merely an instrument of conflict resolution, a tool for homologizing the developments of language and thought? Or do we not instead have to think of it as a permanent revolution that reproduces the conflict on ever-new levels?

Let's look at how Deacon describes the acquisition of language. Instead of the debate about what basic capacities enable us to acquire language, another question takes center stage: what cognitive deficit makes us learn language and which cognitive capacities have to be deactivated to this end? The thesis is that we develop a mental language to compensate for a cognitive lack; for this to succeed, we have to give up another capacity. To explain this thesis, Deacon relies on a semiotic conception of language based on the lingual sign types that are mimetic icons, metonymic indices, and relational symbols. He describes how we acquire lingual sign types and why other species do not.

The perception of icons takes place on the boundary of the sensible capacity for making distinctions and cognitive indistinguishability. To read the wing of a moth on the bark of a tree as an iconic sign, we have to do something a bird that feeds on moths doesn't do, namely differentiate and de-differentiate at the same time. "The interpretative step that establishes an iconic relationship is essentially prior to this, and it's something negative, something we don't do. It is, so to speak, the act of not making a distinction."[36] The bird, therefore, in interpretatively producing iconicity, does *not* do something more fundamental, i.e. distinguish: when I, bird, scan my field of vision, I cannot but see: bark, bark, bark [although "actually" moth, but I, bird, do not notice that, and I do not notice either that I interpret the moth as bark], bark, bark. Unlike human beings, however, I, bird, am not able to recognize this iconicity as such (i.e. as semiotic): bark, bark, moth [which looks like bark and is thus interpreted by me, bird, as an icon of "bark"], bark, bark. Iconicity thus emerges as an act of *not* making a distinction. "Whether because of boredom or limitations, there are times when almost everything can be iconic of anything else (stuff, stuff, stuff ...)."[37]

The cognitive capacity we (unlike the bird) possess and give up to attain the iconic level of language acquisition is the capacity of (not) making a sensible distinction. (Unlike the bird, we are also able to reflect on how significant this capacity is for us—for example by reflecting on the line, "Rose is a rose is a rose is a rose.") Indexical semiotic relations can emerge from relating iconic signs to one another. They establish a connection between an object and its representation, a token. Yet at some point, the acquisition of indexical signs, too, reaches an immanent limit. On the one hand, a language that consists exclusively of indices would not be a language but merely a collection of semantic units without grammar. On the other hand, without relations between the various indices, there would be no order of things. Signs, to put it in Frege's terms, would have reference but they would have no sense. Such a collection of tokens would be anchored exclusively in our memory. Unlike what we do in our habitual use of language, we would have atomistically to define each token individually.

The open question is how grammar is inscribed in such an unordered heap of semantic units. Deacon confronts the problem head-on in decidedly Peircean terms. For him, grammar is not merely a form but a semiotic relation. Grammar institutes a symbolic (and this means: a relational) mediation of meaning and referent. Semiotic relations come in three stages: relations between referents stand in a relation to relations between interpretants. This also clarifies why Deacon resists an orthodox interpretation of Chomsky, whose universal grammar tends toward a dyadic semiotic model of language that includes a grammatical system of rules that is innate and indexical semiotic relations that are to be acquired.

Iconoclasm

We acquire grammar in the construction of triadic semiotic relations, a construction that can only be achieved by way of the procedure we call iconoclasm. Primates cannot learn language because they cannot give up the production of indexical relations (which they can very well be trained to establish). This boundary remains insurmountable. The ever-expanding appropriation of indexical signs like *banana* and *hammer*, *orange* and *knife* does not enable them to distinguish between food and tools. Even if they are shown boxes that contain food at one time, tools at another, this does not usually lead them to form complex symbolic semiotic relations but at most to appropriate one more singular token, one for boxes. For relations between things and relations between signs to be produced, however, the relations between signs and objects have, at first, to be cut: iconoclasm.

The formation of the interpretant primarily takes place negatively, that is, cutting the indexical semiotic relation is the condition for acquiring symbolic relations. Negating indexical semiotic relations is the precondition for and a transitive state in passing from indexical to symbolic reference. We remember the iconoclastic gesture with which Gertrude Stein declared the red of roses to be the meaning of her line, we recall the history of roses in the course of which the perception of red has changed, and we recall cultivators' systematic attempts to capture red. Again and again, we find in the avant-garde's nihilistic and reductive strategies (to which Stein's line belongs as well, a line that seems to be tautological but is in fact recursive) gestures of claiming the symbolic meaning that comes with the rejection of indexical semiotic relationships. The lingual realism of the avant-gardes is, as we can now see, a description of the discovery and establishment of symbolic semiotic relations.

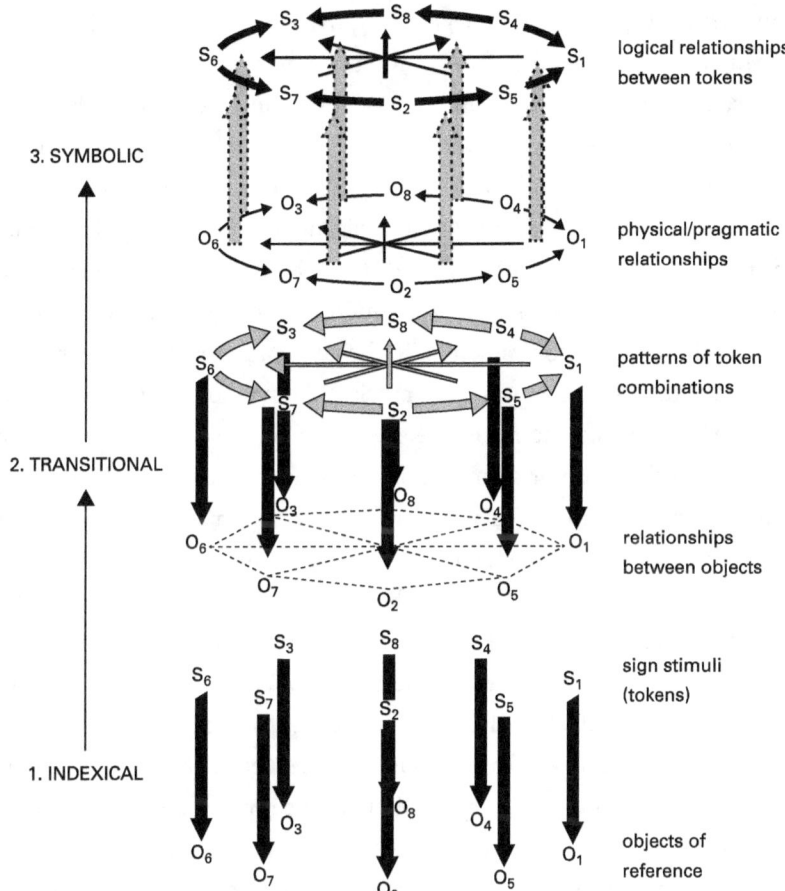

Figure 12[38] Terrence Deacon's semiotics of the brain

We are now also in a position better to understand some stubborn problems in the analytic philosophy of language, problems that arise because analytic philosophy attempts to build language effectively on relations of equivalence. When the definition of reference is based on a theory of truth, both semiotic relations have to be relations of identity. Every semiotic relation that has three positions, however, contains a positive and a negative indexical relation and, in consequence, always contains an irresolvable contradiction. That is why Kripke thinks that true reference is not possible.[39]

The dilemma of the analytic philosophy of language can thus be pinpointed: going back to an iconic semiotic relation leads to an attempt to dissolve the simultaneity of positive and negative equivalences into clear distinctions (instead of clear identities). Accordingly, analytic philosophy laments equivocations—such as the confusion of moth and bark—and, claiming a difference, it attempts to restore the possibility of an identity of denotation and symbolization: moth is moth, bark is bark—that the moth's wings were taken as an iconic sign of the bark is said to be a negligence of semiotic practice that can, in principle, be avoided as long as the distinction is correctly designated. This produces an infinite process of interpretation, a process that cannot, of course, get rid of the semiotic contradiction: in the attempt to reverse the iconoclasm (or to make the iconic relation more precise) the symbolic sign dissolves. It is no longer even possible to recognize a 'simple' icon as such (the way the bird makes the moth disappear as an icon by eating it the moment it distinguishes between bark and moth). This attempt, therefore, remains oblivious of the permanent creation of real referents in the never-ending aimless search for the basis of real reference—for the stuff the world is made of—the way the bird eating the icon also eats a symbolic sign without reflecting on its significance.[40]

At this point, we would like to indicate once more the extent to which this validates deconstructive analyses of literature. The self-denying rhetorical figures found by Paul de Man in Proust's *À la recherche du temps perdu* (and everywhere else)—de Man interprets them as the impossibility for the literary text to reach a conclusive unified sense—would thus be an indication of the parallel staging of two types of signs and their unavoidable contradiction. The unfolding of symbolic semiotic relations can make explicit the negation of indexical semiotic relations on which it is based or merely contain it as covert moment, which it avoids thanks to a subterfuge but never gets rids of.

Relational ontology

Lingual relationality or Thirdness (i.e. the relation of the interpretant) does not go back to a repetition of the indexical relation. When we recall the function of metonymy,[41] we see that this is also the reason why metonymic recursion must not be understood as a twofold or repeated indexical relation. Instead, it must always be posited and negated: iconoclasm.

Looked at from the perspective of the symbolic semiotic relation, the indexical semiotic relation is both positive and negative. It must be negated as an indexical relation in order for the symbolic semiotic relation to be constructed. We recall another moment: only in the semiotic relations of Thirdness that form a part-to-whole relation can oppositions become signs. A semiotic relation with just two positions cannot be an opposition because it could not maintain itself as a negative relation: without a mediating wholeness, it would only be an incoherence.

The referent of Firstness is matter, the referents of Secondness are things, and the referents of Thirdness are relations. The worldview of speculative realism, we believe, is based on Thirdness, in other words: the objects of speculative-realist knowledge are relations. Speculative realism, in this sense, is lingual relationalism. When we look at the relationship between symbolic relations based on Thirdness and relations between things and at the same time consider that indexical semiotic relations can (and to a certain degree must) be negative, we understand how speculative realism can be a *metaphysical* realism that is (like all philosophical writing) a lingual practice without, however, possessing a theory of language. We can also understand how speculative realism could at the same time confront the linguistic turn in philosophy.

Our speculative poetics does not oppose this speculative realism. We rather see it as a necessary complement—it needs a theory of language that reflects the unavoidable correlation of thought, language, and world. Only then can there be a meaningful justification—thanks to *poiesis*—of the realist project of anti-correlationalist thought. From the perspective of *noiesis*, constructions of language and of cognitive capacities go hand in hand. The practice of triadic semiotic relations or the relationalism of the symbolic system is a lingual economization. This makes it possible to account for many more objects (tools) than would ever be possible with indices. Referential procedures acquire an abductive character.

The negative–positive relationalism of symbolic systems leads to a new ontology. Identificatory references, to be sure, are no longer possible without ambiguity, yet at the same time, new referents emerge that we weave into a dense network of relations. By such a *relational ontology* we understand a realism of relations. What language makes visible from now on is no longer the things, which we rather see only in their relations; language gives us the existence of relations to see.

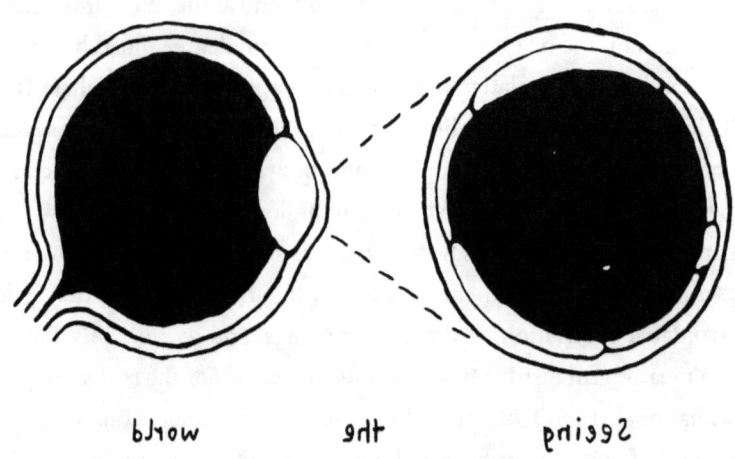

Seeing the world

Epilogue

The Whole Truth and Nothing. But the Truth!

The human being who is conscious of having character in his way of thinking does not have it by nature; he must always have acquired it. One may also assume that the grounding of character is like a kind of rebirth, a certain solemnity of making a vow to oneself, which makes the resolution and the moment when this transformation took place unforgettable to him, like the beginning of a new epoch.

Immanuel Kant

The economy of metanoietic knowledge

With Deacon's reflections on the forgetting of indexical semiotic relations in the service of acquiring symbolic semiotic relations we have returned to the beginning of our study. We began our discussions with an analogue forgetting, a forgetting of earlier processes of understanding. Forgetting seems to have a more profound significance for the experience of metanoia. The metanoietic transformation always links up with formulas of astonishment such as "I don't understand anymore how I could have seen it that way" or with questions such as "Why did I think of it differently back then?" Yet this new I who produces such sentences after having produced the new knowledge the old I knew nothing of does not leave the old I behind as a monad. Metanoia lets us see that our 'old I' has become a part of the new world and that it stands in a relation to it. That is why there are also always sentences produced such as "Now I know why I couldn't think of it before" or questions such as "Why didn't I think of that earlier?"

Metanoia brings about a devaluation, transvaluation, revaluation of all previous knowledge, at least in the form in which it used to be integrated in a coherent whole. It implies, as it were, a potlatch of knowledge, a grandiose shuffling of all that came before. The elements of knowledge lose their earlier significance: some of them become central and all of a sudden appear in a new light, others become banal and lose their former prestige. In this respect, metanoia creates the world anew and differently. Metanoia is the knowledge that there can be totalities in this world totally different from what we thought.

This is the sense in which metanoia is the most radical form of *poiesis*. Yet against the background of our analysis of lingual *poiesis* we not only define metanoia as a change in possibilities for the development of language but also as a fundamental othering of the subject. Here, too, metanoia marks a transition or a radicalization. In a metanoia, we do not simply state in the future perfect that the world constantly changes and that we permanently change in the process. We see a triple shift of subject, thought, and world: a metanoia displaces us into something new (a new world); this places us beyond our previous thought (of the world); and we think (ourselves) in a new world. Accordingly, the (re) introduction of metanoia to philosophy is a double re-entry; we're dealing with two recursive movements in which the radical shift takes place: first the re-entry of the subject into the world, second the re-entry of thought into thought.

Re-entry

Re-entry of the subject into the world

A metanoia resituates us as (new) subjects in the world. As subjects, we enter into the world of which we now know that we have never left it and which has yet become another. This corresponds to the curious rapidity with which we experience the entry of the new. On the one hand, metanoia stands at the end of a long path (in conformity with the heritage of ancient practices of reading and writing). On the other hand (and at the same time) we become aware of it as sudden being-other (this is what its kinship with experiences of religious experiences of awakening consists in). Even if this has not often been thematized, philosophy has always been carried forward by this fascination with a conversion of subject and object.

Re-entry of thought into thought

Metanoia is the well-hidden spiritual core of our philosophical thought and reflection. In this respect, the question of metanoia leads us to the question of the conditions of possibility of thought. We mean this in the fullest sense of the term. Metanoia is a process of thought by which thought develops itself. Thought influences its conditions and creates new possibilities for itself to think or, rather, creates possibilities of thinking another way. For us, this auto-affection is lingual; if we align it with the poetic, we thereby emphasize both the necessity of a critique of language and of a poetics at the same time. In every respect, the experience of metanoia precedes the engagement with *poiesis*.

Sliding hermeneutics

"Every epistemological clarification is tied to an aesthetic decision. What becomes visible in this poetological dimension is the historicality of this knowledge, it is the fact that there are no occasions that, beyond its forms of presentation, in an untouched outside, would await being designated, awoken and made visible by discourses, propositions, existential claims. A history of knowledge cannot be reduced to the history of the objects and referents of knowledge. Every designation of an object at the same time operates a discursive production of this same objective."[1] What Joseph Vogl says about objects in his *Poetics of the homo oeconomicus*, we have described as a process of subjects' othering. For the new epistemes within which we know anything do not exist prior to such an othering. Like the things and objects that it makes its objects, the mind only emerges in the process of investigation. The creative dimension thereby implied is not to be confused with an *aesthetic* decision. It is a *poietic* process, which we have identified as an object of a speculative poetics.

Our speculative reflections on thought were triggered by thinking about metanoia. For what we experience as a metanoia is that coming back to ourselves is not the same as going in circles in our minds. Reading does not turn us into the philologist of the book in our hands, and writing leaves the desk behind when it embarks on its journey.

We've come across the union of reading and writing several times. Does writing do the preliminary work for a reading-metanoia? Does coming back, in writing, to what has been read, does the feedback effect of writing itself make the signifiers slide? Writing is a metonymy because in writing we continue our reading. It brings signs back to themselves in ways that can lead to a fundamental othering. Reading integrates itself into writing, and the new whole the parts get themselves into leads to a permanent sliding.

We've answered the question of what happens in experimental poetic writing by engaging with Hegel's speculative reflections on the relationship between writing and reading. The (first) attempts at writing that come with any metanoia triggered by literary or philosophical readings correspond to the necessity for philosophy to write. Just as writing about an author, about a book, can work towards a corresponding metanoia, every change of mind leads to a full word or pushes on toward a confessional text. Alain Juranville writes with a dose of Lacanian surrealism: "All signifiers have the same signified ('cat' like 'dog' like 'perplexity')."[2] And yet—like language in general—the language in which metanoia takes place is not arbitrary: it practices lingual realism and presents a form of lingual practice that opens up a truth.

There are always writings surrounding a metanoia—notes, a first verse, the diary of a few weeks or decades, agendas, the beginnings of a novel—and none of them ever come to an end. Each such fragment refers to a beginning. Here, then, writing is to be understood grammatologically: it sets a signifier into motion, and there is only ever one act. We change our position and put ourselves in the place of the referent. Only when we assume this position can we mean anything by a signifier. The factual redness that Odd means by "*" can only exist by Odd standing for it. And in just the same way, the factual reality that Derrida means by *différance* or that Kant means by the categorical imperative can only exist because Derrida and Kant stood for it. To lead sense back to itself always implies an elementary authorial act and, in this sense, a full writing that reacts to such a fundamental experience.

Metanoia ≠ aesthetic experience

What conception or dimension of experience is at play in metanoia? It is not, in any case, the everyday use of "gaining experience." Such a concept does not get at lingual *poiesis*, without which referentiality would be impossible and whose fundamental significance has put us on the track of thinking about metanoia. The othering that takes place in a metanoia only emerges in a different aspect of the concept of experience, in the sense of "having an experience." It is about encountering a changing object, an encounter in which we suddenly cross the line into the future.

What we come across at the same time in metanoia is a new subjectivity: the subject has encountered either a knowledge or an object that has changed its reality. This formula could be misunderstood in two ways, each of which can be explained by popular philosophical reflexes. The first is a reflex popular in moral philosophy: metanoia does not imply any witnessing of or participation in an event whose "experience" would have to be kept faithfully (the fetish of Badiou's disciples). The second is a reflex popular in aesthetics: metanoia is not tied to an intense perception of an object (the hobby-horse of politically charged theories of art). We have distinguished metanoia in particular from what an aestheticized philosophy would call sensible thinking. Nonetheless, metanoietic thought is not simply non-sensible, even if sensibility cannot be equated here with perception: sensibility is not the starting point of metanoia; as its product, it is its end point.

To the extent that metanoietic thought creates freedom, freedom attains the domain of our habits. Our body loses its strangeness and stops acting against us. We then "have ourselves" in the strong sense of having arrived in a *habitus*. We no longer react to a precedent address from our senses; instead, our sensibility is the consequence of our (new) intuition. Maybe it all begins with an indulgence of the austerity of the writing it feeds on, perhaps it soon takes on the ascetic form of dry bread, is followed by an empty fridge, and often ignores a freezing apartment.

"Is the self the point to which you return through the long detour of ascesis and philosophical practice? Or is the self an object you always keep before your eyes and reach through a movement that in the end can only be bestowed by wisdom?"[3] The movement Foucault asks about gives rise to the "transformation of *logos* into *ethos*. And *askēsis* may then be defined as the set, the regular, calculated succession of procedures ... The *askēsis* makes truthtelling a mode of being of the subject."[4] In this sense, metanoia recuperates an origin of philosophy as love for wisdom: reading as (temporary) farewell to life, renouncing the riches of the sensible world; reading to become an other; reading to (re)enter (the other) life as this other.

Reading problems

Let's take another look at the connection of metanoia and not-understanding. It can be put in the form of a question: is it not the very difficulty of philosophical texts—and sometimes the incomprehensiblity of literary texts—that provides an important initial impetus for further engagement with an author or a book? Understanding philosophical texts implies an othering of subject and predicate, demands the truth-seeking subject's immersion in the text. This immersion must be all the more radical the more strangely the text speaks to us at first. Metanoia not only constrains us to develop another understanding but has also led us to another theory of understanding.

How do we get from incomprehensibility to understanding? The answer to this very question is provided by the description of the difficulties of speculative reading and of understanding philosophical texts. How is a thought to be understood that is not recognizable by its lingual expression, a thought that is not already part of a code, not semanticized in language and thus not available as signified? This can only be explained by recourse to *poiesis* (i.e. to the potentializing function of language). In the most radical of cases, we understand metanoeitically not only what we have not yet thought but also what language has not yet thought for us either.

It is a perfectly quotidian experience that we do not understand sentences whose thoughts we have not already thought—we then only sense an agreement with the text (and its author). When this happens, we first try to lead the sentence back to itself, usually following up by trying to explain the sentence we did not understand from the context of the paragraph. We can then embed our non-comprehension in the text and try to attain an understanding by increasing the radius of our hermeneutic circle. We continue doing this until we have reached the limit of ourselves and until *poiesis* succeeds in drawing a circle that puts us in the position of the subject of the text. This is how speculative reading begins; this is what is at stake.

Matters ethical (and religious)

Going through puberty with Thomas Bernhard

One day, an adolescent reader, let's say our present-tense specialist, finds a novel lying around in his grandparents' summerhouse. Although he has until then shown no signs of literary affinities—he will later surmise that the subtitle, *Eine Erregung* [*An Irritation*], narcissistically encouraged his volatile character—he begins reading in the minimalistically designed, gray book. Some hours later, he is in the know and an inveterate, cardcarrying, and altogether unique follower of the hero of Thomas Bernhard's novel.

Very quickly, the reflection triggered by *Holzfällen* [*Cutting Timber*] expands in everwidening circles. It leads first to Bernhard's *Der Untergeher* [*The Loser*], then to Schopenhauer and from there to Nietzsche, it leads to Montaigne and the Stoics, to Glenn Gould and Mozart's Haffner Symphony, the only decent performance of which, of course, is the one by Krips and the Vienna Philharmonic. In addition, our reader now knows that he has to leave, that the Viennese are all depraved, and he is certain that one day he will be happy in England. He understands that he is stronger by himself because every coalition is as weak as the ally most ready to compromise. Every day, he feels elevated above those around him, whose collective weakness makes them shy away from the apollonian inexorability of writing books.

Not just because this felt good and continues to feel good—*Holzfällen* must at some point have begun to structure his thought and thereby his whole world, and that has at some point also changed the book: "But Billroth and Schreker (and her companion) are not the only people who make a point of cultivating the people who administer state moneys and state honors in this country: almost all German academics go the same way when once they have *reached years of discretion*, as they say, recanting everything they professed and propagated with the utmost vehemence before the age of twenty-five or thirty as the minimal morality required of the academic, in order to ally themselves with those who dispense state money, state orders, and state pensions. All German academics end up letting themselves be bought out by the state for its nefarious purposes, selling themselves to this vile, unprincipled execrable state, and most of them start off that way. Their science consists solely in working hand in glove with the state—that is the truth."[5]

That the book has begun to structure our reader's thought and world leads to an (equally) circular question: Has he found the book in the grandparents' house and does every reader naturally always find "his" book? Or has the book waited for the reader? Don't all readers only ever find the books they want to find? Have not all books always found their readers, as we ought to say?

No matter how long we think about the primacy of subject and object, in the end, one and the same circle appears. Metanoia's othering does not establish any "meaningful" causal structure; it only ever establishes the circular structure of sense that again and again refers to itself as evidence. Yet metanoia does not leave it at this self-reference, no literary reader sticks with his one author or holy book (but, unfortunately, many a philosophical and, catastrophically, quite a few religious readers do). Circularity, which always refers to itself, also produces an infinite reference. We might trace how sense unfolds, but why it was Thomas Bernhard or whether it couldn't have been something else—this secret the metanoietic Bermuda triangle will never divulge.

Perhaps we keep on reading because every book contains this promise of a metanoietic transformation, the promise of getting us into an elementary epistemic situation in which the object emerges simultaneously with a new subject. Such an othering would, of course, be impossible without the participation of an *other* who changes the status of *subject* and *object* equally. That is why the re-entry of metanoia into philosophy pushes forward beyond a structuralist universe defined by binary oppositions.

Triadic relation

Questions about the objects of our analysis and their procedures of knowledge have, again and again, led us to the speculative question concerning the extent to which we fundamentally think in triads. The constellation subject—object—other, as we saw, defines all knowledge. So far, however, the relationship between object and other is, obviously, ontologically underdetermined, just as the relationship between subject and other seems to be epistemologically underdetermined. Even if psychoanalysis defines the relationship of the subject to an object only via the mediation of an other, it nonetheless seems to make little sense to reproach it with a failure to accept the subject's rationality or sovereignty. Could we not instead credit psychoanalysis with a triadic epistemology? Lacan's concept of the Big Other fits our system insofar as Lacan avoids the Freudian unconscious's one-sided attachment to the subject.

In Lacan's version, a subject's knowing an object is mediated by an other. Up until now, the drift that becomes evident in this process has mostly been understood as an othering of the subject and as a criticism of the possibility of knowledge. But when we construct a triadic epistemic situation, othering— especially an othering of the object—is by no means to be understood relativistically. Quite the contrary: such knowledge has something triumphalist about it, for it promises not only to make things perceptible in their particularity and singularity, but furthermore to capture them in their relationality, their embeddedness in a tightly woven net of references, and their changing in time. In one and the same movement, thought immerses itself in the things and falls into time. "It is possible to *fall* into the heights as well as into the depths [Man kann auch in die Höhe *fallen*, so wie in die Tiefe],"[6] as Hölderlin knew.

We are, however, less concerned here with the fullness of joyful affects that can accompany this triumphal knowledge; we are more concerned with the insight that every profound departure toward knowledge begins with an othering—no matter whether it concerns the decision to become a literary scholar, a philosopher, a neuroscientist, or a psychoanalyst.

Metanoia does not just affect the subject, and it does not merely constitute the subject as the subject of knowledge. It also creates the object of knowledge, in the fullest sense of the term. This is also where we see the reason for its knowledge-instituting potentiality: metanoia begins in the encounter with an other to create a subject and at the same time brings with it an object of knowledge. It is by no means the case that this crisis of the limited calculus of rationality leads to a skeptical position.

Auto-affection

Most of the time, criticism of the idea of pure reason has also been a criticism of the forgetting of language, from Kant's contemporaries (Hamann, Herder) via their Romantic successors (Gerber, Nietzsche) to the present (Heidegger, Derrida). We don't want to criticize the criticism here but instead radicalize one of its many seminal definitions, namely the way in which language theory allows us to think the auto-affection of thought in metanoia. This concerns above all Kant's reflections on the active role the faculty of the imagination—*Was bilde ich mir ein und was denke ich mir dabei? [What do I imagine (myself) to be and what am I thinking?]* (Oswald Egger)—plays in our thought and in our production of world.

"Derangement of the mind" and "imagination" are part of the process of the mind's auto-affection. They go hand in hand, not only in Kant's *Essay on the Diseases of the Head*, but also in the *Critique of Pure Reason*: "Now that which, as representation, can precede any act of thinking something is intuition and, if it contains nothing but relations, it is the form of intuition, which, since it does not represent anything except insofar as something is posited in the mind, can be nothing other than the way in which the mind is affected by its own activity, namely this positing of its representation, thus the way it is affected through itself, i.e., it is an inner sense as far as regards its form."[7]

Metanoia is a procedure of thought by which thought develops itself. The mind influences its own conditions and tries to create new possibilities (of thought) for itself. We understand this auto-affection to be above all lingual; in identifying it, we may get closer again to an aesthetics, but we do not for all that renounce the necessity of a critique of language or the necessity of a poetics. If only because the poetics in question is a speculative poetics, our philosophical question about the conversion phenomenon metanoia is a question about the spiritual dimension of philosophy.

Spiritual philosophy and religion

Let's listen to what Pierre Hadot has to say about philosophical conversions: "More and better than a theory of conversion, philosophy itself has always remained essentially an act of conversion."[8] For Plato and many others following him, only the converted philosopher can ensure the transformation of her fellow citizens, only an act of conversion guarantees the positive changing of state and city.

In his 1968 *Encyclopædia Universalis* entry, Hadot distinguishes between two forms of *conversion*: "*epistrophe*, which signifies change of orientation and implies the idea of a return (return to the origin, return to the self), on the other hand, *metanoia*, which signifies change of mind, repentance, and implies the idea of a mutation and a rebirth."[9] Despite his respect for Hadot, Foucault dissolves such a well-structured definition fourteen years later in his microscopic readings and questionings. Is Platonic *epistrophe*, in its movement from a (lower) world to another (upper) world not fundamentally different from the phenomena of Hellenistic and Roman cultures of the self? What functions are assigned to pure knowledge or, inversely, to the ascetic training of practices? Where is the break with the world situated? Is it a break between subject and object, or does it take place within the subject itself? How does the subject imagine itself—as subject or as object, or both at the same time? When is it a sudden transsubjectivation that snatches a subject away into the transcendence of another world, and when is it a long-lasting and fundamentally inconclusive process of auto-subjectivation?[10]

At the same time, Foucault brings out central definitions and descriptions of philosophical as well as religious and political metanoia, and he draws attention to another aspect of philosophy's spiritual dimension. He describes how, in the nineteenth century, "conversion, this element of technology of the self, was plugged into this new domain and field of political activity, and how this element of conversion was necessarily, or at last exclusively, linked to the revolutionary choice, to revolutionary practice."[11] Stalinist partisan, religious fanatic, fascist psychotic, no matter: no metanoia, no revolutionary.

Religious politics and history

The difference between cognitive shifts that lead to a psychotic breakdown and the shifts of a religious awakening are neither simple nor obvious. The awakening's leading-beyond-thought also has metanoietic qualities. It is no coincidence that radicalized political theories in which "the operation of a mediating term (a 'third')" is seen as a "praxis of political metanoia"[12] likely to borrow from religious metanoia. Theorists from Badiou to Žižek hope to turn every isolated Saul into a part of a Paulinically organized mass.

"Metanoia is not a stage left behind, an 'event' relegated to passivity by the distance of the past tense, but rather an ontological constitution in the Event itself," we read for example in Creston Davis and Patrick Aaron Riches. "Metanoia is henceforth the nonnegative recentering, the absolute (re)turn of all desire to being. As such, metanoia is the ontological (re)turn to the Event as constitutive of eternity and life itself. The Event is the horizon in which metanoia takes hold. It is the happening by which the subject realizes her/himself as subject."[13] Beyond all the excitement adopted from contemporary French philosophies of the event (which have only a limited bearing on finding specific criteria for distinguishing metanoia) the last sentences are particularly interesting. Shifting the Heideggerian concept of the horizon from a *whole time* onto the event as one of its partial moments brings time as a whole into the horizon of the moment. Just one small difference has to be marked here: the event is the nucleus of history—yet the nucleus of time is the moment.

Interconnecting religious and political metanoia brings out the poeticity of metanoietic thought much more than an aesthetic theory ever could. A political impetus transfers the *poietic* qualities of metanoia into practice, whereas an aesthetic impetus seeks to translate them into the autonomy of thought even though the procedure, going back to first principles, might be the same. "This positive unfolding, this sense of being as production, provides a capacity for 'third' term mediation, a capacity required for the metanoic (re)turn to first principles."[14]

It is characteristic of the political tradition of metanoia that it connects the assumption of a meta-position with a return to immanence to create something in the world. As Boris Groys explains: "In the philosophical tradition, such a change of perspective is termed metanoia. The term metanoia can be used to describe the transition from an individual subjective perspective to a general perspective, to a metaposition.... However, metanoia need not be performed in only one direction. Having attained the universal perspective of the good as such, Plato posed the question of how ideas of the good could be embodied in the intramundane state."[15]

The metanoia inspired by Christianity also works toward a reversal. It brings the collective subject it creates, Christendom, into time, as Catherine Malabou explains: "Time is not what it is. It turns, and by its very concept is susceptible to revolution. Negativity is its turning point (*Wendungspunkt*). Christianity brings about time's great 'volte face': 'This new principle is the axis (*Die Angel*) around which the history of the world turns.' (Hegel, *Philosophie der Geschichte*). Christianity is not one moment among many but the *pivot* which brings all into motion, as we can see from the old distinction *ante natum, post natum*."[16] The religious subject (once more) finds itself in a collective that places itself in time which, in turn, unfolds from out of the moment of a turning point.

Going beyond thought: temporality

Strong temporality

Let's look at the figure of the pivot or turning point of time. Change does not simply take place in a chronological time within which we can pinpoint where the change begins. It is thanks to a metanoia that afterward, we understand *what comes before differently*.

We have already given an account of our speaking of "temporality in the strong sense." We mean that the tense structure of the circle results from the lingual structures themselves, from that very recursivity that is constitutive of language and results in a parts-and-whole structure. Recalling Heidegger's definition of time as a circle that starts in the future, we can describe time and the event in the metanoietic circle as entering into a relationship of part and whole.

In metanoia, the moment as part and time as whole display their reciprocal referentiality. To say that part-to-whole relations are genuine relations is to say that none of the terms of the relation exist without the others. There is no moment without time just as there is no time without the moment. What is meant is that a moment placed within the horizon of time only truly acquires temporality if time, too, can be placed within the horizon of that moment.

We're unsure whether it would be better at this point to speak of the "being" of time or to speak of its "sense." Temporality as it reveals itself in a metanoia is a time that has sense. Such a time highlights the moment in which such sense is found. But of course this moment is not self-sufficient. It is nothing without the time with which it enters into a relation. The moment does not return to itself without having taken on the meaning of time as a whole. That, too, is what we mean when we speak of temporality in the strong *sense*.

New reading

Without yet knowing it, we began working on these topics while we were writing another book, a study about the present tense novel. What started with a sudden attention for the seemingly micrological details of tense usage soon turned into an inquiry into temporality, time itself, and into how language shapes the world. In this sense, *Present Tense: A Poetics* and *Metanoia* aren't two different books on two different topics.

Looking back, it is difficult to re-imagine what it was like for someone who was writing *Present Tense* to read the very books that were about to completely change her perception of what writing and reading mean. Yet there must have been a moment in time that involved another time and a new time as a whole, and since that moment, she has been reading differently. How did she get there? It has to do with the novels she has come across lately, which are all written in the present tense. But there's more. The novels she's already familiar with suddenly seem different. And to a certain extent, she also has a new understanding of theoretical texts. Wolfgang Iser's fiction theory, for instance, and his description of textual games in particular, mean something new to her. *Agon*, *alea*, *ilinx*, and *mimicry* are no longer just ways in which texts construct fictive actions taking place in a "fictive world;" they are agencies acting on the reader. Such a process begins with the very first sentence, the line-up of characters, the attribution of names, the depiction of places, the distribution of colors in the sky, the inventory of a shop window, and finally the polishing of the glass pane for the reader. An author opens his portfolio.

These are events in which she as reader participates. Sometimes she opposes the author, and *agon* is dominant; sometimes she is a chance witness of events (*alea*) the text is merely showing her, yet *mimicry* always leaves traces in the text itself.

A good example is Strindberg's *Inferno*—a brilliant fiction in the mind of literary scholars, the diary of a mental breakdown in the mind of psychoanalysts. In the book, Strindberg's alter ego describes the diagnosis of his Swedish doctor—who has grave concerns about the writer's mental health and warns him about his delusions—as a conspiracy. As if by chance, a second doctor appears whom 'Strindberg' trusts and to whom he entrusts the conclusions he has reached in analyzing himself. He feels saved. At the end, his new doctor accompanies him to see his old doctor who almost breaks down.

The setting of the story as a whole is unpleasant. Strindberg's nasty behavior toward his doctor, the base intentions and envy of his literary success he imputes to him—*Inferno* is a text about a soul's twists and turns, a text that charts the dark corners of a character and, no doubt, depicts the obsessions of thinking. But now that she understands the significance of the (present) tense, she also notices something else: the personal pronouns of the two physicians look weird—but of course! She does take another look, just to be sure, but there's really no need: she suddenly knows what that means. No doubt—there is only one doctor!

This is the moment at which *ilinx*, intoxication, comes into the play of reading. She has to be sure she's not mistaken. She rereads every sentence in which either of the physicians is mentioned, rearranges the scenes of the text in her mind—all parts move to different places. And indeed, the perspectivation of the scenes in which both physicians appear simultaneously is off; only one of them is in the picture at any given point. Strindberg must have invented the second doctor as he was writing. He needed an ally, and he needed a conclusion for this unpleasant story that could only have come to an end either with his being committed or with a convincing refutation of all suspicions.

Now the events of the text begin to move, only now does she participate in the book. A cognitive shift takes place. She now sees that at the end of the book, Strindberg by hook and by crook sets up an allegorical reading. It seems that this form of autotherapy was highly effective. Strindberg's *Inferno* crisis, she reads, was the most unsettling event of his psychological biography and did not reoccur on this scale. The author did, in fact, escape from his demons. Writing *Inferno* entailed a post-apocalyptic reality.

What first became apparent as a cognitive shift in the case of Strindberg's present tense novel quickly spreads. A new way of reading leads her to or, rather, immediately accompanies a new way of understanding. Reading and writing for her are no longer ineluctable processes of perception. They involve decisions, they become actions. They become significant, but what they signify does not simply lie in the texts, it shifts according to the position she assumes in reality. She can choose between several options, and each of these decisions has ethical consequences she alone can vouch for. The way in which she understands her environment and herself, too, shifts. She cannot say this happened step by step, incrementally. The way she understood novels was just a part of what her understanding looked like as a whole. The experience she has in reading present tense novels makes it necessary to account for the existence of a phenomenon called the present tense novel and to outline its history. It demands a revision of the concept of literature, of the function poetics performs for language, and it calls for a philosophical account of the role language plays in constituting reality. The comprehensive metanoia that takes place for her thanks to this group of texts requires a language-ontological foundation. In this sense, *Present Tense: A Poetics* is the result of a metanoietic reading experience and *Metanoia* is the result of an attempt to make sense of the space this process opened up.

Science (of con-temporary) fiction

Present Tense: A Poetics differentiated between three forms of shifting that are essential to a "poetics of fiction." We described the shifting of referents, which triggers fiction, as triggering the perception of meaning, in which the semiotic effect of narrative fiction unfolds. A poetics of tense is nothing but a generalized theory of literary fictions, a poetics of the truth of time produced in the reading of tenses.

By the end of the book, we were aware of four methodological principles being at work, even though we did not know that and how these new wholes would become parts of a new theory (of metanoia). These principles are: (1) an experimental poetics of reading; (2) the aspect of finding or inventing concepts; (3) an experimental setup analogous to scientific experimentation; and (4) an empirical aspect of history.

(1) The derivation, in the exact sciences, of a law from empirical data is supplemented by a poietic experiment whose traditional site is experimental writing. The experimental procedures of a poetics have to be brought to bear in reading, for what combines literary practice with practices that create knowledge is a poietic moment: the moment of aiming at something unknown.

(2) Concept formation traces a poietic recursion of the kind described by Gilles Deleuze and Felix Guattari: We "will know nothing through concepts unless [we] have first created them."[17] Our concept "present tense novel" induced a shift of reference: it makes a difference whether we think we're simply dealing with a novel written in the present tense or whether we're reading a present tense novel that acts as a catalyst for a slow but steady shift of dominants, a shift from narration to fiction as the dominant medium of the novel. In the former case, the text is simply read as an example of an aesthetics of estrangement; in the latter, the present tense appears as a tense that guides our reading and constitutes fiction.

(3) By developing a fiction-narratological toolbox and articulating experimental concepts (focus, deictic triad, anteriority, altermodernism), we transformed our material—literary texts written in the present tense—into the phenomenon of the present tense novel. We were thus able to extract our object from the movement of the material and to chart its asynchronous history. The term "metanoia" designates what has changed for us in the process and how that has changed us as concept-forming subjects.

(4) In discussing Jacques Rancière's concept of a *poetique du savoir*, Rüdiger Campe emphasizes that poetics "has a place in knowledge or over against knowledge." In its utopian or seditious deviation from the *adaequatio* of the true word, the "poetological" co-determines "the historicity of knowledge in knowledge and over against knowledge."[18] The success of every singular present tense work challenges poetological knowledge. In each case, literary texts mark the most recent transgression of the boundaries of what narratology and fiction theory know. This pointed us toward a new poetics of history, to the discovery of an unforeseeable past. A new history is just as unforeseeable as the future that sets in with a metanoia.

Before thought

Three things happen in a metanoia almost simultaneously and so quickly that it is hard to state what we notice first or what is most essential—a limit is abolished, the world changes, and something never thought of that way is suddenly true. Perhaps it goes like this: First we notice the change of the world; in metanoia, the world doesn't just appear, it appears *changed*. Then confusion when we become aware of the fact that the "old" world no longer concerns us. But it is (has been) *our* world—doesn't it have to remain ours despite its having changed? And how do we explain its having changed without our having directly influenced it? After all, we just kept going (or just wandered), and everything was as it always was, really.

The last steps we took were no different from all the previous other steps on our path. Yet without noticing, we must have crossed a limit. "That must be it," we think—hence the pathos of having overcome our own thought.

Some kind of vexation, however, remains: Did we ourselves take the decision to go beyond thought? Or have we just been sucked in by a text? But wouldn't we somehow need to want that to happen, too? Perhaps Nicholson Baker can help us understand this better: "Changes of mind should be distinguished from decisions, for decisions seem to reside pertly in the present, while changes of mind imply habits of thought, a slow settling-out of truth, a partially felt, dense past.... 'I wasn't aware of it, but my whole feeling about car-pool lanes (or planned communities, or slippery-slope arguments, or rhyme, or Shostakovich, or whether things are getting better or worse) was undergoing a major overhaul back then.'"[19]

But then we're astonished again. First by the past, which we thought we'd leave *behind* in crossing the line into the future, no longer being the same. We thought to have entered into one concrete world from another, but we see that in trespassing our thought we have shifted all parameters of our thought and that the new world wants to be fully filled by our thought. That is what it means to say that philosophical speculation gets high on the whole, whereas metanoia gets high on the parts.

Metanoia is not speculative in the abstract sense. It is the concrete experience of our own thinking. That is why acknowledging metanoia leads us to a realist epistemology in which we appeal to conditions under which we actually think the world, that is to say in a circular manner. Metanoia is the possibility of changing the world. This possibility was created by thought once thinking had become possible, a possibility of changing itself by thinking, "What if?" The world is no longer as it is by itself; it has to be turned into the world we know it to be in metanoia.

Glossary

Abduction A procedure of logical inference described by Charles Sanders Peirce. Through abduction, one infers facts from facts. Abduction is most frequently encountered in solving crimes and in interpreting literary works. Sherlock Holmes provides a number of spectacular examples. In one case, Holmes infers from an ashtray in a reception room in Buckingham Palace that the Queen of England secretly smokes.

Abductions do not yield unequivocal results because neither the rule nor the connection between the rule applied and the facts is given. Both must be produced, and the singular achievement of abduction is the institution of possible connections. In order to consider Sherlock Holmes's hypothesis to be plausible or even to be surprised by how evident it is, we have to imagine the complicated constellation of agents in a monarchy and, especially, its balancing of publicity and secrecy.

Actualization The process in which the virtual comes into presence. In linguistic theory, actualization usually names the presence in speech of paradigmatic, grammatical structures. What interests us in speech, however, is a potential paradigm that constitutes a poetic moment of speaking and creates not virtual worlds but a new world.

The potential paradigm lies ahead of speaking. We also point out that, as a form of the present, actuality has been hollowed out metaphysically and contrasts with the *strong temporality* of metanoia.

Arbitrariness Ever since Ferdinand de Saussure, linguistics has considered signs to be arbitrary. In examples of arbitrariness such as the statement that "table" says noting about a table, it remains unclear whether the claim is (a) that the semiotic form "t-a-b-l-e" does not look like a table or (b) that the meaning of something like "tableness" can only be a metaphysical idea that causes trouble in every encounter with a table. This is how Henri Micheaux describes a table: "As it stood, it was a table of additions, much like certain schizophrenics' drawings, described as 'overstuffed,' and if finished it was only in so far as there was no way of adding anything more to it, the table having become more and more an accumulation, less and less a table."[1]

Instead, we assume a realist position and argue for the *contingency* of signs. We employ the same argument to oppose philosophical nominalism.

Circle (hermeneutic) Hermeneutics describes processes of understanding as "circular," not unlike drawing a circle with a compass. In order to understand, we first make assumptions about the meaning we seek; we then establish connections with meanings we already possess; and at the end we find the sense we assumed behind us. We employ the 'circle' to describe the emergence of *part-to-whole* relations.

Con-scientia A poetic quasi-etymology of consciousness. We conceive of it as pre-Cartesian thinking with another consciousness. In this conception, consciousness is not the modern form of reflective thought, it is the interior space of thought in which the soul enters into a dialog with God. Thought is this dialog with an other—in this case a divine—consciousness.

We believe that lofty thought is driven by another consciousness and thereby manages to go beyond itself. Metanoia is going beyond one's own thought or the profane epiphany of modern thought. Yet an Other is still present in metanoia and discernible in the *Othering* of the subject that comes with every metanoia.

Contingency Lack of causes, also often used in the sense of chance. As Quentin Meillassoux has it: "*only facticity is not factual—viz.*, only the contingency of what is, is not itself contingent."[2] This is all the more true of the connections between meanings and material phenomena signs produce by means of forms. In our view, there is a contingent connection between thought, language, and world that is not itself contingent.

Conversion Ethical turn. It names a switchover from *logos* to *ethos* as it occurs in metanoia. In our view, language plays a decisive role in every conversion, independently of whether it takes the form of religious prophecy, revolutionary rhetoric, or works of philosophy or literature. Whether I decide to become a Rabbi, join a social movement after reading Marx, or become a Deleuzian or Tolstoyan—in all these cases, I have come across a meaning, and I have given this meaning the form of a change in my view of the world that resulted in a practical, that is to say, ethical conversion. "You must change your life" is not just the last line of a Rilke poem. It is an implication of all poetic writing. Conversion responds to this imperative and constitutes the experience of metanoia—of thinking with another consciousness. An ethical turn comes with an *Othering* of the self (i.e. it implies a break with the old world and the old self).

Exactly effect An experience of the evidence of sense that occurs in reading texts. "That's exactly what Gertrude Stein wanted to say!" or "Exactly! That's what Nancy means by 'corpus'!" What exactly is meant remains unclear. It always derives from the experience of the reader who has entered the position of the subject of the text. When readers succeed in sharing the exactly effect with others, we speak of key interpretations.

In our conception, the exactly effect is a virtual metanoia that mutated into an aesthetic experience and did not make it to become a poetic change of mind and an actual transformation of the world of the subject.

Hermeneutics Theory of understanding, named after Hermes, messenger of the gods and missionary of sense, god of commerce and thieves, of travelers and all those who cross the line, guide to the underworld.

The most important discovery of hermeneutics is the *hermeneutic circle*, a process of sense formation and, purposely deployed, of sense creation.

Iconoclasm Originally the destruction of images. We use the term to name a necessary break within lingual signs. In acquiring a language, learners at some point have to stop associating words with things and instead begin establishing grammatical links between linguistic elements. The word "link" in the preceding sentence may serve as an example. To understand the sentence, it is not enough to understand the connection between the word "link" and a metal object that, in conjunction with similarly shaped metal objects, forms a chain. Only an iconoclastic act interrupting the connection between the words enables us to construct three-dimensional signs that are connected with one another and allows us to understand relations between things. All elements are related to the others only by way of a third element, as in a Borromean ring.

Metonymy A rhetorical figure in which a shifting of meaning along a context (i.e. a contiguity) takes place, for example a shift from a material to an object, as in the case of "glass," or from parts to a whole, as in the case of "a thousand men." Metonymies are formed and understood by means of *abductive* inferences from facts to facts.

In German, for example, "zum Beispiel" (for instance) and "zum Bleistift" (for pencil) sound similar. To understand, however, that "zum Bleistift" is not a slip of the tongue but a joke poking fun at old-fashioned pedantry, one has to make the connection between the employment of pencils in editing and the weakness of examples in scientific prose. Metonymy here is borne by a sound shift.

Metonymy is the master trope of our study. We describe a daring metonymics that allows for the formation of abstract wholes and creates very powerful epistemic situations. We describe cognitive shifts that take place alongside metonymic shifts on the way to ethical conversions, in which metonymists make themselves the individuals of the meanings they created.

Othering Transformation of the self by means of relating to an Other.

Lacanian psychoanalysis describes the fundamental significance of the Other for the self. The *significance* of the Other usually remains enigmatic and leads to alienation. In language acquisition, the subject assumes a certain position vis-à-vis the signifier. Psychoanalytical speaking, like reading literature and philosophy, may change this position and thus bears the potential for an othering of the subject. Systematic experimentation with the tense system, for example, can—as we describe in *Present Tense: A Poetics*—shift the origo of subjects (*I—here—now*) in literary fictions. Othering shifts the constellation of subject, object, and Other, and constitutes a fundamental epistemic situation.

Many scientific methodologies are unaware of the presence of the other in a subject's relationship to an object of knowledge. And most linguists are unaware of the presence of de Saussure in their thinking. Thinking with an Other (*conscientia*) and writing with an Other under the banner "You know (it)" have the greatest potential for leading a subject beyond its own consciousness in a metanoia and for resulting in a *conversion*.

Part-to-whole relations A part-to-whole relation is a real relation, i.e. both, the part and the whole, only exist thanks to their relationship. It consists of at least three elements: a part, a counterpart, and a third element. A whole emerges when the third element relates to the first. This happens through *recursion*. An opposition relationship between two parts only becomes possible within a whole.

The grammatical categories of language relate to each other in part-to-whole relations. Part-to-whole relations can be introduced one into the others without giving rise to paradoxes. Examples of part-to-whole relations include *metonymies*, e.g. the establishment known as bar. Without recursion to the part "bar," the counter, its sense remains incomprehensible and it is difficult to identify a bar.

Plasticity Shapeability. We use 'plasticity' as a metonymic expression for variation and to designate the capacity for shaping and being shaped through *poiesis*. In language, paradigmatics, potentiality, and plasticity combine and allow language to develop itself.

In our study of metanoia, we are particularly interested in the contribution of language to the plastic quality of thinking, which consists in going beyond itself.

Poiesis Creation; the production of something that opens up a space of truth. We speak of poietics rather than poetics to oppose the banalization of poiesis that consists in reducing it to a mere theory of producing artistic artifacts. Poietics emphasizes the aspect of making and yet resists any attempt at separating poetic creation, as mere practice, from theory, seen as the site of truth.

In poiesis, something crosses the line from not-being to being; poietics, in other words, has an ontic dimension. Poiesis constitutes the foundation of our conception of *speculative poetics*, and we argue for both re-poieticizing poetics and poeticizing philosophy. We oppose aesthetics, which bases knowledge on the concept of experience, with a poetic philosophy, and we base knowledge on making—a reconception suggested not only by the productivity of scientific apparatuses but by the cognitive dimension of modern production as well.

Re-entry Metanoia results in the subject's re-entry into the world and a reintroduction of thinking into thought. We see a triple shift of subject, thought, and world: a metanoia transposes us into something new (a new world); this takes us beyond our previous thinking; and we then think (ourselves) as new subjects. This process is recursive and creates the figure of a *whole*, whose parts cannot be had independently of it.

Reference Theories of reference seek to explain how lingual signs refer to reality when the referential function can rely neither on their similarity nor their sensibility. What is referred to is the referent.

Referents are usually thought of as things, for example an apple tree in the case of *pommier*, which is why nouns are seen to be exemplary of lingual signs.

Linguistics is interested in references that reach further such as the ones produced by grammar. Poetics is concerned with shifts of reference in the widest sense—in fiction, for example, or in the radical *creation of reference* that takes place in metanoia—and thus with the creation of (new) references, the institution of lingual signs that refer to (the) world.

Language isn't something linguist-engineers produce; it is the result of everyday semiotic labor. Reference arises poetically in speaking or writing and follows the (ontogenetic) sense of reality that language has. In fashioning new or creative references, *logos* switches over into *ethos* because only their inventor can guarantee this authorial act.

Recursion Recursion is a circular process or structure, for example: "The sentence you are reading refers to itself." Recursion creates a whole when a part goes back to a part, the "sentence" to "itself."

Recursion is a lingual universal—it figures on all levels of all languages—and serves as our guide to the ontology of language: we believe that language is part of the world to which it refers. Language goes back to the world and thereby creates meaning. In the discussion of the epistemological saturation of language, we employ recursion as a counterconcept to reflexivity.

Sign, dimensions of The relations between object, expression, and meaning formed by signs are not "simply" sign-like, nor are they characterized only by the "two" elements they join. Signs, rather, are "three-dimensional." They constitute dimensions of Firstness, Secondness, and Thirdness.

Gertrude Stein's line "Rose is a rose is a rose is a rose" seems to be flatly one-dimensional. Beyond the repetitively tautological reference to an obstinate object named rose, it seems neither to express nor to refer to anything. Yet Stein explains that "in that line the rose is red for the first time in English poetry for a hundred years." How so? we might think. Red isn't even mentioned in the line. Perhaps because (the flower) "rose" and (the color) "rose" share the same sequence of letters? That interpretation requires that we take the expression r-o-s-e into account but also, and more importantly, the implicit difference in color between red and rose. This highlights the contrariness of Secondness that characterizes the second dimension of semioticity.

Only the third semiotic dimension, Thirdness, however, fully elucidates this metonymic movement, which is just as playful as Stein's line. Only when we go back a good 100 years and learn that in the nineteenth century, the colonial importation of "bright red" roses and their systematic hybridization in Europe led to a shift in the coloring of red roses and possible a shift in the color perception of red, do we begin to understand. Today, roses that had been called red are called purple and considered to be either more blueish or more rose.

The meaning of "rose" (and of all other signs) depends on a comprehensive classification—in this instance, of roses and colors—and on historical knowledge about the plasticity of our systems of organization and distinction.

Sliding of the signifier An enigmatic expression of Jacques Derrida's. The signifier is the form of the lingual sign, and it is difficult to see at first how it could slide. In most cases, this sliding is taken to be a sliding of meaning. This view appeals to Derrida's thesis according to which meaning (the signified) is to be criticized as metaphysical and has, in fact, always already been a signifier.

We use the phrase to show that the form of lingual part-to-whole relations is indeed flexible and continually sliding. When the signifier as a whole slides, a metanoia takes place.

Speculative poetics A poetics that is explicitly understood to be a poietics. Picking up on Gustave Guillaume's concept of the potentiality of speech, speculative poetics examines the truth-opening dimension of everyday speech.

Poetic speech creates a potential paradigm of language. Poietics is a speculative tool of language that makes the development of language possible. In emphasizing the genuine epistemic potential of making, speculative poetics also aims at a critique of aesthetics.

Speculative poetics is driven by a criticism of Speculative Realism's forgetting of language. Its interests include Hegel's concept of speculation, Benjamin's speculative poetics, and Whitehead's conception of speculation.

Speculative Poetics has operated as a collaborative research platform since 2012. It is more than a research agenda in literary studies. It implies an investigative attitude that includes the ethical dimensions of work in literary studies. It is guided by the motto: "Follow your speculation!"

Subterfuge *Subterfuges or Unexpected Telling Circumstances*: title of a volume of "procedural discussions" by poet Elke Erb. The movement of the subterfuge resembles the knight's move in chess.

We use subterfuge as a concept of speculative poetics. Subterfuges are a semiotic strategy to convert triadic semiotic relationships into dyadic semiotic models. Three semiotic elements are connected by only two lines such that one sees not a triangle but an angle of signs. Each particular critical discourse is interested in, even obsessed with the problem of the third line that is left out or interrupted. This third line is paced out by means of subterfuges. One example is the philosophical attempt to guarantee a relationship between things and meaning by means of a theory of truth.

Norming expressions by means of logic demands a rigorous lingual discipline and can degenerate into dogmatism. It requires the relationship between things and expressions, like that between expressions and meaning, to be equivalent, it requires the possibility of transforming the ones into the others. The uncritical levelling of the three-dimensionality of semiotic relationships reduces them to mere chains of signs.

The description of subterfuges can shed light on misunderstandings between discourses and on misguided debates about "false friends" (or enemies). One example: the misunderstandings that arise between philosophy and literature when the poetic potential of metaphors clashes with their epistemological potential.

Temporality, strong Strong temporality characterizes the moment of metanoia. It stands out by its transformation of the past. It restructures personal memories, creates an alternative history, and overwrites our ingrained habits. This temporality becomes sensible as an asynchronous present.

Notes

Introduction

1. "Cognitive mechanisms whose existence we must grant independently of any analysis of grammar can account for the origin of grammar. The linguistic mind is a consequence and subcategory of the literary mind" (Mark Turner, *The Literary Mind* [Oxford: Oxford University Press, 1996]: 141).
2. We adopt Deleuze and Guattari's definition of philosophers as *the concept's friends*, as lovers of wisdom: "So long as there is a time and a place for creating concepts, the operation that undertakes this will always be called philosophy, or will be indistinguishable from philosophy even if it is called something else" (Gilles Deleuze and Félix Guattari, *What is Philosophy?* trans. Graham Burchell and Hugh Tominlinson [London: Verso, 1994], 9).
3. Levi Bryant, Nick Srnicek, and Graham Harman, *The Speculative Turn: Continental Materialism and Realism* (Melbourne: re-press, 2011).
4. Michel Foucault, *The Hermeneutics of the Subject: Lectures at the Collège de France, 1981–1982*, ed. Frédéric Gros, trans. Graham Burchell (New York: Palgrave-Macmillan, 2004), 28.
5. Thomas Mann, *Buddenbrooks*, trans. H. T. Lowe-Porter, 1924 (New York: Vintage, 1984), 525 [punctuation modified].
6. Foucault, *Hermeneutics*, 46.
7. Ibid. at 53.
8. Quentin Meillassoux, *After Finitude: An Essay on the Necessity of Contingency*, trans. Ray Brassier (New York: Continuum, 2008), 130 of the e-book.

I. Poetics: Principles of Lingual *Poiesis*

1. Cf. Aleksei Kruchenykh and Roman Alyagrov, *Zaumnaya gniga* (Moscow: [s.n.], 1916).
2. Roman Jakobson, "Closing Statement: Linguistics and Poetics," *Style in Language*, ed. Thomas A. Sebeok, 350–377 (New York: Wiley, 1960), 356.
3. Jakobson, "Linguistics and Poetics," 358.

4 Ibid. at 357–58.
5 Roman Jakobson, "Two Aspects of Language and Two Types of Aphasic Disturbances," *Selected Writings*, vol. II, 239–59 (The Hague: Mouton, 1971), 258.
6 Walter Hirtle, "Introduction: Gustave Guillaume 1883–1960," in: Gustave Guillaume, *Foundations for a Science of Language*, ed. and trans. Walter Hirtle and John Hewson, xi–xviii (Amsterdam and Philadelphia: John Benjamins Publishing Company, 1984), xii–xiii.
7 Guillaume, *Foundations* (Lecture of Dec 6, 1956), 14.
8 To this day, there is in linguistics no subdivision of grammar that could devote itself to the study of this generic dimension of language. This might be the very task of a speculative poetics concerned with that function of language that opens up truth and not, as poetics has traditionally been, with lingual artifacts to be made or even already made. The difference between these two kinds of poetics would be analogous to the difference between morphogeny and morphology or between ontogeny and ontology.
9 John Hewson, "Notes for the Reader," in Guillaume, *Foundations*, xix–xxiv, here xxi.
10 Roman Jakobson and Yuri Tynyanov, "Problems in the Study of Literature and Language," trans. Herbert Eagle, in: *Twentieth Century Literary Theory: An Introductory Anthology*, ed. Vassilis Lambropoulos and David Neal Miller (Albany: SUNY Press, 1986), 32–34.
11 Guillaume, *Foundations* (Lecture of May 23, 1957), 141.
12 Elisabeth Leiss, *Sprachphilosophie* (Berlin and New York: de Gruyter, 2009), 261.
13 Ibid. at 263.
14 Guillaume, *Foundations* (Lecture of Feb 13, 1948, ser. C), 52.
15 Guillaume, *Foundations* (Lecture of Jan 9, 1948, ser. C), 50–51.
16 "From a realistic standpoint, language cannot be interpreted as a whole, isolated and hermetically sealed, but it must be simultaneously viewed both as a whole and as a part." Roman Jakobson, "Parts and Wholes in Language," *Selected Writings*, vol. II, 280–84 (The Hague: Mouton, 1971), here 282.
17 To keep this example simple and intuitive, we here presuppose a totality that is already given to which moth and tree are then referred to as parts. Yet such a part-to-whole relation can also form without our knowing the totality in question (see below on abduction procedures).
18 Cf. Leiss, *Sprachphilosophie*, 264.
19 Ibid. at 283.
20 Ibid. at 262.
21 Roman Jakobson, "Sign and System of Language: A Reassessment of Saussure's Doctrine," *Poetics Today* 2, no. 1 (1980): 33–38, here 33.

22 It is difficult to decide whether the non-referentiality of sounds and their meaninglessness would have to be read as two variants of one and the same arbitrariness. According to Leiss, both aspects of arbitrariness are to be overcome by a theory of grammar tasked with a "dearbitrarization of language" and the creation of a "basis of reference" (Elisabeth Leiss, *Die Verbalkategorien des Deutschen: Ein Beitrag zur Theorie der sprachlichen Kategorisierung* [Berlin and New York: de Gruyter, 1992], 6 and 8). Grammar mediates both ekstases of the lingual signifier and guarantees the transition from a lingual meaning to its referents.
23 Ludwig Wittgenstein, *Philosophical Investigations*, trans. G. E. M. Anscombe (Oxford: Blackwell, 1953), sect. 43:20.
24 Guillaume, *Foundations* (Lecture of Feb 22, 1952, ser. B), 72–73.
25 Daniil Kharms, "Predmety y figury otkrytye Daniilom Ivanovichem Kharmsom [Objects and Figures Discovered by Daniil Ivanovich Kharms]," in: *Polnoe sobranie sochinenii: Proza I stsenki drmaticheskikhprizvedenia*, ed. Valerii Sazhin, vol. 2 (St Petersburg: Akademicheski Proekt, 1997), 306.
26 Jakobson, "Linguistics and Poetics," 356.
27 Ibid.
28 Quoted in Matthias Freise, *Michail Bachtins philosophische Ästhetik der Literatur* (Frankfurt and New York: Lang, 1993), 38.
29 Giorgio Agamben, *The Man Without Content*, trans. Georgia Albert (Stanford: Stanford University Press, 1999), 70.

II. The Analytic Circle: The Lingual Creation of a True World

1 Ulf Stolterfoht, "Funktion folgt Form: Rohfassung," in: *Timber! Eine kollektive Poetologie*, http://timberpoetologie.wordpress.com/tag/ulf-stolterfoht (accessed Jun 23, 2012).
2 Karin Littau, *Theories of Reading: Books, Bodies, and Bibliomania* (Malden: Polity Press 2006), 262 and 107–8.
3 Martin Heidegger, *Being and Time*, 1927, trans. John Macquarrie and Edward Robinson (San Francisco: Harper, 1962), §32:195.
4 Ibid.
5 Ibid.
6 We can already discern a tense-philosophical definition of the circle in Heidegger, where time is twinned with the possible. For Heidegger, time is rooted in the future, which only acquires existence when it is grasped as possibility. Both

self-existentializing possibility and self-fulfilling prophecy obey one and the same mode of speech.
7 Jacques Derrida, *Of Grammatology*, trans. Gayatri Chakravorty Spivak (Baltimore: Johns Hopkins University Press, 1976), 7.
8 Augustinus Aurelius, Bishop of Hippo, *Confessions*, trans. Maria Boulding, 1997, *The Works of Saint Augustine: A Translation for the 21st Century*, vol. I/1, series ed. John E. Rotelle (New York: New City P, 1991–), VIII.29:207.
9 Augustine, *Confessions*, I.9:44.
10 Jacques Derrida, *Spurs: Nietzsche's Styles*, trans. Barbara Harlow (Chicago: University of Chicago Press, 1979).
11 Let us note that the attraction the ancestor of analytic philosophy, Ludwig Wittgenstein, certainly rests on more than the persuasive force of the *Tractatus logico-philosophicus*. It seems reasonable to suppose that the function it performs in founding an entire discourse can be traced back to its strategy of philosophizing by connecting epistemological, language-theoretical, ethical, and ontological discourses: "I might say: if the place I want to reach could only be climbed up to by a ladder, I would give up trying to get there. For the place to which I really have to go is one that I must actually be at already. Anything that can be reached with a ladder does not interest me" (*Culture and Value: A Selection from the Posthumous Remains*, ed. Georg Henrik von Wright et al., trans. Peter Winch [Oxford: Blackwell, 1977], 10). The tradition of analytic philosophy that follows Wittgenstein seems to have thrown away the metanoietic ladder without which anybody could have gotten where they are. Most recently, it has been Peter Sloterdijk who has connected the exactly-effect and metanoia in quite a different way, which is particular significant for our question of how the two are similar (or not). Sloterdijk thinks together the rhetoric of discourses and their performative force: "Nonetheless, once can say that Foucault started from where Wittgenstein left off: showing that entire branches of science or epistemic disciplines are nothing other than complexly structured language games, also known as discourses or discursive practices. Just as Wittgenstein had broken with the cognitivist prejudice in language theory to show much speaking is an act rather than knowledge, Foucault broke with the epistemist prejudice in the theory of science in order to explain how much the disciplines he examined are performative systems rather than "reflections of reality" (Peter Sloterdijk, *You Must Change Your Life*, trans. Wieland Hoban [Cambridge: Polity Press, 2013], 148).
12 Leiss, *Sprachphilosophie*, 58.
13 Ibid. at 278–79.
14 The first Polyantha, however, was created as early as 1875; the genus as a whole encompasses the hybrids of R. chinensis and R. multiflora.

15 Hence Wittgenstein's famous polemic against such an Augustinan conception of language, in which "the individual words in language name objects—sentences are combinations of such names.— ... Every word has a meaning" (Wittgenstein, *Investigations*, sect. 1: 2).
16 Leiss, *Sprachphilosophie*, 57–58. In our analysis of relations, too, we follow Leiss.
17 Karl-Otto Apel, *Transformation der Philosophie*, vol. 2 *Das Apriori der Kommunikationsgemeinschaft* (Frankfurt am Main: Suhrkamp, 1973), 163–64. [Apel does not include this paragraph in the English translation, where it would find its place on 80. See *Towards a Transformation of Philosophy*, trans. Glyn Adey and David Frisby (London: Routledge & Kegan Paul, 1980).—Trans.]
18 Umberto Eco, *Einführung in die Semiotik*, trans. Jürgen Trabant (Munich: Fink: 1994), 30.
19 Igor Smirnov, *Smysl kak takovoy* (St. Petersburg: Akademichesky Proyekt: 2001).
20 Yuri Lotman, *The Universe of the Mind: A Semiotic Theory of Culture*, trans. Ann Shukman (Bloomington: Indiana University Press, 1990). The discussion of "meaning" goes back to the foundational model of structuralist linguistics in the wake of Ferdinand de Saussure; cf. Ferdinand de Saussure, *Writings in General Linguistics*, ed. Simon Bouquet, Rudolf Engler and Carol Sanders, trans. Peter Figueroa, Matthew Pires and Carol Sanders (Oxford and New York: Oxford University Press, 2006).
21 We suspect that this labeling also sheds light on what Meillassoux calls an "empty sign."
22 Viktor Shklovsky, "Art as Device," 6; p. 14 in the Russian original.
23 Symbolic semiotic relations in particular are often said to be based on conventions. We have already laid out some arguments against the assumption that language is arbitrary or that signs are the result of a convention. The specificity of symbols, moreover, seems to us to lie in the fact that symbols differentiate objects by means of relations. The relation of lingual relations to relations between things is often called "homologous." At the same time, the absence of a substantial connection between these relations is interpreted as an indication of their conventionality. What is most important in this context, however, is that there is a difference between the three relations (lingual relations, relations between things, and the relation between the two relations). The three differences influence one another: the differentiation of language, world, and meaning go hand in hand.
24 John K. Sheriff, *The Fate of Meaning: Charles Peirce, Structuralism, and Literature* (Princeton: Princeton University Press, 1989), 69.
25 [*Winkelzüge*—literally, moves at or around an angle.—Trans.]
26 Elke Erb, *Winkelzüge oder nicht vermutete, aufschlußreiche Verhältnisse*

[*Subterfuges, or Unsuspected, Telling Conditions*] (Berlin: Druckhaus Galrev, 1991), 448.

27 Eco, *Einführung in die Semiotik*, 69–70.
28 On this conception of contingency, see also below, 80–3.
29 It was, perhaps, not a coincidence that Saussure chose the name *arbitrarité* when he could have chosen a completely different name (e.g. *pommiarité*). But no matter what other designation he could have chosen, his would still have been contingent, not arbitrary, for at the very least he would have had to remain within the possibilities circumscribed by the alphabetic system.
30 Perhaps the question of signs' similarity or identity did not arise until the advent of modern serial production and serial media (such as film). These create things that are so similar that they lead the ideal of mimesis, which had guided earlier artifacts, *ad absurdum*. When, under the conditions of serial identity, likeness can no longer be thought of as sign-like, the concept of mimesis collapses.
31 Harald Weinrich, "Semantik der kühnen Metapher," in: *Theorie der Metapher*, ed. Anselm Haverkamp, 316–39 (Darmstadt: Wissenschaftliche Buchgesellschaft, 1983), 331.
32 Weinrich, "Semantik der kühnen Metapher," 331.
33 Oswald Egger, *Die ganze Zeit* (Berlin: Suhrkamp, 2010), 553.
34 Gilles Deleuze, *Logic of Sense*, trans. Mark Lester and Charles Stivale, ed. Constantin V. Boundas (New York: Columbia University Press, 1990).
35 Egger, *Die ganze Zeit*, 547.
36 Gertrude Stein, "Sacred Emily," *Geography and Plays*, ed. Sherwood Anderson, 178–88 (New York and Toronto: Villefranche Something Else Press, 1968), 187.
37 Gertrude Stein, *Four in America* (New Haven: Yale University Press, 1947), vi.
38 François Joyaux, *Enzyklopädie der alten Rosen* (Stuttgart: Ulmer, 2008), 124.
39 Peter Harkness, *The Rose, A Colourful Inheritance* (London: Scriptum Editions, 2003), 139.
40 Ibid.
41 Ibid.
42 Rudolf Geschwind, *Die Hybridation und Sämlingszucht der Rosen*, reprint (Hildesheim, Zurich and New York: Olms, 1997), 74.
43 Joseph H. Pemberton, *Roses: Their History, Development and Cultivation* (London, New York, Bombay, and Calcutta: Longmans, Green, and Co., 1908), 70.
44 Harkness, *The Rose*, 248–49.
45 Pierre Joseph Redouté, *Die Rosen: Die vollständigen Tafeln* (Cologne: Taschen, 2007), 173.
46 Ibid. at 139.
47 Harkness, *The Rose*, 138.

48 Redouté, *Die Rosen*, 176.
49 Redouté, *Die Rosen*, 138.
50 Leiss, *Sprachphilosophie*, 196.
51 Ibid, at 173–74.
52 Willard Van Orman Quine, *Word and Object* (Cambridge: Technology Press of the Massachusetts Institute of Technology, 1960), 2.
53 Ibid. at 7.
54 Donald Davidson, "The Method of Truth in Metaphysics (1977)," in *Inquiries into Truth and Interpretation*, 2nd edn, 199–214 (Oxford: Oxford University Press, 2001), here 203–204.
55 Wilhelm Kordes, *Rosen: Züchtung, Anpflanzung und Pflege* (Frankfurt a.d.O. and Berlin, 1932), 37. [This passage, as well as others cited later, is not part of the translation by N. Harvey published under the title *Roses* (London: Studio Vista, 1964).—Trans.]
56 Graham Stuart Thomas, *Climbing Roses Old and New* (London and Melbourne: J. M. Dent, 1986), 49 and 53.
57 Davidson, "Reality without Reference (1977)," *Inquiries into Truth and Interpretation*, 215–225, here 221.
58 Saul A. Kripke, *Wittgenstein on Rules and Private Language: An Elementary Exposition* (Cambridge MA: Harvard University Press, 1982), 21. See also below, 79–80.
59 Ibid. at 77.
60 Bryan Frances, "Saul Kripke (b. 1940)," in: *Philosophy of Language: Key Thinkers*, ed. Barry Lee, 249–67 (London and New York: Continuum, 2011), here 264.
61 Wittgenstein, *Philosophical Grammar*, Pt. I, sect. 41: 83.
62 Charles S. Peirce, "Pragmatism and Pragmaticism" in *The Collected Papers of Charles Sanders Peirce (CP)*, vol. 5, ed. Charles Hartshorne and Paul Weiss (Cambridge MA: Belknap Press of Harvard University Press, 1995), §313: 188.
63 Graham Harman, *Prince of Networks: Bruno Latour and Metaphysics* (Melbourne: re.press, 2009), 125. Harman concludes his description of Pasteur's discovery of microbes with this reversal of the semiotic relation from a predication of properties to the microbes to an attribution of their description to Pasteur. That with his discovery, Pasteur means microbes can also mean that the discovery of microbes refers back to Pasteur's genius. According to Meillassoux, Latour sometimes "severs all links with correlationism in such a way, and does so with much talent and humour. It must be added, of course, that he also uses other elaborate instruments to fight circles" ("Presentation", in: *Collapse*, vol. III, ed. Robin Mackay [Falmouth: Urbanomic, November 2007, reissued December 2012], 423).

64 Bruno Latour, *Pandora's Hope: Essays on the Reality of Science Studies* (Cambridge: Harvard University Press, 1999), 39.
65 Ibid. at 69.
66 Quentin Meillassoux, too, traces signs' semiotic character back to the formation of chains; compare his lecture, "Iteration, Reiteration, Repetition: A Speculative Analysis of the Meaningless Sign," given on April 20, 2012 at Freie Universität Berlin.
67 Within the analytic philosophy of language, this formulation must appear as the height of nonsense even though it is this very philosophy that articulated the knowledge the formula contains as a paradox in the first place.
68 Quentin Meillassoux, *After Finitude: An Essay on the Necessity of Contingency*, trans. Ray Brassier (New York: Continuum, 2008), 130 of the e-book.
69 Quentin Meillassoux, "*Time Without Becoming*," *Spike* 35 (2013): 91–105, here 103.
70 He continues: "Does this mean that the sign is a pure convention that rests only upon the arbitrary identification of various marks? The word 'convention' only masks the problem here. For either the convention identifies distinct *signs*, and in this case it presupposes the notion of sign; or the term 'convention' signifies that I identify two distinct *things*, and in this case, does not yield the unlimited iterability of occurrences. To conventionally identify a material individual x with a material individual y does not produce, in addition to the duality of x and y, their unlimited iterability" (Meillassoux, "Iteration, Reiteration, Repetition," 29).
71 In her *The Future of Hegel*, Malabou addresses the basic features of a speculative ontology of language. This describes the relation between logic and grammar as one in which logic makes way for a temporality of grammar. The problems of predication (such as we raised earlier) are put in the form of statements about reality (in the form of propositions) that promise an increase in knowledge. "The speculative is not only stored lexically. Syntax is equally fundamental, marking the consignment in language of the elementary forms of logic. In the Nuremberg *Propädeutik,* Hegel asserts that the logical categories are, in their immediate form, 'the content of grammar'.... In consequence, for the philosopher, to work on the relation of subject and predicate amounts to an exploration of the *temporal* connections between the philosophical proposition and its grammatical origins" (Malabou, *Future of Hegel*, 169) When Malabou talks about *grammaire*, she does not mean a linguistic model but the notion of grammar in the philosophy of language we've already discussed in Davidson. Like the analytic philosophers, Malabou (following Hegel, Heidegger, Derrida) thinks language is a relation between the lexical and grammar, where grammar means syntax understood as a logic.
72 Eco, *Einführung in die Semiotik*, 77.

73 Strawson, *Individuals: An Essay in Descriptive Metaphysics* (London: Taylor and Francis, 2003), 119.
74 Ibid. at 11.
75 Cf. the concept of spontaneity in Rödl, who writes, for example, "the relationship to an object ... is not *sensory affectation by* but *identity with* the object. First person knowledge is knowledge I have of an object by being that object" (Sebastian Rödl, *Self-Consciousness* [Cambridge MA and London: Harvard University Press, 2007], 124).

III. Speculation: Aspects of a Poetics of Thought

1 Giorgio Agamben, *What is an Apparatus? and Other Texts*, trans. David Kishik and Stefan Pedatella (Stanford: Stanford University Press, 2009), 12–13.
2 Since the sign that is employed here changes its meaning in the process, Guillaume describes the linguistic signifier as "arbitrary [*arbitraire*]." As we saw, however, this is not to be confused with the *dogma* of the arbitrariness of the sign, for what is at stake here is the sign's contingent-contiguous plasticity.
3 Malabou, *Future of Hegel*, 180.
4 Georg Wilhelm Friedrich Hegel, *Phenomenology of Spirit*, trans. A. V. Miller (Oxford: Oxford University Press, 1977), §64:39.
5 Malabou, *Future of Hegel*, 167–68.
6 Hegel, *Phenomenology of Spirit*, §65:39–40.
7 Ibid. at §60:37.
8 Every lexical reading, of course, has to be preceded by a syntactic reading; the juxtaposition of snytactic and lexical reading, therefore, is not an *either/ or* relation.
9 Egger, *Die ganze Zeit*, 547.
10 Hegel, *Phenomenology of Spirit*, §62:38–39.
11 We do not wish to repeat the steps of the dialectical movement here. Instead, we would like to note how Hegel, in his example sentence "God is Being" (*Phenomenology of Spirit*, 59), enthrones the Big Other (God) on the stage of knowledge.
12 Cf. Roman Jakobson and Claude Lévi-Strauss, "Baudelaire's 'Les chats,'" in: Jakobson, *Language in Literature* (Cambridge, MA: Belknap Press, 1987).
13 Giorgio Agamben, "Philosophy and Linguistics," in: *Potentialities: Collected Essays in Philosophy*, trans. Daniel Heller-Roazen, 62–76 (Stanford CA: Stanford University Press, 1999), here 678.

14 Cf. Malabou, *The Future of Hegel*, 39–56 and 184, as well as Jacques Derrida, "A Time for Farewells: Heidegger (Read by) Hegel (Read by) Malabou," in: Malabou, *The Future of Hegel*, vii–xvii, here xi.

15 Agamben, "Philosophy and Linguistics," 67–68.

16 For Valery Podoroga, this shared characteristic is that both approaches are moments of a "poietic ontology" (поэтической онтологии). Valery Podoroga, *Mimesis: Materialy poanaliticheskoy antropology literatury v dvuch tomakh*, vol. 2, pt. 1 (Moscow: Kulturnaya Revolutsiya, 2011), 49 and 434.

17 Günter Wohlfart, Denken der Sprache: *Sprache und Kunst bei Vico, Hamann, Humboldt und Hegel* (Freiburg and Munich: Alber, 1984), 22–23.

18 Hegel, *Phenomenology of Spirit*, §47:27.

19 Howard Caygill, *Walter Benjamin: The Colour of Experience* (London and New York: Routledge, 1997) 34–35.

20 Alain Juranville, *Lacan et la philosophie* (Paris: PUF, 1984), 126.

21 Jacques Lacan, *The Four Fundamental Concepts of Psycho-Analysis*, trans. Alan Sheridan (New York and London: Norton, 1978), 203.

22 Ibid. at 207.

23 Ibid. at 205.

24 Slavoj Žižek, *For They Know Not What They Do: Enjoyment as Political Factor*, 2nd edn (London: Verso, 2002), 164; Žižek is referring here to Heidegger's essay *Hegel's Concept of Experience* (New York: Harper and Row, 1970). [The last sentence of the quote is an insertion added for the German translation of the text: Slavoj Žižek, *Der erhabenste aller Hysteriker: Psychoanalyse und die Philosophie des deutschen Idealismus*, trans. Isolde Charim, 2nd aug. ed. (Vienna: Turia + Kant, 1992).—Trans.]

25 "Das Wiedererkennen des Subjekts in der entfremdeten Substanz zielt nicht darauf, daß es sich ihren Gehalt 'aneignet', daß es ihn als Ergebnis seiner eigenen Tätigkeit durchschaut, im Gegenteil, es erkennt in seiner Mangelhaftigkeit die Wirkung eines Loches, eines Mangels im Anderen, es erkennt in seinem Getrenntsein von der Substanz die Wirkung einer Entzweiung, einer Spaltung im Innersten der Substanz selbst" (Slavoj Žižek, *Der erhabenste aller Hysteriker*, 211–212). [This passage seems to have been added for the augmented second edition of the volume published only in German.—Trans.]

26 Lorenzo Chiesa, *Subjectivity and Otherness: A Philosophical Reading of Lacan* (Cambridge MA: MIT Press, 2007), 6.

27 Jacques Lacan, "La science et la vérité," *Cahiers pour l'analyse*, vol. 1 (1966), 18; translation taken from *Concept and Form: The* Cahiers *pour l'analyse and Contemporary French Thought*, ed. Peter Hallward. Available at: http://cahiers.kingston.ac.uk/concepts/metalanguage.html.

28 Leiss, *Sprachphilosophie*, 2.
29 Ibid. at 265.
30 Meillassoux, *Time Without Becoming*, 91; on his conception of his own philosophizing, compare his *After Finitude*: "The first decision is that of all correlationism— it is the thesis of the essential inseparability of the act of thinking from its content. All we ever engage with is what is given-to-thought, never an entity subsisting by itself. This decision alone suffices to disqualify every absolute of the *realist* or *materialist* variety" (62).
31 Friedrich Hölderlin, "On Judgment and Being (1795)," in: H. S. Harris, *Hegel's Development: Toward the Sunlight 1770 – 1801* (Oxford, Clarendon Press, 1972), 515–16.
32 Umberto Eco, "*Intentio lectoris*: The State of the Art," in *The Limits of Interpretation* (Bloomington: Indiana University Press, 1990), 44–63, here 59. Cf. Uwe Wirth, "Abduktion und ihre Anwendungen," in: *Zeitschrift für Semiotik* 17, no. 3–4 (1995): 405–24.
33 Umberto Eco, "Horns, Hooves, Insteps: Some Hypotheses on Three Types of Abduction," in: *The Sign of Three: Dupin, Holmes, Peirce*, ed. Umberto Eco and Thomas A. Sebeok, 198–220 (Bloomington: Indiana University Press, 1983), here 206.
34 Eco, "Horns, Hooves, Insteps," 206.
35 Ibid. at 207.
36 Ibid.
37 Peirce, *CP* 5.171: 106.
38 Eco, "Horns, Hooves, Insteps," 214.
39 Giorgio Agamben's definition of the paradigm (which is "more akin to allegory than to metaphor") in his book on methodology is quite similar: "while induction proceeds from the particular to the universal and deduction from the universal to the particular, the paradigm is defined by a third and paradoxical type of movement, which goes from the particular to the particular" (*The Signature of All Things: On Method*, trans. Luca D'Isanto with Kevin Attell [New York: Zone Books, 2009], 19).
40 Eco, "Horns, Hooves, Insteps" 220.
41 Charles Sanders Peirce, *Collected Papers of Charles Sanders Peirce*, ed. Charles Hartshorne, Bul Weiss, and Arthur W. Burks, (Cambridge: Harvard UP, 1995), 5.183, pp. 114–15.
42 Ibid. at 114.
43 From a fragment not published in English but included in Charles Sanders Peirce, *Phänomen und Logik der Zeichen*, trans. Bertram Kienzle (Frankfurt: Suhrkamp, 1998), 95.

44 Rüdiger Campe, "Form und Leben in der Theorie des Romans", in: *Vita aesthetica: Szenarien ästhetischer Lebendigkeit*, ed. Armen Avanessian, Winfried Menninghaus, and Jan Völker, 193–211 (Zurich and Berlin: Diaphanes, 2009), 199.

45 Christoph Menke, *Force: A Fundamental Concept of Aesthetic Anthropology*, trans. Gerrit Jackson (New York: Fordham University Press, 2012), x.

46 Caygill, *Walter Benjamin* 36.

47 Menke, *Force*, 12.

48 We share Klaus Weimar's astonishment at the change the expression of beauty underwent in the emergence of aesthetics in Baumgarten: "Beauty is the perfection of sensible knowledge—why does beauty, which traditionally has been an ontological concept, suddenly become a gnoseological predicate? And how does aesthetics lead to beauty? Does it, as a theory of the fine sciences [*schönen Wissenschaften*], lead to knowledge of beauty or does it, as an art of fine thinking [*Schöndenken*], lead to the beauty of knowledge?" (Klaus Weimar, *Geschichte der deutschen Literaturwissenschaft bis zum Ende des 19. Jahrhunderts* [Paderborn: Fink, 2008], 69).

49 Alexander Gottlieb Baumgarten, *Reflections on Poetry*, trans. Karl Aschenbrenner and William B. Holther (Berkeley CA: University of California Press, 1954) §9:39.

50 Ibid. at §18:43.

51 Alexander Gottlieb Baumgarten, *Metaphysics: A Critical Translation with Kant's Elucidations, Selected Notes, and Related Materials*, ed. and trans. Courtney D. Fugate (London: Bloomsbury, 2013). §533:205.

52 Ibid. at §570:214.

53 Ibid. at §575:216.

54 Ibid. at §592:220.

55 Ibid. at §607:224.

56 Ibid. at §610:225.

57 Ibid. at §622:227.

58 Weimar, *Geschichte der deutschen Literaturwissenschaft*, 72.

59 Winfried Menninghaus, *Wozu Kunst?* 234.

60 Peirce, *Collected Papers*, 5.182–92: 133–39.

61 Deleuze and Guattari, *What is Philosophy?*, 197.

IV. Cognition: Metanoia is an Anagram of Anatomie

1 [*Anatomie* is German for *anatomy*.]
2 Immanuel Kant, *Critique of Pure Reason*, ed. and trans. Paul Guyer and Allen W. Wood (Cambridge: Cambridge University Press, 1998), 246–47/B132.
3 Thomas Metzinger, *The Ego Tunnel: The Science of the Mind and the Myth of the Self* (New York: Basic Books, 2009), 50.
4 Here is the *Critique of Pure Reason*'s most famous passage on the subject: "It is, to be sure, a merely empirical law in accordance with which representations that have often follwed or accompanied one another are finally associated with each other and thereby placed in a connection in accordance with which, even without the presence of the object, one of these representations brings about a transition of the mind to the other in accordance with a constant rule. This law of reproduction, however, presupposes that appearances themselves are actually subject to such a rule, and that in the manifold of their representations an accompaniment or succession takes place according to certain rules; for without that our empirical imagination would never get to do anything suitable to its capacity, and would thus remain hidden in the interior of the mind, like a dead and to us unknown faculty. If cinnabar were nor red, no black, no light, now heavy, if a human being were now changeg into this animal shpae, now into that one, if on the longest day the land were covered now with fruit, now with ice and snow, then my empirical imagination would never even get the opportunity to think of heavy cinnabar on the occasion of the representation of the color red; of if a certain word were attributed now to this thing, now to that, or if one and the same thing were sometimes called this, sometimes that, without the governance of a certain rule to which appearances are already subjected in themselves, then no empirical synthesis of reproduction could take place" (229/A100).
5 Metzinger, *The Ego Tunnel*, 26–27.
6 Ibid. at 26.
7 Ibid. at 5.
8 Ibid. at 29–30.
9 Ibid. at 40.
10 Ibid. at 30–31.
11 Ibid. at 19.
12 Ibid. at 33.
13 Ibid. at 42.
14 We resign ourselves here to merely pointing to the recently developed Spatialization of Form Hypothesis (SFH), which presumes "that grammar is a

projection of the basic object schema, it predicts specifically that grammatical competence should employ neurological resources which also figure in the recognition and cognitive analysis of the image schematic structure of ordinary physical objects" (Paul D. Deane, *Grammar in Mind and Brain: Explorations in Cognitive Syntax* [Berlin and New York: Mouton de Gruyter, 1992], 258). In this context, Deane insists that "the OBJECT schema is by origin simply one aspect of the BODY schema," which, in turn, is "the focus of the entire set of image schemas, which integrate information across sensory modalities" (ibid.).

15 Guillaume, *Foundations* (Lecture of Nov 27, 1947, ser. C), 51–52.
16 Guillaume *Foundations* (Lecture of Nov 13, 1944, ser. A), 13.
17 Guillaume, *Foundations* (Lecture of Jan 9, 1948, ser. C), 50–51.
18 Terrence Deacon, "Multilevel Selection in a Complex Adaptive System. The Problem of Language Origins", in: *Evolution and Learning: The Baldwin Effect Reconsidered*, ed. Bruce H. Weber und David J. Depew (Cambridge MA: MIT Press, 2003), 101.
19 Charles N. Li and Jean-Marie Hombert, "On the Evolutionary Origin of Language," in: *Mirror Neurons and the Evolution of Brain and Language*, ed. Maxim I. Stamenov and Vittorio Gallese, 175–206 (Amsterdam: Benjamins, 2002), here 183–84.
20 Terrence Deacon, *The Symbolic Species: The Co-Evolution of Language and the Brain* (London: Penguin, 1997), 112.
21 Ibid. at 194.
22 Ibid. at 195.
23 Ibid. at 116.
24 Ibid. at 121–22.
25 "Behavioral flexibility enables organisms to move into niches that differ from those their ancestors occupied, with the consequence that succeeding generations will face a new set of selection pressures" (Deacon, *The Symbolic Species*, 322).
26 "There are robust correlations between frames of reference used in language and frames of reference used in non-linguistic memory and reasoning, suggesting a major 'Whorfian' effect of language on cognition" (Stephen C. Levinson, *Space in Language and Cognition: Explorations in Cognitive Diversity* [Cambridge and New York: Cambridge University Press, 2003], xix).
27 Philip Lieberman, *The Biology and Evolution of Language* (Cambridge MA: Harvard University Press, 1984), 1.
28 Apel, *Towards a Transformation*, 180–81.
29 Noam Chomsky, *On Nature and Language*, ed. Adriana Belletti and Luigi Rizzi (Cambridge and New York: Cambridge University Press, 2002), 1.

30 Chomsky, *On Nature and Language*, 14.
31 Leiss, *Sprachphilosophie*, 277–78.
32 Chomsky, *On Nature and Language*, 9.
33 Ibid. at 3.
34 Leiss, *Sprachphilosophie*, 259.
35 Ibid. at 258.
36 Deacon, *The Symbolic Species*, 74.
37 Ibid. at 76.
38 Deacon, *The Symbolic Species*, 86.
39 As we now know, this can also be put as follows: Kripke as signifier stands for the truth that true reference is not possible.
40 We do not, of course, reproach the bird for this lack of curiosity.—We cannot, incidentally, know what these signs mean to the bird ("Bird means X by Y"); if ever we were to put ourselves in its place, we might perhaps describe them as *food*.
41 See Chapter 1 above.

Epilogue: The Whole Truth and Nothing but the Truth!

1 Joseph Vogl, *Kalkül und Leidenschaft: Poetik des ökonomischen Menschen* (Zurich and Berlin: Diaphanes, 2004), 13–14.
2 Juranville, *Lacan et la philosophie*, 48.
3 Foucault, *Hermeneutics of the Subject*, 214.
4 Ibid. at 327.
5 Thomas Bernhard, *Woodcutters*, trans. David McLintock (New York: Knopf, 1987), 147. The quote has been modified by replacing "Austria" with "Germany," "artists" with "academics," and "art" with "science." The novel has also been translated by Ewald Osers under the title *Cutting Timber: An Irritation* (London: Vintage, 1993).
6 Friedrich Hölderlin, *Hölderlin, his poems*, trans. Michael Hamburger (New York: Pantheon, 1952), 5; the original can be found in "Reflexionen," *Sämtliche Werke und Briefe*, vol. 2, ed. Jochen Schmidt, 519–22 (Frankfurt: Deutscher Klassiker Verlag, 1994), 519.
7 Immanuel Kant, *Critique of Pure Reason*, 189/B67–68. As for the significance of Kant for an epistemological appraisal of the discourse of derangement, see Oliver Kohns' *Die Verrücktheit des Sinns: Wahnsinn und Zeichen bei Kant, E. T. A. Hoffmann und Thomas Carlyle* [*The Derangement of Sense: Madness and Sign in Kant, E. T. A. Hoffmann, and Thomas Carlyle*] (Bielefeld: Transcript, 2007).

8 Pierre Hadot, "Conversion," trans. Andrew B. Irvine. Available at: http://maryvillecollege.academia.edu/AndrewIrvine/Papers/1488871/Translation_of_Pierre_Hadot_Conversion._Encyclopaedia_Universalis_vol._4_pp._979-81._Paris_Encyclopaedia_Universalis_France_1968 1–7, here 6.
9 Hadot, "Conversion," 1.
10 Cf. Foucault, *Hermeneutics of the Subject*, Lecture of February 10, 1982: First hour, 205–27.
11 Ibid. at 208–09.
12 Creston Davis and Patrick Aaron Riches, "Metanoia: The Theological Praxis of Revolution," in: *Theology and the Political*, ed. Creston Davis, Patrick Aaron Riches, John Milbank and Slavoj Žižek, 22–51 (Durham and London: Duke University Press 2005), here 32.
13 Davis and Riches, "Metanoia," 27.
14 Ibid. at 39.
15 Boris Groys, "The Kingdom of Philosophy: The Administration of Metanoia," in: *The Communist Postscript*, trans. Thomas H. Ford (London: Verso, 2009), 106.
16 Malabou, *The Future of Hegel*, 115. The quote is from Hegel's lectures on the philosophy of world history: "This new principle is the axis on which the History of the World turns. This is the goal and the starting point of History" (*Lectures on the Philosophy of History*, trans. John Sibree [London: Bohn, 1861], 331).
17 Deleuze and Guattari, *What is Philosophy?*, 7.
18 Rüdiger Campe, "Form und Leben in der Theorie des Romans," in Avenessian et al., eds., *Vita aesthetica*, 193–211, here 194.
19 Nicholson Baker, *The Size of Thoughts* (New York: Random House, 1996), 6–7.

Glossary

1 Qtd. in Deleuze and Guattari, *Anti-Oedipus*, 6.
2 Meillassoux, *After Finitude*, p. 130 of the e-book.

Index

À la recherche du temps perdu 158
abduction
    aesthetic perception 122–4
    defined 179
    ethics of 122
    four forms of 113–21
    as a methodical othering 11
    as a *poietic* procedure 111–21
absolute knowledge 106–7
absolute predictions 94–6
acoustic language, and the image 30
actualization, defined 179
actualizing function, of speech 23–4
aesthetics
    aesthetic criticism 128
    aesthetic experience 124, 164–5
    aesthetic mantic art 128
    aesthetic model of language 32, 129–31
    aesthetic *noiesis* 102
    aesthetic perception, abduction 122–4
    aesthetic pleasure, Peirce 124
    aesthetic semblance, and poetic metaphor 74–5
    aesthetics of characterization 128
    and *aisthesis* 103–4
    and arts 125, 130
    in Baumgarten 127–8
    philosophy as 124–7, 133
    and poetics 127–8
Agamben, Giorgio 33, 87, 89, 96–7, 98
aisthesis
    and aesthetics 103–4
    and language development 146
    and language-realist semiosis 100–1
    and *poiesis* 104, 127
    and the reality content of knowledge 99
altered states of consciousness 141
analytic philosophy
    disciplined subterfuges of 73–4
    history of 190n.11
    of language 10, 69–71, 74–6, 78, 80, 101, 138, 151, 157–8
Apel, Karl-Otto 49, 96, 151
arbitrariness
    contingent arbitrariness 57–9
    defined 179
    of lingual signs 28–32
    variants of 189n.22
art(s)
    aesthetic mantic art 128
    and aesthetics 125, 130
    artistic language 32
    non-aesthetic tradition of 104
    and thought 131–2
askēsis 165
Augustine Aurelius 43
author and reader, indistinguishability of 89
auto-affection, of thought in metanoia 169–70
auto-*poietic* accounts, of language 149–51

Baker, Nicholson 177
Baldwin, James Mark 150
Baudelaire, Charles P. 96
Baumgarten, Alexander Gottlieb 126, 127–8, 129
Being 40
Benjamin, Walter 104, 126
Bernhard, Thomas 166–8
Big Other 168 (*see also* othering)
brain
    evolution of the 151
    labor of the 144–5, 146
    and language 148–51
    semiotics of 154–9
Buddenbrook, Thomas 7

Campe, Rüdiger 125, 177
"care of the self" (*souci de soi*) 7
Carnap, Rudolf 70

Charm, Daniel 31
Chiesa, Lorenzo 107–8
Chomsky, Noam 19, 151–2, 153
Christianity, metanoia inspired by 172
    (*see also* religious metanoia)
cogito ergo sum 138
cognition
    and language 132
    and meaning 55
    openness of the cognitive horizon 31
    recursive structure of 141–7
cognitive grammar 153–4
cognitive sciences 135–6
colors, synonyms and the system of 71–3
combination, operation of 24
con-scientia 139–41, 180
concept formation 176
concepts, experimental invention of 131–3
concrete signs 81–2
consciousness
    altered states of 141
    Kant 137, 138
    models of 139–41
    poietic dimension of 144–5
    as the product of the circles created by thought 136
    and situation 142
    theory of 11
    and time 142–3
contingency
contingent arbitrariness 57–9
    creating reference 79–80
    defined 180
    and history 82–3
    language as contingent 29
    and recursion 31, 141–7
    resulting from the recursivity of language 31
contradictions
    and history 82–3
    and signs 80–2
conversion
    defined 180
    metanoia translated as 4, 170
    philosophical 170
correlationist theory, of language 110–11, 131
correspondence, theories of 28
covert knowledge 68–9

creative abductions 114–16, 117, 118, 119
critique, and diacritics 102
Critique of Pure Reason 169

Davidson, Donald 70–1, 75
Davis, Creston 171
de-arbitrarization 29–30
de Man, Paul 41, 158
Deacon, Terrence 11, 148–9, 154–9, 161
deconstruction, and hermeneutics 37–8, 41–2, 55, 57
deconstructive analyses, of literature 158
deductions 112, 117
Deleuze, Gilles 44, 60, 131, 176
denotation, semiotic triangle 48
Derrida, Jacques 37–8, 42, 44, 98, 164
Descartes, René 138–9, 140
development of language 18, 23, 146, 154
diacritics, and critique 102
différance 42
discourses, linguistic and philosophical 5–6
disjunctive synthesis, of hermeneutics and deconstruction 39
dyadic relations 26

Eco, Umberto 11, 49, 56–7, 58, 83, 113, 118, 121
Egger, Oswald 60, 93
empty signs 81–2
Encyclopædia Universalis 170
Epicurus ix–x
epistrophe 170
equivalence, principle of 16
Erb, Elke 56
Essay on the Diseases of the Head 169
estrangement, moment of 126
ethical/religious matters 166–72
ethics, of abduction 122
evolution
    of the brain 151
    of language 21–3, 149–50
exactly effect 44–5, 180–1
existentiales 98
expression angle, semiotic triangle 51
expressions, becoming a sign 47
extralinguistic grammar 153

factiality 10, 80
fiction, science of 176–7

Firstness, semiotic dimensions 52–4, 62, 110, 159
focalization 89
forgetting
    and acquiring symbolic semiotic relations 161
    and unlearning 154–6
Foucault, Michel 7, 44, 165, 170–1
Four in America 61
Frege, Gottlob 58, 69

Gadamer, Hans-Georg 37–8
generative grammar 152
grammar
    and the being of language 17
    cognitive grammar 153–4
    extralinguistic grammar 153
    generative grammar 152
    grammatical semantics 27
    and poetics 33
    as a semiotic relation 156
    universal grammar 151–4
Grammatology 42
Groys, Boris 172
Guattari, Felix 131, 176
Guillaume, Gustave 9, 17–25, 31, 43, 83, 93–4, 97–8, 101, 146–7, 150

Hadot, Pierre 170
Harman, Graham 78
Hegel, Georg W. F. 90–1, 94–5, 102–3, 106, 164
Heidegger, Martin x–xi, 6–7, 40, 98, 106
Heisenberg uncertainty principle 54
hermeneutics
    and deconstruction 37–8, 41–2, 55, 57
    defined 181
    hermeneutic circle 6–7, 9–10, 38–40, 41, 99, 113, 180
    hermeneutical reading 39, 89
    Hermeneutics of the Subject 7
    sliding of 163–4
    violation of hermeneutic rules 87–9
history
    and contingency 82–3
    of knowledge 163
Hölderlin, Friedrich 112, 169
holistic linguistics 17
horizons, concept of 39

Hume, David 68
hypothesis abductions 113

I
    old/new 161
    and thought 137–8, 138–9, 140
iconoclasm 31, 156–8, 181
icons
    perception of 155
    and semiotic triangle 53
identity, principle of 71
imagination 169
indexical semiotic relations 53, 156, 158–9
indexical signs, acquisition of 155
individuals, ontology of, and the lingual things 83–5
inexhaustibility principle 38
Inferno 174–5
Interpretant, the 83, 104
interpretation 91

Jakobson, Roman 9, 15–17, 20, 21, 23–6, 32, 59, 96, 130
Johnson, Dr. 70, 77
Juranville, Alain 105–8, 164

Kant, Immanuel 49, 102, 125, 126, 137–8, 161, 164, 169
Kierkegaard, Søren 87
"know yourself!" (*gnôthi seauton*) 7
knowledge
    absolute knowledge 106–7
    aisthesis and the reality content of 99
    covert 68–9
    fallibility or infallibility of 121
    history of 163
    Kant's critique of 125, 126
    and language 46
    lingual knowledge 68–9
    metanoietic knowledge 161–2
    relational 109
    and semiotics 96
    and sensibility 130–1
Kripke, Saul A. 76, 79, 89, 138, 157

la langue 18, 23, 147
labelings, semiotic triangle/triad 49–52
Lacan, Jacques 105–8, 168
langage spéculative 98

language (*see also* speech)
  acquisition of 148–9, 154–5
  actuality in 19
  aesthetic model of 32, 129–31
  and *aisthesis* 146
  analytic philosophy of 10, 69–71, 74–6, 78, 80, 101, 138, 151, 157–8
  anti-causality of 109
  auto-*poietic* accounts of 149–51
  of the body 130
  and the brain 148–51
  circularity of 110
  and cognition 132
  as contingent and metonymic 118
  correlationist theory of 110–11, 131
  development of 18, 23, 146
  dialectical development of 154
  evolution of 21–3, 149–50
  as a game viii–ix
  la langue 18, 23, 147
  a linguistic ontology of 97–9
  metalanguage 108, 111
  metalingual function of 16–17
  and metanoia 3
  and metonymy 9
  morphogeny and ontogeny of 17–18
  noietic function of 29
  non-poetic language 15–16
  and part-to-whole relations 26–7, 29, 30, 111
  philosophy of 5, 10, 98, 108
  poetic function of 15–17, 23–5, 32, 33, 61, 129
  poiesis of 73, 98, 100
  poietic function of 9, 23–5, 73
  potentializing function of 17–27, 30
  pragmatic theory of 28
  psycho-systematics of 147
  realist theory of 10, 26, 27, 99, 108–9, 154
  and recursion 6–7, 21, 27
  relationism of 109
  and seeing 145
  and senses 145–6
  sensibility of 129
  as a site of knowledge 46
  speculative ontology of 10, 98, 99, 194n.71
  and speech 98
  theory of 5, 8
  and thought 2, 146–7, 148, 150, 154
language-realist poetics, dimensions of 100–1
language-realist semiosis, and *aisthesis*, *poiesis* and *noiesis* 100, 101
Latour, Bruno 78, 79
learning, symbol learning 148
Leiss, Elisabeth 22–3, 26–8, 46, 47, 68, 69, 98, 108, 152, 154
Les chats 96
Lévi-Strauss, Claude 96
lexical reading 92, 93
lexical semantics 27
Lieberman, Philip 150–1
lingual construction, of a true world 37–45
lingual knowledge, covert 68–9
lingual *poiesis* 33, 164
lingual realism 22, 28, 68–9
lingual relationalism, and speculative realism 159
lingual signs 28–32, 46, 155
lingual temporality 41
lingual things, and the ontology of individuals 83–5
lingual Thirdness 68
linguistic ontology, of language 97–9
linguistic turn, in philosophy 61–75, 108–11, 159
linguistics
  holistic 17
  and philosophy 97–8
  poietic 23–8
  speculative 17
literary metanoia 131
literature
  aesthetics of 131
  deconstructive analyses of 158
  knowing of 34
  poetic function of 40
  and structuralism 33
Littau, Karin 38
Logic of Sense 60–1
Lotman, Yuri 32

Malabou, Catherine 83, 90–1, 98, 135–6, 144, 172
materialism, speculative 118
meaning

and cognition 55
formation of 38
holistic context of 45
indexical understanding of 53
sliding of 43
use-theory of 76
Meditations 138
Meillassoux, Quentin 10, 79–80, 81, 109, 110–11, 118
Menke, Christoph 125, 126
Menninghaus, Winfried 130
mereological 27, 95, 101, 145
meta-abductions 116, 118, 119, 120–1
metalanguage 108, 111
metalingual function, of language 16–17
metanoia
  characteristics of 45
  cognitive aspects of 11
  concept of xi–xii, 2–4, 103, 178
  meaning of viii
  term 172, 176
metanoietic becoming 133
metanoietic knowledge, economy of 161–2
metanoietic transformation 8, 161–2
metaphors
  daring 59–60
  and metonymy 60
  new actualization of 65, 67
  and semblance 74–5
  and similarity 17
Metaphysics 127–8
metareflexivity 26
metonymics, daring 59–61
metonymy
  defined 181
  and language 9
  and metaphors 60
  theory of 17
Metzinger, Thomas 11, 124, 136, 137, 139, 140, 141–4, 145, 146, 147
morphogeny and ontogeny, of language 17–18
music, and aesthetic language 130

naive realism 143–6
neurophilosophy 143
neurosciences 135–6, 144
Nietzsche's styles 44
noiesis

aesthetic and poetic 102
and language-realist semiosis 100, 101
noetic plasticity 98
noietic function of language 29
and *poiesis* 104, 127, 146
and realist theory of language 27, 99
nominalism
  of roses 62–8
  weakening of 69–70
non-poetic language 15–16

Object, and Subject 112
objects, othering of 105, 168
ontogeny 9
ontology of individuals, and lingual things 83–5
ontology of relations 109, 158–9
oppositional relations 26
original apperception 137
Other, and the subject 106, 107
othering
  abduction as a methodological 11
  defined 181–2
  and metanoia 44–5, 133, 164, 167–8
  methodical 6–7, 112
  of object and subject 105, 163, 168
  poiesis as 103–5
  of sense 43
  of signifying structures 95
overcoded abductions 113, 117
oxymorons 59

part-to-whole relations
  defined 182
  and hermeneutics 38–9, 41
  language as a system of 30
  and language construction 26–7, 29
  and reading 38–9
  and recursion 110
  and the referentiality of language 111
  semiotic triangle 99
  "switching cards" 34
  triadic 25–6
  and universal grammar 152
Peirce, Charles Sanders 25–6, 34, 45–54, 55, 104, 112, 117–18, 122, 123–4
Phenomenology of Spirit 90, 103
philosophical reading 90
philosophy

aesthetic philosophy 124–7, 133
    as an *alethetics* x
    analytic philosophy. *See* analytic
        philosophy
    epistemic situation of 96
    of language 5, 10, 98, 108
    linguistic turn in 61–75, 108–11, 159
    and linguistics 97–8
    neurophilosophy 143
    poeticizing philosophy 8–9, 122–33
    spirituality of 7, 170–1
    and thought 131, 132
plasticity
    of concepts 103
    defined 182
    plastic reading 98
    plasticité noétique 98
    and the potential paradigm 20
    of sense organs 146
    and thought 136
Plato ix, 170, 172
poetics
    and aesthetics 127–8
    in Baumgarten 127–8
    and grammar 33
    language-realist 100–1
    the Poetic 126
    poetic function of language 15–17,
        23–5, 32, 33, 61, 129
    poetic function of literature 40
    poetic meaning 38
    poetic metaphor, and aesthetic
        semblance 74–5
    poetic *noiesis* 102
    poeticizing philosophy 8–9, 122–33
    poetics of fiction 176
    poetics of tense 176
    poetics of thought 27, 132
    semiotically informed 46
    speculative 32–5, 102, 103, 159, 163,
        170, 184
    undercover 128
Poetics of the homo oeconomicus 163
poetry
    and Baumgarten 127–8
    defined 15
poiesis
    abduction as a *poietic* procedure
        111–21

and *aisthesis* 104, 127
defined 6, 182
of language 73, 98
and language-realist semiosis 100
lingual 33, 164
and metanoia 131–3, 162, 163
and *noiesis* 104, 127, 146
as othering 103–5
poietic circle 67
poietic dimension of consciousness
    144–5
poietic experience 124
poietic function of language 9, 23–5,
    73
poietic function of speech 20
poietic linguistics 23–8
poietic reading 39
poietic triad 54–61
principle of 117
and semiotic poetics 101
political metanoia 171–2
politics, religious and history 171–2
potential paradigm
    actualization—potentialization—
        modalization 19–20
    aspect—tense—mode 18–19
    contiguity—metonymy—recursion
        20–1
potentializing function
    of language 17–27, 30
    speech 18, 23–5
pragmatic theory, of language 28
predicates
    individuals as 85
    as subjects 83–4
predication, signifier of 92–4
predicative reading 90–1, 97
predictions, absolute 94–6
Present Tense: A Poetics and Metanoia 173,
    175, 176
present tense novels 114, 115–16, 173, 175,
    176
principle of identity 71
"Problems in the Study of Literature and
    Language" 21
Proust, Marcel 158
psycho-systematics of language 147
psychoanalysis 108
psychosemiology 31

Quine, Willard Van Orman 70, 77

radicalization, and metanoia 162
Raffmann, Diana 137
Rancière, Jacques 177
re-entry
    defined 183
    of the subject into the world 162
    of thought into thought 162–3
reading
    as an experimental technique 105
    hermeneutical reading 39, 89
    and part-to-whole relations 38–9
    philosophical reading 90
    plastic reading 98
    predictive 90–1, 97
    reading problems 165–6
    speculative 90–1, 97, 105, 166
    syntactic/lexical 92, 93
    and writing 163–4
realism
    lingual 22, 68–9
    naive realism 143–6
    semiotic realism 99
realist theory, of language 10, 26, 27, 99, 108–9, 154
reality, interpretations of 48–9
recursion
    and contingency 31, 141–7
    defined 183
    and language 6–7, 21, 27
    and part-to-whole relations 110
    purpose of 24
    in reading 39
    recursive structure of cognition 141–7
    and self-reference 22–3
    and semiotic triangle 67–8
    and spirit 91
    understanding of 40
reference
    contingency creating 79–80
    defined 183
    and experience/movement 84
reflexivity 21
reistic theory 51–2
relational knowledge 109
relational ontology 109, 158–9
religion, and spiritual philosophy 170–1
religious metanoia 171–2
religious politics and history 171–2
reprogramming 139
Republic, The ix
revolution, readings of 46–7
Riches, Patrick Aaron 171
Romantic literature/music, and red roses 65–6
"Rose is a rose is a rose is a rose./ Loveliness extreme" 22, 61, 66–7, 68, 155, 183
roses, a nominalism of 62–8
Rousseau, Jean-Jacques 1

Saussure, Ferdinand de 58
science
    cognitive sciences 135–6
    of fiction 176–7
    neurosciences 135–6, 144
    semiotics as 96
    and thought 131, 132
Secondness, semiotic dimensions 52–4, 110, 159
seeing, and language 145
selection, operation of 24
self-consciousness 137, 140, 144
self, non-schizophrenic division/doubling of 140
self-reference, and recursion 22–3
self-reflexivity 110
self-representation 141
semblance, and metaphors 74–5
semiosis
    defined 54
    language-realist semiosis 100–1
    subject of 77–9
semiotic dimensions 30, 52–4, 62, 110, 158–9
semiotic poetics, and *poiesis* 101
semiotic realism 99
semiotic relations 6, 47–8, 53, 156, 158–9, 161, 191n.23
semiotic triangle/triad
    closedness of 56
    and icons 53
    labelings 49–52
    and metaphysics of the sign 84
    part-to-whole relations 99
    and recursive movement 67–8
    relations in effect in 47–8, 49–52

and semiotic dimensions 54
and subterfuge 88
symbolization 48, 53
trivalent relation of 45
semiotics
of the brain 154–9
contingent arbitrariness 57–9
and the critique of knowledge 96
Derrida and de Man 55
Peirce 45, 47, 49
as a rigorous science 83
term 10
sense(s)
and language 145–6
othering of 43
sense perceptions 125
sensibility
and knowledge 130–1
of language 129
and semiosis 100
Sheriff, John K. 52–3
Shklovsky, Viktor 51
signification, semiotic triangle 48, 50
signified, and signifiers 58, 61–75
signifier, sliding of the 42–3, 184
signs
acquisition of indexical signs 155
and contradictions 80–2
dimensions of 183–4
empty/concrete 81–2
and form 51
lingual signs 28–32, 46, 155
triadic logic of 45–54
Sloterdijk, Peter 190n.11
space, and time 143, 145
Spatialization of Form Hypothesis (SFH) 199–200n.14
speculative abductions 121
speculative lingual realism 28 (*see also* realism)
speculative linguistics 17
speculative materialism 118
speculative nominalism, and speculative realism 121
speculative ontology of language 10, 98, 99, 194n.71
speculative poetics 32–5, 102, 103, 159, 163, 170, 184
speculative proposition 93–4, 95

speculative reading 90–1, 97, 105, 166
speculative realism 28, 121, 159 (*see also* realism)
speculative thought 103
speculative triad 99–103
speech (*see also* language)
actualizing function 23–4
and language 98
and paradigmatics 20
poietic function of 20
potentializing function of 18, 23–5
and thought 31
spirit, and recursion 91
spirituality, of philosophy 7, 170–1
state of exception, of thought 136–7
Stein, Gertrude 22, 61–2, 66–7, 68, 156
Stolterfoht, Ulf 37
Strawson, Peter 83–5, 104
Strindberg, August 174–5
structuralism, and literature 33
Subject, and Object 112
subject, and the Other 106, 107
subjects
othering of 105, 163, 168
predicates as 83–4
re-entry of into the world 162
Subterfuge or Unexpected Telling Circumstances 56–7
subterfuges
defined 184–5
disciplined, of analytic philosophy 73–4
and semiotic triangle/triad 88
"switching cards" 34
symbol learning 148
symbolic designations 72
symbolic semiotic relations 156, 191n.23
Symbolic Species, The 148–9
symbolization, semiotic triangle 48, 53
syntactic reading 92, 93

Tarski, Alfred 70
temporality, strong 172–5, 185
tense-philosophy, hermeneutic circle 41
Thirdness
lingual 68
semiotic dimensions 30, 52–4, 158–9
thought
and arts 131–2

auto-affection of in metanoia 169–70
dialectical development of 154
and I 137–8, 138–9, 140
and language 2, 146–7, 148, 150, 154
and metanoia 135–6, 162–3, 165
and philosophy 131, 132
and plasticity 136
poietic aspects of 27, 132
re-entry of thought into thought 162–3
and science 131, 132
speculative 103
and speech 31
states of exception 136–7
and world 138–9
time
and consciousness 142–3
and space 143, 145
and temporality 173
triadic epistemic situation 96–7
triadic relations 168–9
truth
and *noiesis* 101
notion of 106
opening up of 83
truth definitions 70–1

Turner, Mark 3
Tynyanov, Yuri 21

uncertainty principle, Heisenberg 54
undercoded abductions 113–14, 117, 118–19
understanding, new 1, 166
universal grammar 151–4
unlearning, and forgetting 154–6
Ur-Theilung 112
use-theory, of meaning 76

Vogl, Joseph 163

Weimar, Klaus 129
Weinrich, Harald 59–60
What is Philosophy? 131
Whorf, Benjamin Lee 150
Wittgenstein, Ludwig 29, 76, 89, 190n.11
Wittgenstein on Rules and Private Language 89
Wohlfahrt, Günther 102
Word and Object 70
writing, and reading 163–4

Žižek, Slavoj 106, 107

www.ingramcontent.com/pod-product-compliance
Lightning Source LLC
Chambersburg PA
CBHW070316230426
43663CB00011B/2151